THE ROSICRUCIAN COMPENDIUM

By Travis Trinca

First published 2026

Temple & Vault Press

ISBN 978-1-7642118-0-2 (Digital Cloth Hardback)
ISBN 978-1-7642118-9-5 (Paperback)
ISBN 978-1-7642118-1-9 (eBook)

All rights reserved. No part of this book may be reproduced or transmitted in any form or by any means, electronic or mechanical, including photocopying, recording, scanning or by any information storage and retrieval system, on the internet or elsewhere, without permission from the author in writing.

© 2026 Travis Trinca

Copyright Notice

Unauthorised copying or distribution of this publication is illegal. It deprives authors, publishers, and booksellers of income necessary to support the creation of new works. Unauthorised versions of publications are also likely to be inferior in quality and contain incorrect information. You can help by reporting copyright infringements and acts of piracy to the author or the local copyright authority.

Images

Every effort has been made to identify and correctly attribute photographic credits. Should any error have occurred this is entirely unintentional.

Cover design: Mitch Savage-Charman
Interior design and typesetting: www.travistrinca.com

To

All who have served the Rosicrucian tradition

CONTENTS

ACKNOWLEDGEMENTS ix
FOREWORD xiii
PREFACE xix
WHISPER OF THE ROSE 3
THE ROSICRUCIAN SOURCE WORKS 11
FAMA FRATERNITATIS 19
    Analysis of the Christian Rosenkreuz story................................. 25
    The case for a historical C.R.C. 35
CONFESSIO FRATERNITATIS 45
    Analysis of the Confessio Fraternitatis 51
THE CHEMICAL WEDDING 57
    Analysis of The Chemical Wedding 65
AUTHORSHIP 81
    Authorship according to Rosicrucian organisations 93
HALLMARKS OF THE R+C 107
    HALLMARK ONE: Service 110
    HALLMARK TWO: The Rosicrucian Pulse 118
    HALLMARK THREE: The Invisible College of the Rosicrucians 131
    HALLMARK FOUR: Rosicrucian Masters 143

THE LOST ROSICRUCIAN SECRET 189
A ROSE BY ANY OTHER NAME 193
OFF WITH THE FAIRIES 209
WAR OF THE ROSES 231
    The Invisible Fraternity and its Visible Critics 233
    Cloaks, Daggers, and Crosses 241
    Across the Atlantic 257
    Echoes in the Chamber 271
    Crown of Thorns 275
AN OPEN LETTER TO ROSICRUCIAN OFFICERS 279
CONCLUSION 283
    The Rosicrucian Secret Revealed 294
REFERENCES 297
APPENDIX ONE: Rosicrucian Groups 311
    Order of the Gold and Rosy Cross (G.u.R.C.) 313
    The Rosicrucians of Toulouse 319
    Kabbalistic Order of the Rose-Cross 328
    Societas Rosicruciana 330
    The Hermetic Order of the Golden Dawn (H.O.G.D.) 335
    The Fraternitas Rosae Crucis (F.R.C.) 339
    The Rosicrucian Fellowship (T.R.F.) 340
    The Ancient and Mystical Order Rosae Crucis (A.M.O.R.C.) .. 345
APPENDIX TWO: Rosicrucian Alchemy 365
APPENDIX THREE: The Rose and the Cross 377
INDEX 380

ACKNOWLEDGEMENTS

This book is the culmination of years of passionate exploration assisted immeasurably by incalculable conversations, fortunate encounters, and chance meetings with many wonderful people. The way in which events and people have come together to help guide this book to completion has truly been a feat of wonder.

First and foremost, my deepest gratitude goes to my beautiful family for their patient love and support. Rahil for supporting me in following my passions even to the point of sacrificing her own. Sophia for always being there to measure my social media presence. And Eli for his enthusiasm that his Dad is a *book writer*. You are my true roses and I love the guinea pig filled garden that we tend together.

To the V. Rev. Fred Shade, not just for his eagle eye, red pen, and endless supply of documents and notes, but also for always being available to any sincere Zelator or Magus; perhaps one day you might even influence me to utilise fewer semi-colons, but it is not this day.

To Dr Sebastiano Della Lena, whose enlightening conversations never cease to bring coherence and structure to my scattered thoughts and ideas.

To the United Grand Lodge of Victoria for their steadfast encouragement of Masonic research. In particular, I wish to thank the Deputy Grand Master RWBro Myles King and Grand Secretary RWBro Bruce Cowie for their fraternal support and for championing the pursuit of Masonic scholarship within our jurisdiction.

To Martin and Kindra Faulks for their support and generosity as publishers and as friends. Their commitment to producing thoughtful and well-crafted esoteric and Masonic books continues to enrich our field.

To Mitch Savage-Charman for his incredible cover design. May it ever remain truly *inevitable*.

To Ian Gladwin for his diligent study of Rosicrucian source works and for providing proofreading and assisting me with the finer points regarding the history of the *Gold und Rosenkreuzer*.

To Samuel Robinson for his assistance in proofreading, *Masters as a Mask: The case of Alois Mailänder*.

To the Brothers and Sisters at *The Symposium of the Rose* for the countless enlightening and supportive conversations.

To the *Victorian Lodge of Research* for their continued support of local Freemasons and advancement of Masonic research.

To Chuck Dunning JR for always recognising the R+C impulse and his great skill in being able to direct others to recognise the same. You are a beacon for our tradition and I am so happy that you agreed to provide the foreword to this book.

To Drago Dragojlovic for his wise counsel and for always recognising the mystical in everything.

To Michael Osborne for the enlightening conversations, helpful advice, and for helping readers to recognise the spirit of the Rosicrucian tradition.

To the Fratres and Sorores at Harmony Lodge for their unending service to the R+C. You took in a stray wanderer from the darkness, made him one of your own, and helped him discover gifts and abilities he never knew he had.

To the Fratres at *Demiurgus College No. 3*, whose incredible wine and cheese driven conversations exemplify the true spirit of Rosicrucianism.

And to all the silent workers tending to the Rosicrucian flame: may your unseen labours continue to illuminate the path for those who seek it.

FOREWORD

This book will not only help you learn more about Rosicrucianism, but through it you will learn more about the soul of a man who has been touched and changed by that tradition's spirit. In the process, you are likely to learn more about yourself as well, perhaps recognizing something compelling behind his words that lives in you too.

One of the blessings of technology is that it can so easily facilitate connections between people. Travis Trinca and I have only known each other online, and yet even through the limitations of laptop computers and cell phones separated by many thousands of miles, there has been a welcome recognition of resonance between our souls. In some ways, that's not at all surprising because we are both students of Rosicrucianism and Freemasons. Still, these commonalities don't guarantee the deep feelings that our hearts associate with words like *brother* or *sister*, *frater* or *soror*. In addition to speaking of experiences, perspectives, and values with each other, we need to hear things in each other's voices, see things in each other's faces. In this way, we can come to know that we're not only like-minded, but also kindred spirits rediscovering our oneness with each other and the Divine. I am grateful to know Brother Travis in this way, and I'm excited to welcome you to get to know him better through this wonderful book.

When Travis first shared with me his intention to write *The Rosicrucian Compendium*, I felt something stir. It was not simply interest, but recognition — a sense that something long hoped for was finally coming into being. In a world full of books on esotericism that either romanticize or over-analyze, this one has struck me as aiming for something more grounded and more precious: clarity without arrogance, breadth without dilution, and perhaps most importantly, sincerity without preachiness.

Over the years, I've had the good fortune to walk alongside many fellow seekers on Rosicrucian paths — some in formal initiatic orders, others in quieter solitude. What often binds us is not just a shared set of symbols or language, but a deeper calling: to be transformed inwardly, and to serve the world in some way as a result of that transformation. It is rare to find a book that speaks to the scholar, the aspirant, and the adept with equal care, but Travis has done just that.

His journey, which he recounts with honesty and humility, is one that mirrors so many of our own – the early stirrings of a hidden call and the disorientation when first trying to trace that call through books and organizations that don't quite fit. And eventually, the emergence of an authentic synthesis that honors the diversity of the Rosicrucian landscape while remaining faithful to its essence.

One of the first things that struck me in reading the manuscript was Travis's ability to frame the path with poetic clarity. He writes:

It felt less like a discovery and more like a recognition; something remembered rather than learned.

Those of us who've walked this path know that feeling well. It's not about conversion to a doctrine, but awakening to something already stirring in the soul.

This book isn't a manifesto. Nor is it a dry academic catalogue. It is, as Travis himself says, a compendium — a living map of ideas, figures, and traditions that have shaped the Rosicrucian current over centuries. In that way, it reflects the compendium that was the vault of Father C.R.C. But even more than that, it is a work of service. It invites the reader not merely to learn *about* Rosicrucianism, but to reflect, to feel, and perhaps even to remember something ancient yet personal that stirs in the heart. In short, it is the book I wished for when I was first investigating the Rosicrucian movement decades ago, and one that I will be happy returning to as I continue along the way.

Time and again, Travis captures the Rosicrucian spirit in fresh, yet faithful language. In a passage I highlighted with admiration, he writes:

> *True Rosicrucianism is not about titles or charters... it is about listening to an inner call to become more fully human and help others to do the same.*

That phrase — *to become more fully human* — lies close to the heart of the Great Work as I've come to know it. And throughout this book, Travis returns again and again to the theme that our value lies not in esoteric trappings, but in the lived application of compassionate wisdom. As he puts it so aptly:

> *The real work occurs inwardly and relationally. It happens when the teachings are lived; not just studied. When the heart is opened; not just the intellect.*

In my own writing and teaching, I've emphasized the necessity of bringing head and heart together — of balancing insight with caring, knowledge with presence, theory with practice. This book walks that line beautifully. It both challenges and consoles. It asks hard questions and leaves space for subtle replies. It neither idolizes nor dismisses the past or the present while speaking of the future with both caution and optimism.

The emphasis Travis places on *service* may already be apparent from the previous quotes. Yet it deserves special highlighting among the many things that inspire my confidence in this text. In fact, he lists service as the first of four hallmarks in the Rosicrucian tradition. Placing this motive and intention at the fore clarifies that aligning with the Rosicrucian spirit is not merely an intellectual pursuit, a matter of organizational membership, ceremonial recognition, or even the practice of rituals, prayers, and meditations. Each of these things certainly has a valued place within the tradition. But their true value is in their potential to transform our lives into greater expressions of our oneness with the Divine, with Nature, and thus with all others. Such lives are recognizable by greater love, and with it a stronger drive to meet others with respect, empathy, and caring in action. Travis has great conviction that commitment to service is not only what transforms us as individuals, but also what will transform Rosicrucianism's future and its impact on the world.

Whether you're someone newly curious about Rosicrucianism or a longtime student of its mysteries, you'll find something here worthy of your attention. You may not agree with every perspective presented, and that's as it should be. But if you approach this book with sincerity, openness, and a willingness to wrestle with mystery, I believe you'll be changed by it in positive ways.

To Travis, I offer my sincere thanks, not only for the monumental labor of research and writing, but for the care, humility, and living spirit that breathes through these pages. This is not just a book *about* Rosicrucianism. It is one of Rosicrucianism's most fragrant new blossoms.

By the Cross and Rose,

Chuck Dunning
May 26, 2025

PREFACE

My first book, *The Temple and the Vault*, was a labour of love. In fact, its approximation to the gestational process of a human was so close as to be almost poetic. It took a little over nine months to complete the draft manuscript. During this period, I was like an expectant parent. I would go to sleep thinking about the manuscript and I would wake up thinking about it as well. It was a journey of sleepless nights, moments of joy, occasional frustration, and feelings of wonder. But the process was worth every word. The ease and flow with which the manuscript came together left little doubt in my mind that it was the right thing to do.

It was to be a project that had a purpose. A project that could clarify and refocus the ideals of initiatic traditions. A project that could assist those earnest aspirants towards an initiatic home. Did it achieve this purpose?

Initiatic traditions are...well...traditional. They are prone to conservation. What were the chances that initiates of these traditions might find The Temple and the Vault to be more of an exposé? During the writing process, I did have to grapple with one significant challenge: *how much, is too much*? It was a delicate balancing act to try to find the *Golden Mean* between maintaining curious mystery and bringing forth informative coherency. In some cases, I simply opted to paraphrase initiatic stories. However, in most other cases, I opted for near word-for-word copying from passages of original ritual texts. This was never meant an exposé. Quite the opposite. I wanted to ensure that the reader would be able to both distinguish between my own musings and the authentic ritual source as well as demonstrate that my own findings were grounded in the tradition itself, and not simply the product of absent-minded fantasy.

Fortunately, judging by the response to the book, many readers received the message that I was intending to express.

The whole process, from writing, to publication, to promotion was highly rewarding. But I always felt like there was something missing.

It always felt like that this book was simply a start. A stepping stone to something much larger. Something that sits behind all initiatory traditions; and which was only touched upon in The Temple and the Vault.

Naturally, the book was followed by many presentations, podcasts, interviews, etc. And time and time again I found myself becoming engaged in conversations about *Rosicrucianism*.

Over the course of my adult life, I've been called upon to prepare many presentations, lectures, workshops, and discourses on esoteric subjects, ranging from *A(lchemy)* to *Z(aphnath-Paaneah)*! Given my personal interests, I routinely introduce Rosicrucian concepts and ideas. Naturally, one of the common questions I receive is *What is Rosicrucianism?* Such a simple question deserves a simple answer. But if we look at how the Rosicrucian tradition has manifested itself, it quickly becomes apparent that answering such a question can at times prove challenging.

Rosicrucianism has become many things to many people.

A scholar of the Western Esoteric Tradition might state that Rosicrucianism is a philosophical tradition which combines Hermeticism with alchemical symbolism.

A member of an initiatic Rosicrucian society might state that Rosicrucianism is a practical mystical path that teaches ancient wisdom and cosmic laws to help individuals achieve mastery of life.

Preface

A Gnostic might state that Rosicrucianism is a path to divine knowledge which aims at unveiling the inner spark and liberating the soul from material illusion.

A Christian Pietist might state that Rosicrucianism emphasises spiritual renewal and aligning life with God's will through prayer and meditation.

An Alchemist might state that Rosicrucianism is a movement that integrates alchemical symbolism and practices into a broader mystical philosophy aimed at the spiritual transmutation of the individual.

A historian might state that Rosicrucianism was a precursor to the *Age of Enlightenment* and influenced early members of the Royal Society.

Truly, Rosicrucianism is all of these things. But it is also *so* much more.

When considering whether to write this book, I was met with a moment of hesitancy. I had a very definite vision of how this book should look. It should be encyclopaedic in nature and contain all the elements that make up Rosicrucianism. It should inspire in the reader a recognition of the Rosicrucian spark. It should be accessible by the academic as well as the initiate. It should provide an unbiased understanding of Rosicrucian groups, whilst upholding their individual integrity. And most importantly, it should aim for enchantment and not cynicism. *Can this be achieved?*

This book is an ambitious undertaking. It is intended to be a one-stop for all Rosicrucian seekers, be they curious of the sociology of the German Rosicrucian movement of the seventeenth century or if they are an Officer of a contemporary initiatic Rosicrucian organisation. This book takes no favourites and will hold no specific organisation to be superior or inferior to any other. This book is intended to be, as its name suggests, a *Compendium* of Rosicrucian knowledge.

It would be misleading for me to state that I had taken no inspiration from the highly regarded book, *Freemasons for Dummies* by Christopher L. Hodap; a book that I had always hoped to see in Rosicrucian form. Indeed, it is this author's sincere wish that The Rosicrucian Compendium becomes a valuable read for all those interested in Rosicrucianism, no matter their background.

However, it does not aim to be revelatory in nature, exposing the secrets of specific Rosicrucian groups. Each Rosicrucian path has its own distinct character and cultural identity, and it is not my place to presume authority over traditions that many readers may know more intimately than I do myself. Instead, it is my intention to provide a robust overview to all of the major themes, doctrines, and concepts that constantly engage the curiosity of Neophytes and Adepts across the vast spectrum of Rosicrucian practice. But more importantly, to assist in illustrating that which makes Rosicrucianism so enchanting. This book is written in service of the broader Rosicrucian tradition.

As we explore its major themes, I will occasionally draw upon doctrinal perspectives from specific Rosicrucian organisations. This should hopefully help us to observe the richness and diversity of the tradition as a whole. At times, these comparisons may also reveal points of divergence between groups. When this occurs, I will strive to identify common ground where possible, and where such unity cannot be found, I will respond from the standpoint that I feel best serves the higher ideals of the Rosicrucian path.

Travis Trinca
Melbourne, Australia
2025

WHISPER OF THE ROSE

There are moments that alter the trajectory of your life's journey. Often, these occur without warning. Quiet events that ripple outward until you look back and realise everything that followed, began with a *whisper*. My introduction to the Rosicrucian tradition was one such moment. I was only a teenager when I was introduced to the term, *Rosicrucian*. It was only a short mention, buried in a conversation about adjacent topics such as secret societies and hidden knowledge. But it struck me with unusual force. It felt less like a discovery and more like a recognition; something remembered rather than learned. Perhaps a part of me recognised then, my life was changing.

From that moment onward, the Rosicrucian tradition began exerting a pull on my attention. In those early years, I read what I could. Most of what I could find was rather superficial or speculative in nature. Put simply, it didn't align with the call I felt. It wasn't until I was twenty-one that I formally joined my first Rosicrucian organisation: *The Ancient and Mystical Order Rosae Crucis* (A.M.O.R.C.). Here, I found myself among a community of seekers, some of whom shared a similar desire for *Light*. And it wasn't just the rituals and history that kept me engaged. It was sincere curiosity. That was the beginning of what has now become a twenty-year journey down multiple Rosicrucian paths, including leadership roles in more than one Rosicrucian organisation.

As my experience in the Rosicrucian tradition matured, so did my questions. Why do different Rosicrucian groups present such divergent views regarding the same tradition? Why do some Rosicrucian initiates not appear to have the same connection or perceive the same depth in the tradition that I had glimpsed? And most relevant to this book, why do so many writers, both academic and esoteric, treat the Rosicrucian tradition with such cynicism or dismissiveness, as though it were but a footnote in history or relic of pre-enlightenment thought? I began to suspect that the heart of Rosicrucianism was being overlooked.

This book is my attempt to correct that.

This book is not meant to be a simple history or commentary. It is a guide. One shaped from lived experience, thorough research, and many conversations with fellow seekers, including high-ranking members from across the Rosicrucian landscape: *The Ancient Mystical Order Rosae Crucis, Societas Rosicruciana, Fellowship of the Rosy Cross, Builders of the Adytum*, as well as other initiates that follow more personal or Gnostic paths. These conversations have been at times inspirational, and at other times quite candid, and even challenging. They revealed not only the strengths and intentions of each tradition, but also the misunderstandings they often held, particularly about each other. Yet beyond these differences, a shared resonance can be glimpsed; a sense that something real, vital, and subtle is being preserved. A truth guarded by both the individual as well as by the tradition from which each claimed alliance. And it was in this shared resonance that that faint Rosicrucian whisper can be heard. A whisper that calls from beyond, not only individual organisations, but time and space as well.

If this book does anything new, it is to approach the Rosicrucian tradition, not as a lineage to be defended, nor a mystery to be decoded, but as a living current that expresses itself through ideas, symbols, stories, and most importantly, people. This book seeks to understand Rosicrucianism, not just by its historicity, but by its fruits. The inner transmutation it initiates, the virtues it cultivates, and the kind of person it can develop.

The Rosicrucian source works of the seventeenth century are usually cited as the starting point of the Rosicrucian tradition. However, as you will see throughout this book, the real impetus of the Rosicrucian tradition began long before this period. In truth, the Rosicrucian tradition is timeless. Nevertheless, the influence of these works upon the Rosicrucian tradition cannot be understated. They are strange texts. Anonymous, symbolic, and at times contradictory. They read more like spiritual provocations rather than the manifestoes that they are usually cited as being. And within them lies a radical vision: an invisible fraternity without dogma, devoted to service, healing, and understanding the relationships which exist between *Man, Nature,* and *God*. This vision has inspired centuries of seekers, mystics, scientists, artists, and idealists. Though, not always in the same way.

One of the primary challenges in writing this book is attempting to reconcile the *ideal* with the *actual*. Many who claim the Rosicrucian name do so with sincerity but diverge vastly in practice. The Rosicrucian epithet has encompassed a variety of disciplines such as alchemy, Kabbalah, mystical Christianity, esoteric psychology, and ceremonial magic. Some emphasise tradition and lineage, whilst others prioritise inner work and the cultivation of intuition. This diversity can be both a strength and a source of confusion. To truly understand the Rosicrucian tradition, we must look beyond these outer trappings and consider the underlying values.

For me, these values are defined by a few key qualities, such as humility, service, and sincerity. True Rosicrucianism is not about titles or charters. It is not about amassing passwords and gestures. It is about listening to an inner call to become more fully human and help others to do the same. Such a statement might seem odd. But to the Rosicrucian, human potential is far greater than many might realise. This calling expresses itself in different ways depending upon the culture, century, or individual. But the *pulse* remains.

This book is structured to offer both clarity and depth to the Rosicrucian tradition. It does not aim to set out down the same tired worn-out paths offered by previous Rosicrucian commentators. Nevertheless, we will find ourselves inhabiting the same locations and periods and meeting some of the characters already well-known to Rosicrucian philosophers. But we will not be engaging with them in the same way.

We will take time to examine the narratives of Christian Rosenkreuz, before moving on to a contemplation and analysis of the themes, symbols, and historical context of the Rosicrucian source works. We will then explore the *authorship* question, before considering a set of *hallmarks* that I believe best reflect the Rosicrucian spirit in action. These hallmarks are not drawn from any organisational doctrine, but from lived observation: from what I have seen, experienced, and quietly tested.

In later chapters, we will explore a lesser-known, but absolutely vital subject to understanding the Rosicrucian tradition; *esoteric didactic literature*. In fact, this might just be the very first exploration of the importance of esoteric didactic texts considered from a Rosicrucian perspective. The *elemental* creatures discussed in texts such as *Zanoni* and *Comte de Gabalis* spark wonder and imagination. They were critically acclaimed by Rosicrucian leaders and passages from these texts have silently crept into some of the rituals of contemporary Rosicrucian organisations. These texts are often neglected in academic treatments, yet they have played a critical role in shaping modern Rosicrucian thought and practice.

Following the awe and wonder of these fictional narratives, we will then have the tools ready to pull-up our bootstraps and march into the muddy waters of Rosicrucian rivalries. From the early attacks of the seventeenth century, to rivalries in the occult revival, to modern disputes across the Atlantic, and into the internet age. Only by facing these shadows can we be prepared for the next step of the Rosicrucian tradition. One which *you* may be called upon to assist with.

Finally, this book closes with a personal appeal to Rosicrucian leaders and students alike. It is a call to manifest the heart of the tradition. For while Rosicrucianism has utilised hierarchical structures, degrees, and rituals, these are but only vessels for communicating the tradition to seekers. The real work occurs inwardly and relationally. It happens when the teachings are lived; not just studied. When the heart is opened; not just the intellect. The Rosicrucian tradition has much to offer, but only *if* it remembers what it is.

I will not pretend to have all of the answers. This book is not the final word on the Rosicrucian tradition. It is *a* guide, not *the* guide. It is a conversation. Some readers may find here confirmation of what they have always felt. Others may find a challenge. But I would encourage you to approach this book with the spirit of a Rosicrucian, by approaching it with sincerity, a willingness to learn something new, and perhaps most important of all, curiosity. I am not the first to write on the subject, nor will I be the last. But what I do hope this book achieves is something that I feel too few have attempted. To bring together heart and mind, insight and scholarship, enchantment and clarity. The Rosicrucian tradition deserves to be taken seriously. It is a living spiritual impulse that has touched countless lives over the centuries, often quietly and in silence.

So, let us walk together and listen for the *Whisper of the Rose*.

Like all good initiatic narratives, the mythos of the Rosicrucians relates the journey of a sincere protagonist. When the Rosicrucians first announced themselves in Germany in the early seventeenth century, they did so through a series of anonymously printed source works, usually referred to as *manifestoes*. The bulk of the *biography* of the protagonist is revealed in the first of these works, usually referred to simply as the *Fama Fraternitatis*[1]. But the lesser used full title does give us an indication as to the target audience of this work: *to the heads, estates, and scholars of Europe.*

---
1 The full title is, *General Reformation of the whole wide world besides the Fama Fraternitatis or Brotherhood of the Highly Praiseworthy Order of the R. C. To the heads, estates and scholars of Europe* (German: *Allgemeine und General Reformation der ganzen weiten Welt beneben der Fama Fraternitatis Oder Brüderschafft des Hochlöblichen Ordens des R. C. An die Häupter, Stände und Gelehrten Europae*).

If we look at the many commentaries, letters, and discussions which followed the early Rosicrucian announcements, we find that the target audience had both received these messages and found them intriguing, even if there was not a universal support for the ideas being presented.

Perhaps one of the earliest responses to the Rosicrucian source works was from Adam Haslmayr, a Paracelsian physician, who published a reply to the Rosicrucian brotherhood in 1612[2]. Haslmayr would even pass on a copy of the Fama Fraternitatis manuscript to his friend Prince Augustus of Anhalt-Plötzkau, a prominent figure in the Holy Roman Empire. Prince Augustus was so taken that he would even initiate a search for the brotherhood. And he would soon be joined by others.

Many of the Neoplatonic ideas being presented in the early Rosicrucian source works resonated with the Paracelsian physicians of the time. Michael Maier was a German physician and alchemist who had a great influence on the Rosicrucian furore powering its way through Europe. A physician by trade, Maier attempted to strike a careful balance between the traditional Galenic medicine and contemporary Paracelsian medicine which, due to its reliance upon correspondences between worldly and supernatural forces, was not often appreciated by the fellow practitioners of Maier's Lutheran faith. Naturally, Maier became supremely interested in alchemy and began his pilgrimage throughout Europe to learn all he could of the Royal Art. Eventually, he was recruited as personal physician to Rudolf II (as were many other Kabbalists, alchemists, and astrologers). So aligned were Maier's values with the Rosicrucian cause (Waite A. E., 1887, pp. 268-282) that he even authored a whole book, called *Themis Aurea*, which elaborated upon the six fundamental laws of the *Fraternity of the Rosy Cross* as first outlined in the Fama Fraternitatis.

---

2 Although the Fama Fraternitatis was not published until 1614, it was already being circulated in manuscript form.

Another physician and alchemist who was supportive of the Rosicrucian movement was Robert Fludd who would write three papers defending the Rosicrucian movement. Maier and Fludd were known acquaintances and it was perhaps Maier's instigation that led Robert Fludd to write his third paper in defence of the Rosicrucians. It has also been speculated that Maier may have introduced Fludd to the Rosicrucian brotherhood (Craven R. J., 1968) although proof of this is outstanding.

Robert Fludd's three-volume series on the *History of the Macrocosm and the Microcosm,* an ambitious trilogy of works that was incomplete upon his death, shows a tremendous concurrence of thought between Fludd and the anonymous Rosicrucian authors.

But not all responses to the Rosicrucian movement were positive. The French polymath and Catholic priest, Marin Mersenne led the fight against the Rosicrucians. In contrast to the Rosicrucian worldview which embraced a mystical and esoteric approach to knowledge, Mersenne was a scientific rationalist whose ideas were promoted in reputable scientific circles, such as his own *Académie Mersenne*, which fostered open debate among scientific minds. The Rosicrucians, by contrast, claimed elite knowledge that was hidden away from the general populace. No doubt his disfavour for the Rosicrucians would have been further amplified by his own religious worldview, which the Rosicrucians were decidedly against.

It was not just Catholics, but even Lutherans found the Rosicrucian message to be problematic. Lutheran Alchemist Andreas Libavius would become a prominent critic of Rosicrucianism, denouncing the Rosicrucian manifestoes as promoting heresy (Yates, 2003, pp. 69-70).

These several examples illustrate that the budding Rosicrucian movement was certainly successful in reaching their intended target audience, including academics, physicians, alchemists, theologians, and even those in positions of political power. But the reception was by no means universally appreciated.

THE ROSICRUCIAN SOURCE WORKS

*P*ick up any book on Rosicrucianism and you will quickly learn about how Rosicrucianism was born from several anonymously printed documents commonly referred to as *manifestoes*. In each resource on the topic, you will come across the same repeated facts. There were three manifestoes. These were printed in Germany between 1614-1616. The authors were anonymous. It is not my intention to bore the reader with trivial information that they may have come across multiple times before. But as this work is aiming to present a *compendium* of Rosicrucian knowledge, it would be challenging to ignore the facts of the matter.

The good news for the experienced Rosicrucian thinker reading this work however is that I do not intend to simply repeat the same information, for in fact, I believe (and will explain with ample evidence) that many of the so-called *facts* that we might be familiar with are in dire need of review.

Just how many source works are there?

For those of you that may have been reading the room of Rosicrucian academia of recent years, you will note that there has been quite ample discussion on just how many Rosicrucian source works there actually were. Traditionally, they have been thought of as a trilogy of works:

the *Fama Fraternitatis, Confessio Fraternitatis,* and the *Chemical Wedding of Christian Rosenkreuz in the Year 1459*. But there were also texts written around the same time that contained similar messages, or which were presented in a similar way. As such, you may have come across references to there being more than three source works.

Some of the most notable Rosicrucian works from the time-period in which the Fama Fraternitatis arose include:

- *The Mirror of the Wisdom of the Rosy Cross* (Latin: *Speculum Sophicum Rhodostauroticum*) (1618) by Theophilus Schweighardt Constantiens (likely a pseudonym for Daniel Mögling (1596-1635);

- *The Silence after the Cries* (Latin: *Silentium Post Clamores*) (1617) by Michael Maier (1568–1622);

- *Parabola* (1625) by Hinricus Madathanus (pseudonym for Adrian von Mynsicht) (1590–1638);

- *The Pegasus of the Firmament* (Latin: *Pegasus firmamenti*) (1619) by Josepho Stellato (pseudonym for Christoph Hirsch (*1577-1653*);

- *A Letter from the Brothers R.C.* (1651) by Thomas Vaughan (often known by the pseudonym Eugenius Philalethes (1622-1666).

In addition, since the publication of the Fama Fraternitatis in 1614, there have been groups and individuals who have taken it upon themselves to develop similar manuscripts, in a spirit designed to be a follow-up to those seventeenth century Rosicrucian source works.

For example, the largest and most well-known Rosicrucian organisation, *The Ancient and Mystical Order Rosae Crucis* (A.M.O.R.C.) has developed three additional *manifestoes* since 2001, so according to the *canon* of that tradition, there are six Rosicrucian source works. But whilst these contemporary Rosicrucian source works serve a purpose, they are often intrinsically attached to the specific tradition from which they emanated. This is not a rebuttal of the contents contained within these texts; not by any means. In fact, I find A.M.O.R.C.'s *Positio Fraternitatis* from 2001 to be, not only inspired, but incredibly relevant, especially considering the time-period in which it arose. But in this present work, which aims to transcend any outer Rosicrucian group, it will not be considered and discussed as a part of our present analysis.

There are also arguments for considering fewer-than-three Rosicrucian source works. Some scholars contend that *The Chemical Wedding of Christian Rosenkreuz in the Year 1459* differs so significantly from the earlier two texts, that it could hardly be considered a foundational Rosicrucian source work. Some proponents of this position claim therefore that only two Rosicrucian source works should be recognised. An even more extreme perspective suggests that only the Fama Fraternitatis qualifies as a so-called *true* source work.

So, how many source works are there really? Ultimately, does the exact number matter? For the purposes of this analysis, I will treat the Rosicrucian tradition as encompassing a trilogy of core works. The argument for this stance is straightforward: these three main texts have significantly influenced the development of the Rosicrucian tradition up to the present day. Some may argue that this is a self-fulfilling prophecy because Rosicrucian commentators have consistently repeated the same trivia that there are three Rosicrucian *manifestoes*. This might be true, but these works' undeniable impact also cannot be ignored.

For those that are interested in the Rosicrucian milieu in which the Rosicrucian movement began, I would encourage you to seek out additional writings from this period, some of which have been noted above (but in this case, might I suggest my personal favourite, *A Letter from the Brothers R.C.* which appeared in a work by Thomas Vaughan, called *Lumen de Lumine*).

So although there are more than three Rosicrucian source works, for our present analysis, we will examine the trilogy of works which has been most influential upon shaping the Rosicrucian tradition. But before we get started on an overview of these works, let us briefly touch upon something that might just challenge some of our pre-conceived notions. Do the works of the Rosicrucian trilogy accurately depict *manifestoes,* as they are so often referred?

Manifesto, Treatise, or Allegory

Before we challenge the labelling of the Rosicrucian source works, we must first clarify the meaning of the term *manifesto.* Merriam-Webster defines a manifesto as, "*a written statement declaring publicly the intentions, motives, or views of its issuer*" (Merriam-Webster, 2024). The term itself is rooted in the Latin *manifestus,* meaning, "*plainly apprehensible, clear, apparent, evident*" (etymonline.com, 2024).

At first glance, the Fama Fraternitatis and Confessio Fraternitatis seem to fulfill the basic definition of a manifesto. The Fama Fraternitatis outlines the origins of the *Fraternity of the Rosy Cross,* while the Confessio Fraternitatis declares its intentions and ideals.

We will go into a thorough synopsis and analysis of each of the Rosicrucian source works in the following chapter, but for now, we can say that both texts superficially appear to be public declarations, but closer examination reveals their allegorical nature. This challenges their classification as straightforward manifestoes, as their primary aim was not so much to communicate practical goals, or recruit members, but to provoke thought, inspire spiritual reflection, and critique contemporary society.

A key complication arises from the fact that there is no concrete evidence to suggest the existence of a physical Fraternity of the Rosy Cross at the time these documents were written. The Fraternity of the Rosy Cross, as depicted in the texts, seems to function more as a metaphorical ideal rather than a literal organisation. As we will soon see, individuals associated with the preparation and distribution of the source works often declined to claim actual membership in the fraternity.

To these authors, becoming a Rosicrucian was likely seen as an aspiration rather than a formal affiliation. This distinction was no doubt observed nearly three centuries later by Dr. Franz Hartmann, who captures this perspective succinctly when he states,

> *To call a person a Rosicrucian does not make him one, nor does the act of calling a person a Christian make him a Christ. The real Rosicrucian or Mason cannot be made; he must grow to be one by the expansion and unfoldment of the divine power within his own heart. The inattention to this truth is the cause that many churches and secret societies are far from being that which their names express.* (Hartmann F. M., 1888)

If the Rosicrucian Brotherhood exists primarily as an allegorical construct, can their writings be accurately considered as manifestoes in the traditional sense? The absence of the term *manifesto* from the title pages of the Fama Fraternitatis, Confessio Fraternitatis, and the Chemical Wedding of Christian Rosenkreuz in the Year 1459 is also noteworthy here. This is another piece of evidence that demonstrates that the authors may not have intended these works to serve as manifestoes, in the traditional sense. The Rosicrucian foundational texts certainly appear to provide more of a philosophical discourse than any direct proclamation. While the works might superficially align with the concept of a manifesto, their allegorical depth and symbolic intent extend far beyond this definition.

Perhaps then, we might consider that the Rosicrucian source works have been mischaracterised as manifestoes. But if we reject this definition, what should we call them instead?

One plausible argument is that these works might be better defined as *treatises*. According to Merriam-Webster, a treatise is, "*a systematic exposition or argument in writing including a methodical discussion of the facts and principles involved and conclusions reached*" (Merriam-Webster, 2024).

Certainly, both the Fama Fraternitatis and the Confessio Fraternitatis align with this definition to some extent. They do present systematic arguments and ideas addressing religion, science, and philosophy. They also include reflections on humanity's place in the cosmos and an esoteric interpretation of the natural world; including humanity's place within it. However, their multilayered symbolism, riddles, and allegorical storytelling suggest they are more than simply structured arguments or philosophical discourses. And The Chemical Wedding of Christian Rosenkreuz in the Year 1459 presents as nothing of the sort and would naturally require its own classification.

But there is one definition that is both broad enough to encompass the complete Rosicrucian trilogy and additional Rosicrucian texts of this era as well as being specific enough to be a useful description. To this end, I would suggest that these works simply be considered as *allegories*. Turning to Merriam-Webster once again, an allegory is defined as, *"the expression of truths or generalizations about human existence by means of symbolic fictional figures and their actions"* (Merriam-Webster, 2024). It has not been uncommon to consider The Chemical Wedding of Christian Rosenkreuz in the Year 1459 as an allegory. But the other two works of the trilogy have perhaps evaded this definition due to the way that they have presented themselves as literal proclamations. However, as we will now see in the forthcoming synopses and analyses, these are not proclamations in a literal sense, but primarily allegorical narratives crafted to explore the mysteries of nature and the universe.

One final point, in my commentaries I have relied upon *The Rosicrucian Trilogy: The Three Original Rosicrucian Publications in new translations* (2016) by Godwin, McIntosh, & McIntosh and published by Red Wheel/Weiser, which I believe to be the best translations yet available.

FAMA FRATERNITATIS

The first of the Rosicrucian source works was published in Kassel, Germany in 1614[1] under the full title of *General Reformation of the whole wide world besides the Fama Fraternitatis or Brotherhood of the Highly Praiseworthy Order of the R. C. To the heads, estates and scholars of Europe* (German: *Allgemeine und General Reformation der ganzen weiten Welt beneben der Fama Fraternitatis Oder Brüderschafft des Hochlöblichen Ordens des R. C. An die Häupter, Stände und Gelehrten Europae*). Hereafter referred to as *Fama Fraternitatis*[2]. Whilst there has been debate about which documents should be considered as part of the canon of the Rosicrucian source works, there has been mostly universal agreement that this document be included.

The Fama Fraternitatis presents the story of a poor German monk of noble birth known as Christian Rosenkreuz. The Fama is where we get the bulk of the *biographical* information related to Christian Rosenkreuz. In this text we learn about his family, childhood, studies, and travels. We also learn about the formation of the *Fraternity of*

---

[1] Handwritten copies were already in circulation from at least 1610, but the first published copy appeared in 1614.
[2] Over the centuries, several versions have appeared in various languages. Christopher McIntosh has put together perhaps the most complete and modern translation based upon a comprehensive cross-analysis of various versions. This can be found in The Rosicrucian Trilogy by Godwin, J., McIntosh, C., & McIntosh, D. P.

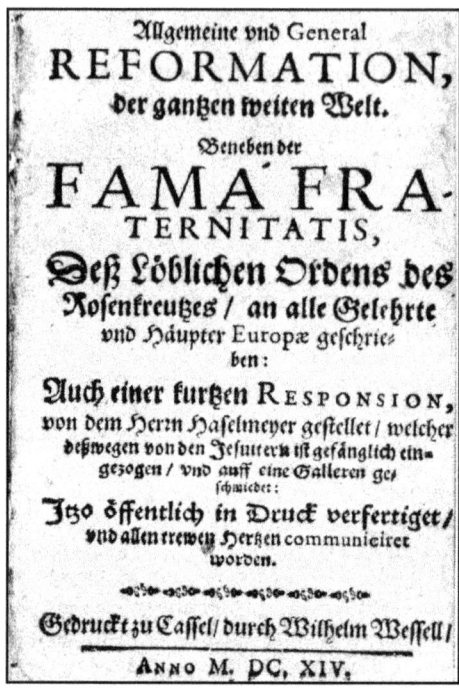

The title page of the original publication of the Fama Fraternitatis showing its complete title indicating its target audience.

the Rosy Cross and its governing rules. The text then culminates in the discovery of his tomb which is filled with enough symbolic detail to keep esotericists and Rosicrucian philosophers thinking and discussing its rich symbolism for centuries to come. The text is certainly a spiritual allegory and the likelihood of Christian Rosenkreuz having been a historical figure is not only unlikely, but his biography is contradicted within the foundational Rosicrucian texts themselves (although, I would think it foolish to rule out a historical persona entirely).

At the core of the Fama Fraternitatis, we find a story, quite simple in its details, but whose message appears to have struck just the right sympathetic chord to elicit a response from the audience to whom it was intended. This story has been related in detail in multiple commentaries, some of which have strayed from the actual document itself. Some authors have sought to overlay their own Kabbalistic, numerological, alchemical, or personal convictions on top of the narrative, sometimes to prove its primordial truth, but more often to bolster support for their own doctrinal systems.

In my own sincere efforts to not lead the reader astray from the original narrative, I will commence with a brief summary of the story that can be objectively supported from the foundational document from which the synopsis is drawn.

However, it is recommended that you seek out a copy of the Fama Fraternitatis should you wish to read the source in its entirety. To this end, I thoroughly recommend the version presented in *The Rosicrucian Trilogy* (2016) by Godwin, McIntosh, & McIntosh.

As an additional remark, it is important to note that the name of the protagonist in the story does differ throughout the foundational Rosicrucian documents. For the sake of consistency, I will be using, *Christian Rosenkreuz*. However, keep in mind that neither the Fama Fraternitatis nor the Confessio Fraternitatis use the name Christian Rosenkreuz but rather variations such as *CR, CRC, Father Christian*, etc. There is indeed a valid discussion in Rosicrucian academia about whether Christian Rosenkreuz and the mentioned variations of CR/CRC/Father Christian are representative of two different personas. This author maintains that in nearly all circumstances, the names can (and should) be considered synonymous.

The Story of Christian Rosenkreuz

At the age of five, a poor boy of noble birth, Christian Rosenkreuz was placed in the care of a monastery in Germany. Whilst in his youth he became acquainted with both Greek and Latin. By his *own fervent plea* he and a companion would embark on a pilgrimage to the Holy Sepulchre in Jerusalem. On the way to Jerusalem, they are detained in Cyprus where his companion would pass away following a brief illness. Undeterred, Christian continues on when he himself is detained in Damascus with an illness of his own. Whilst here, he learns of a group of wise men who live in a faraway land called *Damcar*[3]. These wise men apparently knew all of the secrets of the Nature. The thought of making their acquaintance impressed our protagonist so much, that no longer was his desire to pilgrimage to Jerusalem, but to the East to find these wise men.

3   In some early versions of Fama Fraternitatis, this city was referred to as *Dhamar*. It is likely that Damcar was a mistake on the part of an early copiest that continued to be repeated in subsequent versions and translations. Dhamar is a city in Yemen known during this period as a centre of Islamic studies and sciences.

At the age of sixteen, he would eventually find these men, who had long been expecting him and even knew his name. They taught him all manner of knowledge which had been hitherto hidden away from man. The wise men entrusted to Christian their sacred book; the *Book M*. Over the course of three years, Christian would study with these wise men and translate the Book M from Arabic into Latin. He would then continue on his return journey back to Europe, hoping to instruct the leaders of Europe with the new information he had received, in the hopes of bringing about a new reformation; a return to a true Christianity.

On his way back to Europe, Christian would make several more stops, acquiring new skills and knowledge along the way. His next stop would be in Egypt where he would study the flora and fauna. Then he would then sail the Mediterranean towards his next stop in Fez, Morocco. The people of Fez were said to be gifted in mathematics, physics, magic, and Kabbalah. However, their magic was *not altogether pure* and their Kabbalah had been *tainted by their religion*. Whilst here, he also made acquaintance with the *Elementary Inhabitants* who revealed to him *much of what they knew, just as we Germans could do among ourselves if we had sufficient unity and a passionate and earnest desire to search* (for further discussion on *Elemental creatures* and their importance to the Rosicrucian tradition, see the chapter *Off with the Fairies: Rosicrucian didactic literature*).

By the time Christian arrives back in Europe, he is no longer a boy, but a grown man. Christian seeks out the religious leaders to instruct them with all that he has learned. Despite acknowledging his genius, the religious leaders of Europe were quick to dismiss him. Being in a position of authority and power, there was no need to acquiesce the status quo to a new world order, seemingly unaffected by the turmoil present in the society which Christian so earnestly wished to relieve.

Undeterred, Christian would return to his homeland, where he would gather some disciples around himself. Together, they established the very first Rosicrucian Order; *The Fraternity of the Rosy Cross.*

The Fraternity of the Rosy Cross had six governing rules.

1. That none of them should profess any other thing than to cure the sick, and that gratis;

2. None of the posterity should be constrained to wear one kind of habit, but to follow the custom of the country;

3. Every year, upon the Day C., they would meet together at the house Sancti Spiritus, or write the cause of their absence;

4. Every Brother should seek a worthy person to succeed him after his death;

5. The word CR should be their seal, mark, and character;

6. The Fraternity should remain secret for one hundred years.

This Rosicrucian brotherhood would operate in secret. Amongst their plans, they hoped to bring about a new Christian reformation that proclaimed a return to a true Adamic Christian wisdom. This coming new age was imminent, and was being foretold not only by prophecy, but was being heralded by signs present in the night sky as well as signalled by the political and religious events being observed throughout Europe. The Rosicrucian Brotherhood were simply acting as assistants to this effort of a *"general divine and human reformation* (Godwin, McIntosh, & McIntosh, 2016, p. 30)" by providing their "*hidden aid to the good cause* (Godwin, McIntosh, & McIntosh, 2016, p. 30)". Whilst the Rosicrucian brotherhood as a group were operating in secrecy, they were actively preparing for a future moment when they would reveal themselves to the world to help usher in a new era.

Christian Rosenkreuz would eventually die in 1484 at the age of 106. The details of the illustrious founder and his location were kept secret from the members by the elders of the Fraternity. Three generations after Christian Rosenkreuz's death, in 1604, a member of the Fraternity would unwittingly stumble upon a hidden door whilst performing some renovations on the house Sancti Spiritus. Upon opening the door, he would discover the vault (or tomb) of their illustrious founder along with all of the Rosicrucian secrets.

The vault is a meticulously designed repository of Rosicrucian knowledge intended to preserve the brotherhood's teachings as well as guide future generations. Even if the original brotherhood were to disappear, it could be reconstituted using the knowledge contained in the vault alone. It is heptagonal in shape and illumined by its own internal sun. The vault is divided into three sections: *the upper* (illuminated by its own inner sun), *the middle* (containing chests in the wall filled with various scientific and artistic instruments), and *the floor* (divided into multiple triangles which described the rulership and power of the base regent).

In the centre of the vault was a round altar covered with a brass plate bearing the inscription: "*A.C.R.C. This compendium of the universe I made during my lifetime as a tomb for myself* (Godwin, McIntosh, & McIntosh, 2016, p. 27)." Beneath the altar lay the body of Christian Rosenkreuz, remarkably *undamaged and completely undecayed*. In his hands was a book, written on gold parchment, called the *Book T*, which was the one of the most important treasures of the brotherhood, second only to the Bible.

The Fama Fraternitatis closes with an appeal for readers to relay their responses, and although the brotherhood would not announce their identities, they would take care to read the opinions of those who took the time to respond, no matter the language employed by the writer.

Analysis of the Christian Rosenkreuz story

It is common to refer to the Fama Fraternitatis and Confessio Fraternitatis as *manifestoes;* public declarations of the Fraternity of the Rosy Cross. Whilst it is true that these documents were publicly printed and circulated, they were never actually referred to as *manifestoes* in their original German. In fact, the foundational Rosicrucian documents can be observed to have a much broader purpose then simply a public declaration. For instance, the Fama Fraternitatis acted as a social critique, commenting upon various aspects of society, including religious institutions, political structures, and established scientific practices. It also acted as an open invitation to the learned of Europe to join with them and offer their assistance for the advancement of humanity.

But if we keep in mind that much of the content contained within the Fama Fraternitatis and Confessio Fraternitatis are of an esoteric nature, we might also conclude that they serve as a spiritual allegory. Rather than recruiting members in a literal sense, these texts aimed to connect with individuals who resonated with its ideals on a personal philosophical level. Its depiction of a secret brotherhood dedicated to learning and societal improvement were useful ways to plant seeds of change, encouraging readers to *join* this *fraternity* in spirit, even if not in a formal sense. The text speaks to those who, like Christian Rosenkreuz, seek hidden knowledge.

As such, the real value that the foundational Rosicrucian texts can provide to us today comes from their contemplation. Whilst the pages that follow elucidate some meaning behind the Fama Fraternitatis let me be clear that I do not ask that readers simply supplant existing conclusions with my own, but rather use the ideas presented as seeds for your own contemplation and meditation.

The journey of Christian Rosenkreuz can be separated into three distinct sections: *The Aspirant, The Initiate,* and *The Adept.*

The Aspirant

The opening lines of the Fama Fraternitatis tell us that young Christian was born poor but of noble heritage. While it is technically possible to be of nobility and live in poverty, these two conditions often exist in opposition. Nobility is typically associated with wealth and status. Humanity finds itself in a similar predicament; we are of noble birth as we possess a divine spark, yet we are seemingly disconnected from our divine source, in a sort of spiritual poverty. Christian Rosenkreuz is more than an archetype in this narrative. He is an evolving character. Despite his divine pre-condition, he is not outwardly perfect but must work to refine his character; remove the dross to allow his inner divine nature to shine forth.

Christian Rosenkreuz embarks on a journey to the East in search of spiritual knowledge. During this journey, the Aspirant discovers his true nature, deepest desires, and life's purpose, shedding unnecessary aspects of himself along the way. He learns many things, but the ultimate spiritual knowledge he seeks is eventually found and is represented by the Book M. The Fama Fraternitatis is filled with many acronyms and riddles for us to solve. Without any clear advice from the authors, many of these can only be speculated upon. Some commentators have suggested that the Book M might be short for *Book of the World* (Latin: *Liber Mundi*). By viewing the Book M as the Book of the World, it suggests that the wisdom Christian Rosenkreuz sought and ultimately found was not confined to esoteric writings alone but extended to the understanding of the natural world and the cosmos. This perspective proposes the universe as a living, breathing *manuscript* of divine truth; revealing the interconnectedness between Man, Nature, and God. And whilst it may not be possible to state with certainty that the Book M means Book of the World, it would appear to be quite an apt proposal, given the context of how it is received and used throughout the narrative.

The Initiate

By the time Christian leaves Damcar/Dhamar, he is no longer a boy, but rather a young adult. An *Initiate*. As in every initiation, the initiate must return to the world. And so, it is with Christian. But the world no longer seems the same. The people are sick and in need of healing. Of course, the world is not truly different...the Initiate is. Like many initiates of the mysteries throughout history, Christian makes a stop in Egypt where he learns about the *Flora and Fauna*, suggesting that he is now at liberty to utilise the wisdom contained in the Book M to investigate the hidden mysteries of Nature; a *practical* application of the *theoretical* knowledge which he has recently acquired. Continuing on with his exploration of Nature, Christian continues on to Fez where he learns about the *Elementary Inhabitants*. This is a curious admission in the text and would have been one of the few hints to potential readers regarding the underlying values held by the anonymous author/s. Christian's study of the subtle forces and intelligences that govern the natural world is certainly in keeping with his continuing practical application of the Book M into the hidden mysteries of Nature, but it also indicates the Paracelsian values of the writers. In the Paracelsian worldview, these Elemental creatures, whilst not human, do have some human-like attributes and are able to appear to us and reveal to us the hidden Mysteries of Nature. But they could also be mischievous and even dangerous. Working with such forces requires someone initiated into a certain knowledge and capability.

But what about their magic being not *altogether pure* and their Kabbalah having been *tainted by their religion*? To answer this question, we must first come to an understanding about what would be an *untainted* Kabbalistic doctrine versus a *tainted* doctrine; at least according to the intended meaning of the author/s. However, I will state upfront that this analysis will likely not be appreciated by some readers, especially those that have a very well-established Kabbalistic understanding. In fact, it would require us to assume that the Kabbalah as presented by a myriad of Rosicrucian societies is not altogether the same as the Kabbalah that was respected by the author/s of the Fama Fraternitatis. However, this need not be a controversial opinion, but like many contemporary fields of study, the meaning has drifted over time.

Some Rosicrucian commentators have suggested that the use of Kabbalah in Fez may have been overly syncretic, incorporating aspects of Islamic cosmology and practices that conflicted with the Christian worldview of the Rosicrucian authors. While this explanation aligns with the critical comments on Islam contained in the Confessio Fraternitatis, I wonder how the author/s would perceive the Kabbalistic doctrines present in more recent, post-*Hermetic Order of the Golden Dawn* Rosicrucian organisations.

The Kabbalah of this period is best understood through the lens of traditional Rosicrucian philosophy. This Kabbalah is much more simple and differs markedly from later Hermetic reinterpretations, which are thick with infinite correspondences, endless gematria, and sprawling syncretic scaffolding. As regards to the mechanics and practicality of this Kabbalah, it is usually used as a substitute for what we might term today as esoteric science or metaphysics. In this respect, I suspect that they would prefer a more simple Neoplatonic cosmology focused upon the emanation of creation from Unity and only occasionally inferring a pathway of return. This streamlined and unified approach might have resonated more with the original Rosicrucian world vision.

Christian eventually returns to his homeland, the residents of whom he tries to heal; both spiritually and physically. At first, he tries in vain for not everybody is ready to pursue this path. The recently initiated Christian surrounds himself with a small group of disciples to assist him in the Great Work of *healing* the world. This therapeutic work is not necessarily confined to physical healing but is broader in scope to encompass healing that divide which exists between who we appear to be and who we actually are; that is, healing the divide between our inner and outer self. Having attained the Philosopher's Stone, it is now Christian's responsibility to assist others in realising their own true Divine state.

The Adept

At this stage of the journey, Christian Rosenkreuz has transitioned fully into the archetype of the *Adept*, embodying mastery over the spiritual, philosophical, and natural sciences he has painstakingly studied and integrated. Curiously, it is here that the Fama Fraternitatis begins to refer to him as *Father Christian*, perhaps reflecting the role he assumes as a spiritual teacher, guide, and guardian of wisdom for the fledgling Rosicrucian fraternity.

However, Father Christian's new role is not without challenges, as the ultimate completion of his mission requires a profound act of renunciation: his death to the world.

This sacrificial act is not a final end. It is an act of transmutation. A further rarification of the alchemical process that ascends beyond the need of a physical body. Christian's death represents the ultimate purification and sublimation of matter into spirit. His undecayed body within the vault serves to emphasise that this death is not one of corruption or decay but one of transcendence. It serves to illustrate the Rosicrucian ideal: the preservation of divine wisdom and the eternal nature of the soul. The vault itself mirrors the human body as a vessel for the divine spark. Christian Rosenkreuz, now the Adept, leaves behind a legacy not of personal glorification but of Service.

Through this final transformation, Father Christian entrusts the continuation of his mission to those who come after him. The responsibility shifts from the individual to the collective, from the personal enlightenment of Christian Rosenkreuz to the communal work of the fraternity and its adherents. The Adept understands that while individual achievement is necessary, it is only through collective effort that the Great Work can reach its fullest expression.

The lesson from the Adept is clear: enlightenment and mastery are not endpoints but responsibilities. To house a divine spark is not enough; we must nurture and share it. Just as The Philosopher's Stone transmutes that which it comes into contact.

The path of the Adept reminds us that the Great Work is not only the refining of the self but also the uplifting of others, an eternal and shared quest to bridge the human and the divine into a living expression: *The R+C*.

The Vault of C.R.C.

The Vault of Christian Rosenkreuz is perhaps one of the better-known residual themes extant in contemporary Rosicrucian traditions that has been sourced from the Fama Fraternitatis. Some Rosicrucian organisations have even utilised this space as an initiatory space. For example, both the *Societas Rosicruciana* and *Hermetic Order of the Golden Dawn* utilise the Vault of C.R.C. as the location of their Second Order workings. However, in other Rosicrucian organisations, the vault is more symbolic representing a mirror of our own *inner temple*, urging us to explore, protect, and ultimately reveal the divine mysteries within ourselves. Like with the previous section, my analysis of the Vault of Christian Rosenkreuz will not be limited to any particular tradition. Rather, I will attempt to provide a more universal understanding. Unfortunately, this may mean that I will naturally leave out some minor details, that whilst important within a specific tradition, may be trivial in the greater Rosicrucian tradition which this book aims to serve.

The author/s of the Fama Fraternitatis describe the Vault as a *compendium of the universe* and a *miniature world, corresponding in all motions to the greater one*. As such, the Vault of Christian Rosenkreuz, represents the microcosm of the Cosmos. Its tripartite structure- the *Upper*, the *Middle*, and the *Lower*- illustrates the link between the divine, psychic, and earthly realms, providing insights for those who seek to comprehend the mysteries within. In such a way, it may be viewed like a Mandala; a visual representation of the cosmos with a universal ontology.

Therefore, following the tripartite structure of the vault, we will analyse it by looking at each part individually.

The Upper

The Fama describes the roof of the vault as being illuminated by an inner sun and states,

> *Of the ceiling you will not hear anything more from us at present, save that it was divided by triangles running from the bright centre toward the seven sides. But what was inside should rather be seen by your own eyes, rather than be received by our description.* (Godwin, McIntosh, & McIntosh, 2016, p. 27)

The refusal to describe the ceiling in detail underscores the limitations of language in conveying spiritual truths. We are indeed dealing with an allegorical space. It is beyond the description of words. The vault's roof becomes a metaphor for the transcendent nature of divine knowledge; something that must be personally experienced rather than intellectually dissected. It resonates with the initiation rites of various esoteric traditions, where the seeker is temporarily deprived of sight (or understanding) to encourage the awakening of an inner perception. Just as a Masonic initiate is hoodwinked so that his *heart may conceive before his eyes may be permitted to discover*.

We also see a curious similarity between the vault and an astrological horoscope. An astrological horoscope positions the Sun in the centre and shows the Sun's position relative to other heavenly bodies, most notably, the seven classical planets and the twelve signs of the Zodiac. In astrology, the relative positions of the bodies are mapped and the angles between the bodies are noted. In astrology, these angles are usually called *aspects*. Some aspects may be considered harmonious, and others may be considered opposing. We need not get into a detailed study of astrology, other than to note that a harmonious and beneficial relationship between two-bodies can be considered when the angle between them is approximately 120°, or a third part of a circle, and is thus called a *trine*. For our purposes in analysing the Vault of Christian Rosenkreuz, we only need to take note that the Sun being divided into seven triangles extending towards the seven sides is alluding to the perfect balance that exists between the microcosm and the macrocosm. Essentially, if this were a tomb, it would be the final resting place of an individual who represents the embodiment of perfection.

The Middle

Following the astrological correspondences above, it might be natural to consider that the seven sides might allude to the seven classical planets. And whilst this would not be an incorrect assessment, it would be limited. We should consider that the writer/s of the Fama Fraternitatis were quite knowledgeable in many fields of art and science and were trying to appeal to a broad audience. As such, whilst they do refer to the classical planets, the scope should be widened to encompass a broader appreciation. Also, this is a holistic space, so even those correspondences that the author/s may not have been familiar with, whilst not being anticipated, may still be very worthy for our consideration. For example, we could even extend this meaning to encompass the seven major psychic centres of the human body.

The middle section of the vault is a psychic space that bridges the earthly and the divine, symbolising the role of human life as the intermediary between the material and spiritual realms. This central area serves as a metaphor for our dual-nature; poised between heaven and earth we are truly dwellers between two worlds. It calls upon us to explore and understand the connections between our physical reality and our spiritual aspirations.

This is a place where the boundaries between that which is known and that which is unknown are blurred, thus encouraging contemplation and introspection. In this space, we can use reason and intuition to help us reveal the Hidden Mysteries of Nature and Science.

Within the chests contained in the walls we find the speculative tools of all science and art. Microscopes and looking glasses are the speculative tools for us to reflect and look within to discover our true nature. Likewise, musical instruments and bells are the speculative tools by which we may be permitted to hear the whisperings of Self, residing deep within our being.

Similarly, within the captivating Hermetic mandala-like illustrations conceived by the Rosicrucian philosopher Robert Fludd, one can discern the Liberal Arts and Sciences positioned at the crossroads of the Microcosm and Macrocosm.

The Floor

The floor was divided into multiple triangles and described the rulership and power of the base regent. Only those who feared God could read this to obtain the heavenly antidote. The author/s of the Confessio Fraternitatis likewise urge the reader to study the Book of Nature as being essential to revealing the *Word of God*[4]. Similarly, the physician Paracelsus (who was held in high regard by the Rosicrucian source work authors) stated that all things expressed in some way a unique signature by which to appreciate their essential nature (Waite A. E., 1894, pp. 171-194). Therefore, the Vault of Christian Rosenkreuz contains the signature by which could be obtained the knowledge of health (in the broadest sense). Or as the Fama Fraternitatis calls it, the *Heavenly Antidote*.

The Rosicrucian philosopher is not a hermit. Far from advocating escapism, the Rosicrucian tradition emphasises active

---

4 "*The Book of Nature is opened wide before the eyes of all, though few can either read or understand it*" (Confessio Fraternitatis- Reason Twenty-Two).

participation in the world. The tools and signatures within the vault serve as reminders that the philosopher's duty is to heal and transform, bridging the divide between humanity and its divine origin. The floor represents the practical application of the divine knowledge we have gained in our journey.

In its entirety, the vault serves as both a sanctuary and a catalyst for spiritual evolution, a timeless reminder of humanity's potential to bridge the gap between earth and heaven.

Perhaps it is for this reason that the Fama Fraternitatis states,

> ...were the whole Order or Brotherhood to perish, it would be possible, even after many centuries, to reconstitute it from this unique vault. (Godwin, McIntosh, & McIntosh, 2016, p. 28)

The case for a historical C.R.C.

Whilst most commentators of the Rosicrucian tradition have associated C.R.C. as an allegorical character, this is not universally agreed upon. In fact, some commentators have speculated that some of the details of C.R.C. and his journey may actually represent historical events, locations, and people.

Rudolf Steiner, the founder of Anthroposophy and commentator on Rosicrucianism spoke on several occasions about Christian Rosenkreuz being both a *historical* individual and a *spiritual* archetype. He asserts that Christian Rosenkreuz was a real person who lived in the thirteenth century and was chosen to undergo an advanced initiation. This initiation was not through any particular school but instead was guided by twelve advanced spiritual beings who represented the highest wisdom of humanity. This process transformed him into a vessel of cosmic wisdom, making him the bearer of a renewed form of esoteric Christianity that would shape the future of human spiritual evolution.

Steiner emphasises that Rosenkreuz's initiation served a broader purpose. He became a kind of spiritual beacon whose influence would guide the development of Western esotericism and certain individuals who resonated with the stream or tradition which he represented. This role continued beyond his lifetime through the Rosicrucian movement, which Steiner describes as an ongoing spiritual impulse rather than a fixed institution, suggesting that Rosenkreuz's presence can still be felt by those who attune themselves to this current of wisdom.

At the same time, Steiner portrays Christian Rosenkreuz as an archetype or ideal, representing a model of human spiritual attainment. He argues that his being and teachings were meant to prepare humanity for the modern age, in which individuals would seek knowledge through direct inner experience rather than reliance on external authorities (Steiner, 1912). Thus, according to Steiner, while Rosenkreuz was a historical figure, he also represents an ongoing living spiritual presence.

Within contemporary Rosicrucian organisations, speculation as to the historicity of C.R.C. has also extended to his tomb. One curious theory as to a physical location for the Tomb of C.R.C. had been proposed by A.M.O.R.C., but was quickly forgotten. Nevertheless, there is indeed some merit to the theory that is worthwhile exploring.

In July 1937, a periodical of A.M.O.R.C. called the Rosicrucian Digest published an article announcing *'A very wonderful discovery'* having been made in Germany. This discovery was said to be none other than the possible site of the Tomb of Christian Rosenkreuz. This announcement was accompanied by an illustration of a strange looking natural rock formation with several man-made carved out structures.

Only a small amount of information was provided in the Rosicrucian Digest about this discovery.

Accompanying the image, we find the description,

> *Has the mythical tomb of Christian Rosenkreuz become an established fact? Is the above illustration the actual tomb of the legendary character, Christian Rosenkreuz?* (The Rosicrucian Digest, 1937)

In short, the article announces that some German investigators had been doing some excavations on a site when they located the remains of a Temple that had been carved into the side of a mountain. Inside was to be found the relics of a stone coffin that had at one stage been sealed inside a cave.

Some of the remaining relics as well symbolical figures carved into the rockface were identified and were said by the author to be recognisable to Rosicrucian students who determined that this was a Rosicrucian site, possibly even the Tomb of Christian Rosenkreuz itself.

However, this article closes by stating,

For very excellent reasons we cannot reveal at the present time the precise location of this intensely interesting discovery. (The Rosicrucian Digest, 1937)

What would it have been like to be a sincere Rosicrucian initiate in 1937, being told this cryptic information, and then having nothing to follow up? What a cliffhanger!?

As this narrative was not to be continued in later editions of A.M.O.R.C. periodicals nor in any A.M.O.R.C. teaching materials, you could be forgiven for thinking that this site and story was all a work of fancy. Christian Rosenkreuz is *generally* regarded as an allegory by the organisation. But there is a little more to this story than at first meets the eye. And it has the potential to shift the perspective of the Fama Fraternitatis narrative as a work of allegorical fiction.

Firstly, the illustration that was used was not actually a work of imagination but was of a real archaeological site located in North Rhine-Westphalia, Germany (near to the Teutoburg Forest). This site is called, Externsteine. Between 1881-1933, the site had undergone several excavations.

Today, researchers have concluded that the Externsteine site had been occupied by humans during several distinct periods, the first of which is dated to at least the eleventh century. Primarily, it would appear that this site had been one of religious significance, evidenced by religious bas reliefs. There are also some celestial correspondences, with one section being aligned to the rising sun of the Summer Solstice. It was perhaps due to this solar arrangement as well as the site being primarily carved out of a mountainside that led one lay researcher to dub the site a *Germanic Stonehenge*. In 1932, the Externsteine site underwent a third excavation, and it was likely during this excavation period that the site caught the attention of an A.M.O.R.C. officer in Germany.

An image provided in an A.M.O.R.C. publication purporting to show the location of the Tomb of Christian Rosenkreuz.

Externsteine as it appears today.

Unfortunately, however, there were other powers in Germany at the time who enjoyed glorified tales of an exotic history. In 1933 we find further investigations being overseen by the *Third Reich* under the direct guidance of *Heinrich Himmler* who was serving as President of the *Externsteine Foundation* where the site was studied in an attempt to locate anything of value to German folklore and to no doubt strengthen the Nazi claim to an ancient prehistory. As such, much of the research of this period was less of an attempt at objective research and more of an attempt to direct greater support towards Nazi ideology. As such, it is perhaps not surprising that A.M.O.R.C. later distanced themselves from the claims made in this Rosicrucian Digest article.

A.M.O.R.C. likely chose to distance itself from the claims made in the 1937 Rosicrucian Digest article due to the complex historical and political context surrounding the Externsteine site. By the mid-1930s, the site had become entangled with Nazi-era myth-making which sought to appropriate the site for ideological purposes. Any association with Externsteine risked being misinterpreted or co-opted for purposes contrary to A.M.O.R.C.'s principles. Additionally, as A.M.O.R.C. traditionally treated C.R.C. as a figure primarily of allegorical value, endorsing the discovery of a supposed physical tomb might have also contradicted its established teachings. Rather than engage in a potentially controversial narrative, one that could be seen as speculative at best and politically sensitive at worst, A.M.O.R.C. likely found it prudent to simply let the story fade into obscurity.

Nevertheless, despite the ideological scrutiny endured during the Nazi-era, the Externsteine site boasts a fascinating history; one that is worth investigation from researchers interested in the history of the Rosicrucian tradition.

One noteworthy chapter in the life of the Externsteine site unfolds in 1469 when it served as a Christian hermitage, aligning its historical timeline with the later years of the protagonist featured in the Fama Fraternitatis. Remarkably, during this epoch, there are indications that the Externsteine site may have functioned as a potential pilgrimage location for Christian devotees who, unable to embark on the arduous journey to Jerusalem, sought spiritual fulfillment closer to home. It is intriguing to note that in the Fama Fraternitatis, C.R.C. initially envisioned his pilgrimage leading him to the Holy Sepulchre. Later, he redirected his quest, focusing on uncovering the enigmatic wise men of Dhamar/Damcar and their mysterious sacred book.

Today, the Externsteine site is the centre of Neo-Pagan Walpurgis pilgrimage.

Curiously, several hours west of Externsteine we have another local legend which shares some parallels to the legend of C.R.C. According to German folklore, Emperor Frederick Barbarossa did not die in the Third Crusade but instead retreated into a subterranean chamber beneath the Kyffhäuser Mountains, where he remains in a deep slumber. The legend of Kyffhäuser and Emperor Frederick Barbarossa share several thematic similarities with the legend of C.R.C., particularly in the motif of a hidden figure sleeping in a sealed chamber, awaiting the right time to reawaken and restore balance to the world. He is said to sit at a stone table, his red beard growing ever longer, winding around the table. Periodically, he awakens and asks if the ravens still fly over the mountains. If they do, it means his time to return has not yet come. One day, according to local German folklore, when the world is in great need, he will rise and lead Germany into a golden age (Suedharz-Kyffhaeuser.de, 2021). Whilst there is no known connection between the narratives of Barbarossa and Rosenkreuz, the similarities between the two at least indicate the popularity of such legends of folklore amongst the local populace and provides us with another explanation as to why the legend of the Fraternity of the Rosy Cross was so persuasive.

Another case for a historical C.R.C. that gained traction in some European and North American Rosicrucian circles involves an individual by the name of Christian von Germelshausen. This case was popularised by *Gary Lee Stewart*, the Imperator of the *Confraternity of the Rose + Cross* (C.R+C.). This story is sourced from the works of French writer Maurice Magre who first discusses the Christian von Germelshausen narrative in his work *Magician, Seers, and Mystics*.

The narrative relates that a young boy, Christian von Germelshausen, was the last surviving member of the noble Germelshausen family following the Albigensien crusade in the Languedoc region in southern France. The young boy was carried away from the family's burning castle by a monk and they sought refuge in a local monastery (Magre, 1932, p. 114). From here, the young von Germelshausen would participate in a journey very similar to that of C.R.C. in the Fama Fraternitatis. In fact, many of the events, locations, interactions are described exactly as from the Fama Fraternitatis. Such a high level of correspondence between the characters of C.R.C. and von Germelshausen would be remarkable, if it were not for that fact that the von Germelshausen narrative appears to be sourced purely from Magre's book and does not seem to have any basis in historical reality. Maurice Magre's book is a lovely read, but it must be kept in mind that it does provide a more romantic legendary account of the magicians, seers, and mystics which it discusses.

In time, it is likely that additional historical figures will be discovered whose lives loosely conform to the events and settings described in the Fama Fraternitatis. We will also likely discover parallels between the C.R.C. narrative and certain mythic events described in German and northern European folklore. Some scholars have already noted a celestial basis to much of this folklore (Johnsen, 2014) (Volker, 2021), and so an astro-theological foundation for the C.R.C. narrative is certainly possible.

Yet, in pursuing such correspondences, we must guard against fanaticism or the temptation to treat symbolic narratives as literal history. The primary value that Rosicrucian initiates can gain from the story of C.R.C. is not to be found in its historicity, but in the sympathetic chord that this allegory strikes within us to elicit an inner alchemical transmutation. The C.R.C. narrative endures, not just in the past, but within us.

A sculpture of Frederick Barbarossa taken from the Kyffhäuser Monument.

CONFESSIO FRATERNITATIS

*T*he second work of the Rosicrucian Trilogy was published in Kassel, Germany in 1615 under the full title of *The Confession of the Fraternity R.C to the Learned of Europe* (Latin: *Confessio Fraternitatis R.C. ad Eruditos Europae*). Hereafter referred to as the *Confessio Fraternitatis*.

It was actually published with another document, *A brief consideration of the secret philosophy written by St. Philip à Gabella, and now together with the Confession of the Fraternity of R.C. published in Casselli, in the year 1615* (Latin: *Secretioris Philosophiae Consideratio brevis a Philipp à Gabella Philosophiae St. conscripta, et nunc primum una cum Confessione Fraternitatis R.C. in lucem edita Cassellis. Anno post natum Christum MDCXV)* often shortened to simply, the *Consideratio Brevis*.

Despite its name, the *Consideratio Brevis* actually makes up the bulk of the complete book, being fifty-four pages of the complete sixty-seven page compilation. The Consideratio Brevis borrows liberally from an important work of the English alchemist John Dee; *Monas Hieroglyphica*. In fact, this will not be the only inspiration taken from John Dee within the Rosicrucian source works as we will see again in the next chapter regarding *The Chemical Wedding of Christian Rosenkreuz of the Year 1459*.

Few copies of the original Latin edition of the Confessio Fraternitatis exist. As a result, many of English translations of this work have been based upon a slightly flawed German version published in 1652. This 1652 version is often referred to as the *Vaughan Version,* named after the Welsh philosopher-alchemist Thomas Vaughan (who often used the pseudonym Eugenius Philalethes). However, it is not actually known if Thomas Vaughan was ever responsible for this translation, or if this was a case of someone using his name. In any case, the name has stuck.

Title page of the combined, Secretioris Philosophiae Consideratio brevis a Philipp à Gabella Philosophiae St. conscripta, et nunc primum una cum Confessione Fraternitatis R.C. in lucem edita Cassellis. Anno post natum Christum MDCXV) often shortened to simply, the Consideratio Brevis from which the Confessio Fraternitatis first appears.

Whilst the Fama Fraternitatis contained the story of C.R.C. and the foundation of the Fraternity of the Rosy Cross, the Confessio Fraternitatis outlines the mission, principles, and worldview of this Rosicrucian brotherhood. It is in this that we learn of the *modus operandi* of the fraternity. We learn of their values, their methods, their hopes and aspirations for mankind.

Over the course of thirty-seven *Reasons* (Latin: *Rationes*) the a philosophical sickness and that the Rosicrucian fraternity have a cure. The Reasons are not explicitly delineated within the text but can be deduced as representing the sentences ending with full-stops or question marks in the original Latin text (following the initial introductory address to the reader).

The Confessio Fraternitatis asserts that a new age was beginning, and it was now time to share the genuine Rosicrucian secrets; but only to the worthy. Or as it states in Reason Thirty-Seven of the Confessio Fraternitatis,

> *But do not disturb our sacred silence with your clamor if you merely want to satisfy your curiosity, enticed by the gleam of gold; nor (as we would emphasize) if you are virtuous now, but could be seduced by unexpected affluence into a soft, lazy, indulgent, and complacent existence. Consider rather that, although there is a medicine that cures all ills, those whom God chooses to disturb, afflict, and punish with diseases are not given this opportunity. Although we could instruct and educate the whole world and free it from endless troubles, we are not made known to anyone unless God permits it. It is impossible for anyone to enjoy our benefits against God's will. He will sooner lose his life in searching for us than attain felicity by finding us.*
> (Godwin, McIntosh, & McIntosh, 2016, p. 51)

In the opening pages, the author/s state that this document is intended to elaborate upon the Fama Fraternitatis,

> *However, for the sake of the learned we have seen fit to explain more fully what was obscure in the Fama...*
> (Godwin, McIntosh, & McIntosh, 2016, p. 43)

The document declares the Rosicrucian fraternity's aim to reform the world through spiritual enlightenment, scientific progress, and moral improvement. It emphasises that their mission is divinely inspired and aligns with God's will, intending to restore humanity to a state more in keeping with the harmony of nature and the Will of the Creator.

The Confessio Fraternitatis doesn't just outline the ideal state that the fraternity hopes to see mankind return to, but also provides the fraternity's opinion on how humanity came to be in its current disastrous state. Therefore, the fraternity also criticises the corruption and greed of contemporary institutions, notably religion, science, the arts, and politics.

Of religion, the Fraternity is quick to criticise multiple institutions. It reprehends the actions of the Catholic church and Islam by stating,

> *We hate the blasphemies of both East and West (i.e. Mohammed and the Pope) against our Lord Jesus, and offer to the Emperor our prayers, our secrets, and our great store of gold.* (Godwin, McIntosh, & McIntosh, 2016, p. 43)

The fraternity portrays the Catholic church as tyrannical and being led by the Pope who is accused of being both morally and spiritually deceptive. They even go so far as to align the Pope with the Antichrist, and they predict that the complete annihilation of the Papacy will soon come about with the coming new age; which the Rosicrucian fraternity heralds.

While the author/s seem aligned with the Lutheran cause, they also critique the Reformation for not going far enough. They call for a more comprehensive reformation, one that addresses not only theological issues but also encompasses science, medicine, and all aspects of human life.

The fraternity regarded science and the arts as branches of philosophy. However, the growing instability of the world has cast these disciplines into darkness, overshadowed by falsehood, obscurity, and servitude.

Alchemy, particularly the transmutation of metals, is seen as secondary to understanding of the Mysteries of Nature; a knowledge that transcends mere material manipulation.

Regarding politics, the author/s outline their preference for a system of government utilised in Damar (Damcar in the Fama Fraternitatis) *who live under a political system far different from the other Arabs.* For in Damar, *the wise predominate, and the king allows them to make other laws*, revealing a preference for a system of government where learned individuals hold political authority, aligning with the broader Renaissance ideal of philosopher-kings.

As such, the fraternity pledge their allegiance to the Holy Roman Emperor, the most powerful secular ruler in Europe at the time, whom they feel is best suited to the role of ruling in the coming new age.

The Confessio Fraternitatis highlights the fraternity's commitment to secrecy, stating that they operate anonymously to avoid persecution and to focus on their work without external interference. They promise eventual public revelation but stress that their wisdom is accessible only to those prepared to receive it.

Central to their philosophy is a balance of spiritual and material pursuits. The Confessio Fraternitatis praises the advancements of science and human understanding but warns against pride and misuse of knowledge. It calls for humility, purity of intention, and dedication to the common good as prerequisites for genuine progress.

The document rejects material wealth, emphasising that the Rosicrucian fraternity seeks no personal gain or worldly power. Instead, their wealth lies in spiritual knowledge and the improvement of mankind.

In summary, the Confessio Fraternitatis is a bold declaration of a new era, where divine wisdom, natural philosophy, and moral virtue converge to uplift humanity. It calls upon the worthy to join their cause and promises profound change for those willing to embrace their cause.

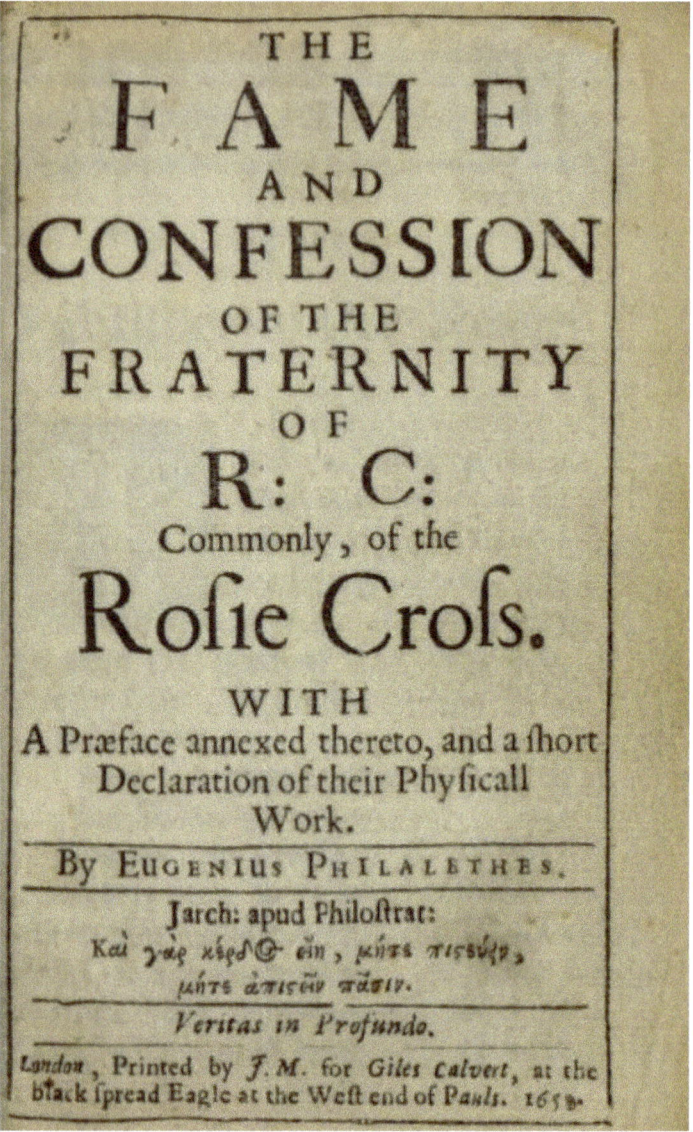

Title page of The fame and confession of the Fraternity of R.C., commonly, of the Rosie Cross and attributed to Eugenius Philalethes. Although the portion of the Confessio Fraternitatis contained therein is a rather poor translation, until recently this was the only copy readily available to many Rosicrucians. As such, these errors carried over into most reproductions of the text provided in the twentieth century.

Analysis of the Confessio Fraternitatis

The Confessio Fraternitatis is the neglected middle-child of the Rosicrucian Trilogy. It does not contain the Indiana Jones-esque treasure hunting spirit incorporated in the Fama Fraternitatis. Nor does it contain the rich alchemical symbolism found within The Chemical Wedding of Christian Rosenkreuz in the Year 1459. However, this text contains perhaps the most comprehensive (if still often enigmatically veiled) insight into the aspirations and hopes for society held by the anonymous authors of the Rosicrucian source works.

The Confessio Fraternitatis preaches a return to Adamic wisdom; a true and original Christianity. The writer/s urge the reader to study both the Bible and Nature (both books considered revealers of the Word by the authors).

In this manifesto, very little information is provided regarding the biographical details of Christian Rosenkreuz. Reason Eight does state that,

> *Concerning the first part, we judge that our father Christian's meditations embrace everything invented, refined, and propagated since the world's beginnings out of human ingenuity, divine revelation, the ministry of spirits or angels, the sagacity of mind, or the experience of daily observation. We reckon that if Almighty God should decree the destruction of the entire body of literature, Christian's work alone would serve as the new foundation of the sciences, on which posterity could erect a new citadel of truth. It might well be easier to do so than to repair such a ruined structure, enlarging a courtyard here, letting light into rooms there, and altering the doors, stairs, and other things that represent our intentions.* (Godwin, McIntosh, & McIntosh, 2016, p. 44)

Whilst Reason Fifteen relates that Father Christian lived to be 106 years old. Both Reasons further reinforce the notion that we are dealing with a text which is presenting a spiritual allegory, rather than a historical figure.

There are suggestions within the Confessio Fraternitatis that the Rosicrucians, being dissatisfied with the formality and intellectualism of both Catholic and Protestant traditions, sought a more personal and experiential approach to spirituality.

The Rosicrucian source works, commentaries and discussions, whether apologetic or censorious have led to this period of Rosicrucian history as being dubbed *The Rosicrucian Furore*. In addition to the political turmoil (as discussed earlier in this book) there were also the more prophetic Rosicrucian messages, many of which were pseudoepigraphically ascribed to Paracelsus. In these prophecies, the Holy Roman Empire was frequently symbolised by an eagle, while Bohemia (or Luther) was represented by a lion, Saxony by a dragon, and Bavaria by a bear. Some prophecies foretold a scenario in which a lion would seize the sceptre from the eagle, symbolising a potential future where Lutheranism might prevail in popularity over the Catholic Church (Gilly, 2000).

We can see evidence of this prophecy in Reason Fourteen of the Confessio Fraternitatis, when referencing the Pope,

> *...his annihilation is reserved for our age, when he will be clawed to pieces and the lion's roar will end his braying.*
> (Godwin, McIntosh, & McIntosh, 2016, p. 47)

To the esoterically minded or the Rosicrucian apologist the lion here represents The Fraternity of the Rosy Cross (or Christ). Here we can also begin to see Rosicrucian philosophy undergoing a transformation, transitioning from a tale of an initiatic quest to manifesting as a tangible group with distinct political ideologies.

The Confessio Fraternitatis also provides the author/s opinions upon the art of alchemy. Many commentators have used these points to enforce their opinions on alchemy when writing about the Rosicrucians. However, we need to be careful not to confuse the alchemical thoughts of later Rosicrucian movements with the Rosicrucian movement of this era. The Confessio Fraternitatis presents a nuanced and critical view of alchemy, distinguishing between its true purpose, being the pursuit of knowledge and spiritual enlightenment through the study of Nature, and its perversion, the greedy pursuit of material wealth through deceptive practices.

For instance, the author/s explicitly differentiate between the *transmutation of metals* and the *knowledge of Nature*, stating that while the former is a *noble [a] gift of God*, it doesn't necessarily lead to the latter. They argue that a deeper understanding of philosophy, encompassing the study of Nature, surpasses the mere ability to manipulate metals.

The author/s prioritise the study of Nature as the true path to wisdom and enlightenment, suggesting that alchemy should be approached as a means of understanding the natural world rather than simply a pursuit of material wealth. This perspective aligns with the broader Renaissance interest in natural philosophy and the belief in Nature as a *book* to be deciphered.

The authors warn against the *vile books of the pseudo-chemists*, who exploit the *curiosity of the credulous* for profit, using *monstrous figures and riddles* to deceive and mislead. They distance themselves from such practices, offering instead a *simple and lucid explanation of the secrets*. This distinction highlights their belief in an ethical and sincere approach to alchemy, free from deception and exploitation.

Regarding these *pseudo-chemists,* the author/s do identify a specific individual,

> *Our age has produced many of this type: one of the foremost is the "Amphitheatrical" comedian, a man most ingenious in deceit.* (Godwin, McIntosh, & McIntosh, 2016, p. 51)

The *Amphitheatrical comedian* here is clearly the famed alchemist, Heinrich Khunrath (taking reference to his 1609 work, *Amphitheatrum sapientiae aeternae*). Surprisingly, many twentieth century Rosicrucian organisations either missed this clear reference or else disagreed with the assessment of the Fraternity of the Rosy Cross, for in many Rosicrucian organisations of this era we find various positive praises and considerations of Khunrath's work.

The authors reiterate their rejection of those who seek the Fraternity of the Rosy Cross solely for material gain, emphasising that true seekers should be motivated by a genuine desire for knowledge and spiritual growth. They warn that those who are driven by greed or a desire for a *soft, lazy, indulgent, and complacent existence* will not find what they are looking for, reinforcing that, according to the Fraternity of the Rosy Cross, true alchemy requires, effort, purity of intention and commitment to higher ideals.

Confessio Fraternitatis

THE CHEMICAL WEDDING OF CHRISTIAN ROSENKREUZ IN THE YEAR 1459

Once more Jesus spoke to them in parables, saying: "The kingdom of heaven may be compared to a king who gave a wedding banquet for his son. He sent his slaves to call those who had been invited to the wedding banquet, but they would not come. Again he sent other slaves, saying, "Tell those who have been invited: Look, I have prepared my dinner, my oxen and my fat calves have been slaughtered, and everything is ready; come to the wedding banquet." But they made light of it and went away, one to his farm, another to his business, while the rest seized his slaves, maltreated them, and killed them. The king was enraged. He sent his troops, destroyed those murderers, and burned their city. Then he said to his slaves, "The wedding is ready, but those invited were not worthy. Go therefore into the main streets, and invite everyone you find to the wedding banquet." Those slaves went out into the streets and gathered all whom they found, both good and bad; so the wedding hall was filled with guests.

'But when the king came in to see the guests, he noticed a man there who was not wearing a wedding robe, and he said to him, "Friend, how did you get in here without a wedding robe?" And he was speechless. Then the king said to the attendants, "Bind him hand and foot, and throw him into the outer darkness, where there will be weeping and gnashing of teeth." **For many are called, but few are chosen.**

Matthew 22:1-14 (NRSVA)

When I wrote *The Temple and the Vault*, I provided a thorough overview of the Rosicrucian mythos, which was primarily sourced from the Fama Fraternitatis with some additional minor points from the Confessio Fraternitatis. As the purpose of that text was to discuss the initiatic journey of the allegorical founder of the Fraternity of the Rosy Cross, it was quite unnecessary to discuss the third source work of the Rosicrucian trilogy; *The Chemical Wedding of Christian Rosenkreuz in the Year 1459*.

However, now it would be completely remiss of me to not outline and detail this important, if somewhat controversial text.

But before we can commence an esoteric analysis of this text, it is important that we ground ourselves in the narrative itself. This will better assist the esoterically minded in appreciating its importance and value.

In 1616, the third manifesto of the trilogy appeared. Written in German, The Chemical Wedding of Christian Rosenkreuz in the Year 1459 (German: *Chymische Hochzeit Christiani Rosencreutz anno 1459*) presents an allegorical tale quite unlike the previous source works. Rife with esoteric symbolism and written with an adept understanding of alchemy, The Chemical Wedding of Christian Rosenkreuz in the Year 1459 is a text which still confounds esotericists today.

The Chemical Wedding of Christian Rosenkreuz in the Year 1459 unfolds over the course of seven days, with each chapter representing a single day. At the close of the first three days, the narrative transitions into a dream sequence. The protagonist and narrator of the story is Christian Rosenkreuz, who guides the reader through the events of his journey.

The story begins on Easter Eve with Christian Rosenkreuz reflecting upon the great mysteries which the *Father of Light* had allowed him to glimpse. Amidst a violent storm, a striking woman appears, adorned in star-studded blue robes, golden wings covered in eyes, and holding a trumpet. Without uttering a word, she hands him an invitation to a royal wedding. Then, with a resounding trumpet blast, she takes flight leaving the whole mountain upon which Christian resides trembling in her wake.

Christian Rosenkreuz recognises the significance of the wedding invitation delivered by the mysterious woman. This, he realises, is the very event foretold in a vision seven years earlier and confirmed by his planetary calculations. However, the invitation carries a warning: the path to the wedding is fraught with peril. The invitation was stamped with a *delicate cross* and the motto *in hoc signo + vinces* (English: *In this sign + thou shalt conquer*).

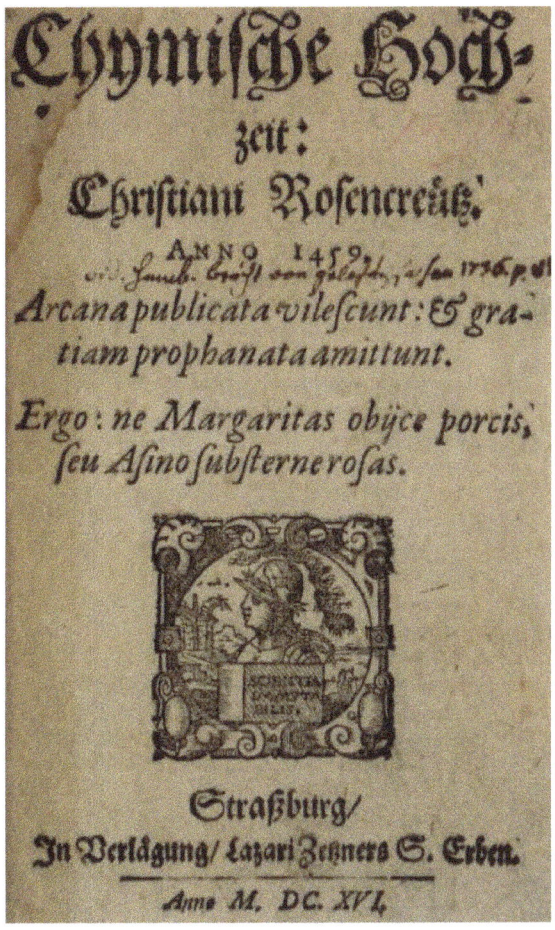

Title page of The Chemical Wedding of Christian Rosenkreuz in the Year 1459.

On the second day, Rosenkreuz embarks on his quest, armed with a few carefully chosen items. Exiting a forest and entering a meadow, he discovers a sign affixed to a tree. It outlines four potential paths to reach the royal castle, each path presenting its own unique challenges:

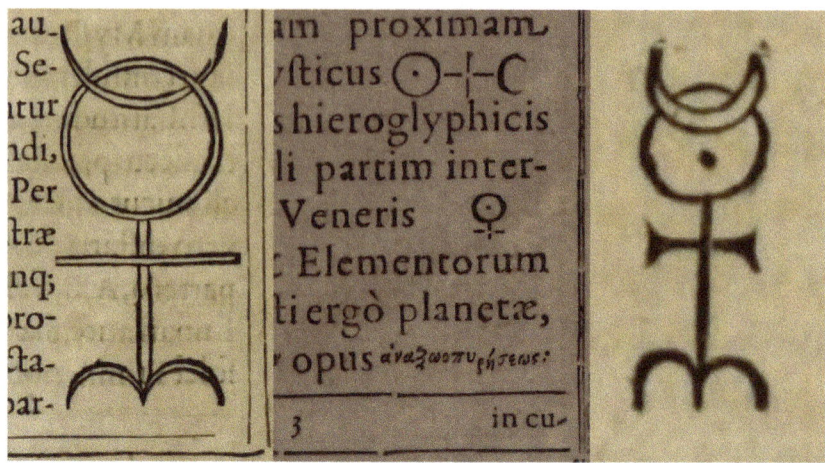

From left-to-right, contrasting the Hieroglyphic Monad of John Dee (1591), Consideratio Brevis (1615), and Chemical Wedding of Christian Rosenkreuz in the Year 1459 (1616).

1. **The Short Path** – Dangerous but direct.

2. **The Long Path** – Flat yet winding, requiring a magnet to avoid losing one's way.

3. **The Royal Path** – Rarely achievable, yet the most rewarding.

4. **The Consuming Path** – A journey for incorruptible beings alone.

As Rosenkreuz ponders his choice, he shares a piece of bread with a dove, only to witness a raven attack the bird. Chasing them in an attempt to save the dove, he inadvertently chooses the second path[1].

The road leads him to three gates, each guarded by a stern gatekeeper demanding a token for entry. Rosenkreuz offers his rose, prayer book, and salt to gain access. Along the way, he notices cryptic symbols and inscriptions, hinting at the deeper meaning behind his journey.

---

1 This is not explicitly stated but can be inferred from the text. For example, "There appeared to be many by-ways, but thanks to my compass I avoided them. I turned not a footsbreadth from the meridian, although the path was sometimes so rough and unkept that I was quite unsure of it. On the way I thought constantly of the dove and the raven, but could not fathom their meaning (McLean & Godwin, 1991, p. 15)".

Once inside the castle, Rosenkreuz's excitement turns to dismay as he encounters a variety of boastful and frivolous guests. Maybe these invitations are not as special as he first thought. Questioning his own worth, he prepares for the ultimate test: a weighing ceremony overseen by a radiant Virgin. The Virgin would then become a major character in the narrative and acts as the guide for the guests over the next several days. She announces that the guests will be judged to determine who is worthy of attending the royal wedding. Rosenkreuz, fearing his unworthiness offers to abstain from the ceremony to which the Virgin agrees.

On the third day, Rosenkreuz watches as emperors, kings, scholars, and charlatans face judgment. Many, despite their grand claims, are found wanting. The unworthy guests are punished according to the severity of their unworthiness. Some are simply sent away whilst the worst faced capital punishment. Despite having abstained from the ceremony, Rosenkreuz is asked to participate anyway, but simply as a test in good faith. No punishment would be exacted should he be found wanting. To his surprise though, Rosenkreuz passes all of the tests and is rewarded with velvet garments, a laurel wreath, and the Golden Fleece bearing a flying lion; symbols signifying his acceptance into a mysterious Order.

The worthy guests are taken on a tour of the castle's wonders, from ancient royal tombs to a vast library. They engage in riddles and philosophical discussions, each revealing their wit and understanding. Rosenkreuz solves a riddle posed by the Virgin, uncovering her true name.

The fourth day brings a symbolic cleansing ritual. The guests bathe in a fountain inscribed with words attributed to Hermes, receive new clothing, and are gifted a second Golden Fleece adorned with precious stones and symbols of the sun and moon.

The guests are presented to the King and Queen, who sit in a room of unimaginable splendour. The Queen herself is of unsurpassable beauty.

The guests then witness a series of allegorical plays, depicting the struggles between good and evil, and the story of a maiden who is crowned queen, falls from grace, and is ultimately redeemed.

Following the play, the guests become witness to a gruesome ceremony in which six royal figures willingly undergo a ritualistic beheading. Their blood is collected into a golden chalice. Following this, the executioner is also beheaded, with his head and axe carefully placed in a small chest.

Although shaken by the scene, Rosenkreuz and the other guests are reassured by the Virgin. She instructs them to remain calm and declares, "*The lives of these now rest in your hands; and if you follow me, you will witness this death bring life to many.*"

Retiring to his bedroom, Rosenkreuz gazes out of his bedroom window just as midnight strikes and sees a vast lake illuminated by the moonlight. Seven ships arrive to the castle, and the six coffins along with the chest from the earlier ceremony are carefully loaded onto the ships.

Early on the morning of the fifth day, Rosenkreuz finds a vault where he beholds the *most precious thing ever created by Nature*. Upon opening an unlocked door and descending some stairs he finds a room with a bed draped in fine curtains. Drawing back the curtains, Rosenkreuz is struck by the glorious sight of *Lady Venus*, unclothed and of breathtaking beauty. A small, winged Cupid appears and admonishes Rosenkreuz for his presence, for this vault was meant to be locked. However, Cupid admits that this was partially his own fault as he had accidentally forgotten to lock the vault the night before. Cupid also reveals to him that Lady Venus is actually his mother. The guests then leave the royal castle and accompany the six coffins and chest on the boats and sail towards a square island upon which stands the *Tower of Olympus*.

On the sixth day, Rosenkreuz and his companions work in the Tower of Olympus to resurrect the King and Queen through various alchemical operations. These alchemical procedures become more refined as Rosenkreuz and the guests ascend the seven levels of the tower.

In order to ascend each level, the guests are assigned either a rope, ladder, or wings. Rosenkreuz acquired the ladder, and whilst at first being upset that he did not obtain the wings, which seemed to make it easy to ascend, he would eventually find the ladder to be quite useful, even if rather clunky and large.

Upon reaching the seventh level they commence some prayer before moving on to the final stage of the work; a resurrection ritual.

For the resurrection ritual, the six royals' corpses are required. A golden globe is used to collect water from a fountain. This water is then heated by sunlight which produces a solid resembling an egg. From this, a bird hatches, which is cleansed and prepared in a bath.

In a final ritual, the bird drinks from a fountain, attacks a white snake, and consumes its blood. Some of the ingredients produced from the alchemical operations are placed in little moulds and formed into two small homunculi. These two homunculi, one male and one female, are nurtured with blood until they grow to full human size. A trumpet is then placed onto their mouths and directed towards an opening in the ceiling. Fire then descends through the trumpet and into the homunculi thus bringing them to life; revealing them to be the reborn King and Queen. The revived King and Queen are in a more glorious form then before; their beauty being even beyond that of Lady Venus. The royal couple are then clothed and placed into thrones. The royal couple then express their sincere gratitude to the workers for their labours.

On the seventh day, the guests are inducted into the *Knights of the Golden Stone*. Each knight was asked to write their name and Rosenkreuz writes:

Summa scientia nihil scire.
Fr. *CHRISTIANUS ROSENKREUTZ,*
Eques aurei Lapidis:
Anno 1459[2]

---

2   English: *The height of knowledge is to know nothing. Brother Christian Rosenkreutz, Knight of the Golden Stone. In the year 1459.*

Rosenkreuz and the guests then prepare to depart the castle. Rosenkreuz finds himself riding with the King, who praises him as a man chosen by God. However, when the King expresses concern after learning of a recent trespasser who stumbled upon Lady Venus in her chamber, Rosenkreuz wrestles with his conscience and ultimately confesses his guilt.

Although the King admires Rosenkreuz and dearly wishes to pardon Rosenkreuz for his crime, he is bound by ancient rules. As punishment, Rosenkreuz is sentenced to become the castle's gatekeeper. Rosenkreuz accepts his fate with humility. He bids farewell to the King and Queen and is led to an opulent bedchamber to spend the night, fully expecting to be gatekeeper in the morning.

The manuscript ends abruptly with a note lamenting the loss of two pages, leaving the ultimate fate of Rosenkreuz shrouded in mystery.

Analysis of The Chemical Wedding of Christian Rosenkreuz in the Year 1459

The preceding is meant to be a brief synopsis of the story. It would be worthwhile seeking out a copy of the full-text should you desire to read the text in its completeness.

The Chemical Wedding of Christian Rosenkreuz in the Year 1459 is a challenging work. I would be wary of any person who claims a complete understanding of the text. In fact, it is almost as if the text itself defies a simple holistic explanation.

Of this text, the eminent alchemical author Adam McLean writes:

> *Its hidden mystery seems always just one step beyond our comprehension. The more we puzzle over it and appear to clear up one point, another layer of mystery arises from our new understanding of the symbolism, and occludes its meaning even deeper. Many esotericists despair of ever grasping its inner content, but all who work with this allegory come to respect the profound and masterly achievement of the creator of this elegantly sculpted symbolic tale.* (McLean & Godwin, 1991)

Christian Rebisse in his analysis notes that the tenth treatise of the *Corpus Hermeticum* describes an ascent towards the summit of Olympus[3] (Rebisse FRC, 2016), suggesting that the author/s of the text may have drawn from this concept in forming their own mystical allegory of the *Tower of Olympus* as a literary device used to describe a striving for spiritual and philosophical elevation or advancement. Certainly, there does appear to be enough similarity in meaning here to suggest such a consistency.

---

3   "For god does not ignore mankind; on the contrary, he recognizes him fully and wishes to be recognized. For mankind this is the only deliverance, the knowledge of god. It is ascent to Olympus. A soul becomes good only in this way, though it is not good (forever) but becomes evil. By necessity it becomes so. (Copenhaver, 2000, p. 33)"

Nevertheless, we must be cautious, for many interpreters, driven by their own eagerness to unravel the meanings within this narrative, often end up projecting their own philosophies and biases onto the text. This tendency has led to a wide range of interpretations, some of which must stray from the original intent of the work; assuming there was ever a single definitive meaning intended. While I will attempt to explore and shed light on some of the layers of meaning within this tale, it is important to acknowledge the inherent challenges this presents. The Chemical Wedding of Christian Rosenkreuz in the Year 1459 is a richly symbolic and enigmatic text and I do not claim to offer a simple or definitive explanation. Instead, my aim is to provide perspectives that might help readers navigate its complexities, while recognising that its ultimate truths may remain elusive and open to personal interpretation.

Even in light of the words of the book's likely author Johannes Valentinus Andreae (see the next chapter regarding authorship) we may still reach valid interpretations that were not anticipated in the drafting of the original work. As Umberto Eco declares in the postscript to his celebrated work *The Name of the Rose*, *"A narrator should not supply interpretations of his work; otherwise he would not have written a novel, which is a machine for generating interpretations*[4]*."*

The Chemical Wedding of Christian Rosenkreuz is rich with references to theology, mythology, and literature, weaving these elements into its narrative. The author/s of the work were clearly individuals of considerable academic depth and intellectual curiosity. Their extensive knowledge of classical and religious texts, as well as their ability to synthesise diverse traditions, is evident throughout the story. This intertextuality certainly adds additional layers of complexity.

Therefore, I would read my comments here not as something authoritative, but as a seed from which to build your own personal understanding and to reflect upon your own personal alchemical journey.

---

4   Thank you to *Bro Michael Shirk* for pointing out this quote to me.

Will the real Christian Rosenkreuz please stand up?

Christian Rosenkreuz, the enigmatic figure at the heart of Rosicrucian lore, remains a perplexing and multifaceted character. We will take an opportunity in a future chapter to explore the potential historicity of this character, but for now, it is worth noting that Christian Rosenkreuz, the protagonist of The Chemical Wedding of Christian Rosenkreuz in the Year 1459 bears little resemblance to the *CR/CRC/Father Christian* character of the Fama Fraternitatis and the Confessio Fraternitatis.

The earlier texts portray CR/CRC/Father Christian as a sage-like figure; the visionary founder of the Fraternity of the Rosy Cross. He is presented as a man of immense wisdom, deeply engaged in spiritual, scientific, and artistic advancements of his time. His wisdom is so profound that the character takes on quite a legendary status. From dates in the Fama Fraternitatis and Confessio Fraternitatis we can determine CR/CRC/Father Christian was born in 1378 and died in 1484[5]. This long life certainly adds to the legendary quality of the character.

In contrast, the Christian Rosenkreuz character of The Chemical Wedding of Christian Rosenkreuz in the Year 1459 comes across as a more human and fallible character. He is someone at the mercy of the events taking place in the narrative, rather than the instigator of the events themselves.

The only date provided in The Chemical Wedding of Christian Rosenkreuz in the Year 1459 is the date from the title, which coincides with when the protagonist was made a *Knight of the Golden Stone*. In this story, Christian is presented as an elderly but not supernatural character. In fact, there appears to be no explicit connection to the extraordinary lifespan or achievements attributed to the CR/CRC/Father Christian character.

---

5   *"It would be worthwhile examining that whole period from 1378, when our Christian was born, until today, seeing how much change in the world he witnessed in his 106 years of life, and how much he left after his blessed death to be experienced by our fathers and ourselves. But brevity compels us to leave this to another time."*

The sharp contrast between these two representations suggests that these texts may not be referring to the same individual. Or at least they are presenting the same character with a multiverse-like interpretation[6].

So, what is going on here? Was Christian Rosenkreuz ever intended to be a consistent character across the Rosicrucian source works? Or was he intended to be a flexible archetype, adapted to fit the themes of each text?

One argument is that the differences in character representation could reflect an evolution of priorities by the Rosicrucian author/s. The Fama Fraternitatis and Confessio Fraternitatis emphasise the establishment of a mystical brotherhood, detailing their vast knowledge, and utopian ideals. Whilst The Chemical Wedding of Christian Rosenkreuz in the Year 1459 seems to relate an individual spiritual and alchemical transformation, employing a narrative that is rich in allegory; but much less concerned about organisational identity.

Was there ever a grand master plan behind the trilogy? Were the Rosicrucian author/s responsible simply playing a game of 4D chess beyond the ken of us mere mortals? Or perhaps the question of *who* Christian Rosenkreuz was is of less importance than the impact of his story. No matter the case, later movements calling themselves *Rosicrucian* would take this story in all of its contradictory glory, add to it other characteristics and pseudo-history, and develop traditional histories and ritualistic traditions for their organisations, leaving us today with a complicated patchwork of elements. It is for this reason that I tend to advise Rosicrucian students to simply view the protagonist across the trilogy as just, *Christian Rosenkreuz*.

---

6   Any Hollwood writers feel free to hit me up to develop a CRC character for your next superhero franchise!

The Chemical Wedding 69

Where is the Wedding?

Perhaps the most obvious thing one might notice after completing a reading of The Chemical Wedding of Christian Rosenkreuz in the Year 1459 is that the name is a bit of a misnomer. The story of The Chemical Wedding of Christian Rosenkreuz in the Year 1459, while containing the word *wedding* in the title, does not actually depict a literal wedding ceremony; at least not in the traditional sense.

So what could the author/s have possibly meant by this? They could have quite easily called the story *The Alchemical Journey of Christian Rosenkreuz* or something similar. Or perhaps there is an esoteric meaning to the title's name.

The work could be understood to be an alchemical allegory in which the *wedding* represents the process of alchemical transmutation, and the events and characters are symbolic representations of various alchemical concepts and stages.

The Chemical Wedding of Christian Rosenkreuz in the Year 1459 resists being pinned down to any single interpretation. In fact, many of the symbols used in the narrative may be engaged with on multiple levels, be that emotionally, spiritually, or philosophically.

The allegorical symbolism in The Chemical Wedding of Christian Rosenkreuz in the Year 1459 discusses themes often found in later Rosicrucian philosophy, particularly those explored by the German Rosicrucians of the eighteenth century, such as can be found in *The Secret Symbols of the Rosicrucians* (German: *Geheime Figuren der Rosenkreuzer*). For example, one relevant image from The Secret Symbols of the Rosicrucians with the heading *The Hermetic Philosophy* reveals that *The Source of Miracles* (Latin: *Fons Miraculorum*) is born from two opposing energies represented by the balance of solar and lunar symbols depicted in the image by the Sun and Rose opposing the Moon and Lily with written references to the *Rose of Sharon* and the *Lily of the Valley*. The triangle where these energies converge contains the statement, *Sanguinary animals are a spiritual rose. Bright, silver, milky drops from the white Lily of the Valley of Josophat*[7] (Latin: *Sanguinalis animala Rosa Hicrichuntia Spiritualis. Lucida, argentea, lactealstillata ex candida Lilia in Valle Josophat*). This suggests a transformative alchemical process in which corporeal elements (blood, body, and earthly matter) are alchemically refined, paralleling the symbolic imagery of The Chemical Wedding of Christian Rosenkreuz in the Year 1459. This allegory aligns with the speculative alchemical process sometimes depicted as a spiritual or philosophical *wedding* where the lower (earthly) Self unites with the higher (spiritual, divine) Self.

A conjunction of opposites is commonly depicted in Alchemical literature as a wedding between a Red King and White Queen, such as in this image from the Rosarium Philosophorum.

---

7 A full pdf copy of this text with English translations can be found here: https://www.rosicrucian.org/secret-symbols-of-the-rosicrucians (as of 15/12/2025).

The Chemical Wedding

In fact, both The Chemical Wedding of Christian Rosenkreuz in the Year 1459 and works like The Secret Symbols tend to share a thematic preoccupation with the union of complementary or opposing symbols. This is a fundamental alchemical principle sometimes referred to as the *Union of Opposites* (Latin: *Coniunctio Oppositorum*)- the sacred marriage where duality dissolve into unity.

In The Secret Symbols, this union is often represented visually by the Sun (often associated with gold, the masculine, and spirit) and the Moon (silver, the feminine, and soul).

The references to the *Rose of Sharon* and the *Lily of the Valley* here, though borrowed from the *Song of Solomon*, are heavily reinterpreted and imbued with an esoteric meaning that is unique to the Rosicrucian tradition. While these phrases originally appear in a poetic and allegorical context within the *Song of Solomon* (often attributed to King Solomon) they are rarely used in their original Biblical sense by Rosicrucian philosophers.

In the Song of Solomon, the Rose of Sharon and Lily of the Valley are poetic metaphors, often interpreted as expressions of beauty, love, and spiritual longing, and sometimes seen as symbols of Christ or the Church in Christian theology. However, within Rosicrucian and alchemical traditions, these symbols take on layered meanings that are often far removed from their original context.

In Rosicrucian philosophy, the Rose of Sharon and Lily of the Valley are transformed into symbols of duality and harmony. The Rose representing those fiery, active, and solar qualities linked to spirit, divine love, and passion, while the Lily signifies the cool, passive, and lunar qualities associated with purity, soul, and receptivity. The reconciliation of these masculine and feminine, solar and lunar, active and passive forces is a common occurrence in alchemical-Rosicrucian literature.

A similar conjunction of Roses and Lilies can also be found in the Magician Tarot card which contains a variety of similar opposing but complementary symbols. It can also be observed in ritualistic traditions, such as with the placement of the Celebrant and Exponent within the *Societas Rosicruciana* tradition.

This reinterpretation is part of a broader esoteric practice of adapting Biblical language and symbols to convey mystical or alchemical concepts. It's important then to recognise that while these symbols borrow the language of the Song of Solomon, their meaning in Rosicrucian and alchemical traditions is distinct. Consequently, the Rosicrucian usage should not be conflated with their original Biblical meanings.

From the Secret Symbols of the Rosicrucians.

The Rose and the Lily together symbolise the alchemical goal of balance and integration, forming the *marriage* central to the alchemical work. This then helps us to understand the description of the second Golden Fleece received by Rosenkreuz on Day Four:

> On it hung a heavy piece of gold picturing the sun and moon opposite one another. On the reverse was this saying: "The moon's light shall be like the sun's light, and the sun's light shall be seven times as bright. (Godwin, McIntosh, & McIntosh, 2016, p. 122)

The Divine Feminine

A similar spiritual conjunction of rose and lilies appear in the theosophical writings of Jakob Böhme (1575-1624), whose mysticism grew from the same cultural milieu as the Rosicrucian source works.

Böhme quite often employed floral imagery to describe metaphysical processes. The rose and lily were two common metaphors which he used.

For instance, in *The Way of Christ,* Böhme describes an experiential process of awakening that can arise from our own efforts to *Know Thyself*. The blooming forth of understanding that can arise from this process, he compares to the lily,

> *A Man must wrestle till the dark Center that is shut up tight, breaketh open, and the Spark lying hid therein kindleth and from thence the noble Lily-Branch sprouteth, as from the divine Grain of Mustard-Seed as Christ saith*. (Böhme, 1624, p. 96)

The rose was a complementary symbol that Böhme often associated with the Wisdom of God, which he called, *Sophia* and represented by a virgin. Sophia was frequently depicted in the center of a rose garden or else holding a rose and offering it as a metaphor for divine revelation, as in the following quote from *The Three Principles of the Divine Essence,*

For the Virgin [the Wisdom of God] has graciously bestowed a Rose upon us, of which we will write in such Words as we behold in that Wonder; and we cannot [write] otherwise, but our Pen is broken, and the Rose taken from us, and then we are as we were before the Time [of our Knowledge;] whereas yet the Rose stands in the Center of Paradise, in the Hand of the Virgin, which she reaches forth to us, in the same Place where she came to us in the Gate of the Deep, and proffered us her Love, when we lay on the Mountain towards the North, in the Strife and Storm before Babel, which [Virgin] our earthly Man has never seen nor known.

Therefore we write out of a School, wherein the earthly Body (with its Senses) never studied, nor never learned the A, B, C[8]; for in the Rose of the Virgin we learned that A, B, C, which we supposed we could have learned from the Thoughts of the Mind; but that could not be, they were too rough, and too dark, they could not comprehend it. And therefore the earthly Body must not learn in this School, and its Tongue cannot raise itself up to it; for the Mind of this School stood hidden in the Gate of the Deep, in the Center. Therefore we ought not to boast of this School at all, for it is not the proper one of the Senses [or Thoughts,] and Mind of the earthly Man; and if we go forth from the Center of the noble Virgin, then we know as little from this School as others; just as it was with Adam when he went out of the Paradise of God, into the Sleep of being overcome, then at his awaking in this World he knew no more of Paradise, and he knew his loving Virgin no more. (Böhme, 2016)

To Böhme, roses and lilies were also associated with apocalyptic times signifying the end of an era. This he referred to as *rose and lily times* (Schmidt-Biggemann, 2004, p. 352).

---

8   It is worth pointing out that the cover page for *The Secret Symbols of the Rosicrucians* describes the text as a *Simple ABC book for young students practicing daily in the school of the Holy Ghost.*

Finally, and perhaps most importantly here, Böhme frequently describes that the human soul's highest calling was to undergo a mystical union with Sophia. He described this as a spiritual wedding, where one might encounter Sophia as an eternal Virgin and Heavenly Bride. This marriage signifies the Soul's restoration to its divine state,

> *If ever he will obtain the Love and Marriage of the noble Sophia, he must make such a Vow as this in his Purpose and Mind. For Christ Himself saith, He that forsaketh not Wife and Children, Brethren and Sisters, Money and Goods, and all that he hath, and even his earthly Life also, to follow Me, is not worthy of Me. Here Christ meaneth the Mind of the Soul, so that if there were any Thing that would keep the Mind back from It, though it should have never so fair and glorious a Pretence or Show in this World, the Mind must not regard it at all, but rather part with it than with the Love of the noble Virgin Sophia, in the Bud and Blossom of Christ, in His tender Humanity in us as to the Heavenly Corporality. For this is the Flower in Sharon, the Rose in the Valley of Jericho, wherewith Solomon delighted himself, and termed it his dear Love, his chaste Virgin which he loved; as indeed all other Saints before and after him did; whosoever obtained Her, called Her his Pearl.* (Böhme, 1624, p. 12)

And just like the symbolic nuptials depicted in The Chemical Wedding of Christian Rosenkreuz in the Year 1459, Böhme's wedding to Sophia exemplifies a conjunction of opposites.

Böhme started writing after a mystical experience in 1610. His initial writings were circulated privately, and the bulk of his publications would appear in the 1620's. As such, it is highly unlikely that Böhme was an influence on the Rosicrucian source work authors as the Fama Fraternitatis had been already circulating in manuscript form from at least 1610.

However, we can state that both Böhme and the Rosicrucian movement both emerged from the same intellectual and cultural background. Both were influenced by German Lutheran mysticism, alchemical and hermetic traditions, Paracelsian medicine and cosmology, and apocalyptic and millenarian expectations.

So, does this symbolism clarify the meaning of the wedding in The Chemical Wedding of Christian Rosenkreuz in the Year 1459? Partially, yes. The wedding can be read as a symbolic representation of the alchemical union, both in the material sense (as with gold and silver) and the spiritual sense (the marriage of Soul and Spirit). However, just as with interpretations of The Secret Symbols of the Rosicrucians or the Tarot, authoritative interpretations of The Chemical Wedding of Christian Rosenkreuz in the Year 1459 resists any simple or reductive conclusions and we must remain cautious when interpreting such a nuanced esoteric work.

While it's tempting to reduce the story to a straightforward spiritual metaphor, such as the union of Christ Consciousness (the *Bridegroom*) with the human conscience (the *Bride*), such an explanation also risks oversimplifying the text and ignoring a more broad appreciation.

Abrupt ending

Another peculiar aspect of the story is its sudden and abrupt ending, which leaves readers without a clear understanding of the final outcome of Rosenkreuz's adventure. Steven E. Markham, in his excellent analysis, suggests that Rosenkreuz's fate may not have been as pessimistic as it initially appears. He points to earlier scenes and events that seem to foreshadow a more noble and uplifting conclusion for the protagonist, even going so far as to propose an unpublished eighth day (Markham, 2019, p. 248).

This is an interesting proposal, and whilst I am personally not of the opinion of their being a missing eighth day, I cannot help but consider a possible optimistic ending.

The Chemical Wedding

It is also possible that the missing pages were simply lost or damaged during the transmission or publication of the text. Johannes Valentinus Andreae did claim in his autobiography to having written a text with the title *Chymische Hochzeit* (English: *Chemical Wedding*) in his youth. This explanation, though more mundane, aligns with the fact that no complete version of this potential proto-manuscript has ever been found.

Alchemy

The Chemical Wedding of Christian Rosenkreuz in the Year 1459 presents us with very few explicit references to a physical laboratory alchemy, leading to the reasonable conclusion that what is being hinted at is perhaps something more philosophical. However, that is not to say that there are no references to a physical operation.

Take the dream sequence from Day One as an example. When Rosenkreuz falls asleep on Day One, he recounts being trapped in a dark, oppressive tower alongside countless others, all bound by heavy chains. The captives suffer as they crawl over one another in the pitch black, increasing their collective misery. Suddenly, majestic trumpets and drums sound, and a small amount of light enters the tower as its ceiling opens. A grey-haired old man addresses them, offering a chance at freedom. A rope is let down seven times, and those who can hold on are pulled out.

The captives scramble in desperation, but many fail to grasp the rope due to their heavy chains, weak hands, or interference from others. After multiple attempts, only a few are rescued. On the sixth attempt, the rope swings toward the narrator, who seizes it and is pulled out, despite suffering a head injury during the process and bleeding. Joy overwhelms the narrator, overshadowing the pain of the wound.

Once the seventh pull concludes, freeing the most captives, the tower's roof is closed, leaving the remaining prisoners in despair. The freed individuals are gathered by an old woman and her aged son, who count and record their names.

The old woman, expressing sorrow for those left behind, orders the fetters of the freed to be removed. She gives each a golden medal as a token, bearing the symbols of a rising sun and the inscription "D.L.S." (*Deus Lux Solis; Deo Laus Semper*[9]). The freed are instructed to glorify God, aid their neighbours, and keep their experiences secret. Despite his wounds and limping, Rosenkreuz is encouraged by the woman to see his imperfections as a reminder of his journey. Trumpets sound once more, waking the narrator from the dream.

Considering this dream, it is not difficult to envision the locked tower as a metaphor for an alchemical flask, with the chaotic scene of the captives symbolising the base elements of matter, unrefined and in turmoil. The trumpets and kettledrums may then represent the roaring sounds of a furnace, signalling the application of heat, a vital step in the alchemical process. The tower, or flask, is subjected to the transformative power of fire, controlled and orchestrated by the grey-haired old man, who may symbolise the alchemist or the guiding principle of wisdom and order.

The captives' struggles to grasp the descending rope align with the process of purification and separation in alchemy. Only the strongest and most prepared components (symbolised by the individuals who successfully hold onto the rope) are extracted from the chaotic mass. These *saved guests* could represent the refined materials, freed from the impurities of the base material, and now ready to progress to the next stage of the *Great Work*.

The dream's imagery, from the fetters symbolising the restraints of base nature to the final liberation of select individuals, could be interpreted from a physical or spiritual perspective. This dream sequence could suggest a chemical transformation just as readily as an inner purification, where the individual must overcome challenges, discard impurities, and endure suffering to achieve spiritual refinement and enlightenment. The painful wounds could

---

9   God, the light of the sun; Praise always to God.

be read as marks of an arduous life journey, reminding us that transformation is not without sacrifice, but may also represent a physical discolouration caused by a refined material having been scraped and losing a portion of its outer layer.

Nevertheless, despite this, and several other passages which could allude to a physical operation, the text ultimately leaves us wanting of any method or *recipe* with which to perform any laboratory alchemy. So whilst there is room for the consideration of allusions to physical alchemy, these are more speculative in nature, rather than operative.

From these brief considerations, it should become abundantly clear that The Chemical Wedding of Christian Rosenkreuz in the Year 1459 is an allegory using alchemical metaphors. In keeping with this consideration, on Day Three Rosenkreuz solves the riddle revealing the Virgin's true name. Whilst the protagonist does not announce her name, he does suggest that he solved the riddle. Fortunately, the writer/s of this text provided the riddle in the narrative, and it did not take long for readers to copy Christian Rosenkreuz and determine that her name is *ALCHIMIA*. The method of solving this riddle has been revealed in several places, perhaps most recently in *Markham's Brotherhood* where the author has gratefully provided the working out should you wish to reproduce it yourself (Markham, 2019, pp. 168-170).

AUTHORSHIP

*D*espite the many responses to the Rosicrucian source works, no author has yet been identified, although multiple candidates have been proposed. Certainly, there were a great number of practical reasons for denying intimate associations with the Rosicrucians. Not all reactions to the messages expressed in the Rosicrucian source works were positive. Critical responses ranged from the source works being a childish joke to claims that the Rosicrucians were devil-worshippers.

Michael Maier

Whilst seemingly sympathetic to Rosicrucian values, Michael Maier would deny being a Rosicrucian.

Michael Maier states in his *Themis Aurea* that many have accounted the fraternity as heretics, necromancers, deceivers and disturbers of the Commonwealth and posits that many of these criticisms come from wealthy apothecaries who were suffering a financial loss as a result of people turning away from their exotic and needlessly expensive *alchemical* remedies, which was in turn encouraged by the growing Rosicrucian influence (Maier, 1656, pp. 130-131). Self-preservation would wisely dictate distancing oneself from such claims and powerful enemies.

Throughout Themis Aurea, Maier displays a very intimate understanding of Rosicrucian philosophy. Whilst he mostly uses impartial language, he does on occasion use possessive terms such as *"our Fraternity"* (Maier, 1656, p. 121) which could suggest a closer personal connection. Maier's alignment with Lutheran ideals and Neoplatonic philosophy, along with his evident familiarity with Rosicrucian concepts, make him a compelling candidate to consider as an author or significant contributor to the Rosicrucian source works. His writings also reflect his engagement with the themes and principles associated with the Rosicrucian movement.

However, on the last page of Themis Aurea, Maier finally admits his *insufficiency to reach the worth of the Fraternity R.C.* This admission, while seemingly modest, raises questions about the extent of Maier's direct involvement with the Rosicrucian movement. Was this a sincere declaration of his outsider status, or could it have been a strategic disclaimer meant to distance himself from the movement and by extension, avoid any undue harm which might befall him for maintaining such an association?

Whilst his intellectual and philosophical alignment with the principles of the Rosicrucian movement is undeniable, the lack of explicit confirmation of his direct participation leaves room for continued debate among scholars. Nevertheless, whether as a direct participant or an influential observer, Maier's contributions remain significant in the context of early Rosicrucian literature.

Robert Fludd

Robert Fludd also denied being a Rosicrucian, despite accusations by critics.

Another notable figure that we have already mentioned earlier in this book, but is well worth bringing up in this section, is the physician and mystic Robert Fludd. Fludd and Maier were contemporaries and are known to have had a professional relationship.

Fludd wrote three apologies[1] in defence of the Rosicrucians and there is some suggestion that Maier may have played a role in instigating Fludd to compose his third defence. Some contemporary Rosicrucian organisations even speculate that Maier may have even facilitated Fludd's introduction to the Rosicrucian brotherhood, though definitive evidence for this claim remains elusive (Craven R. J., 1968).

Robert Fludd authored a series of works called *Summum Bonum*. However, when authoring these works, Fludd chose to use the pseudonym, *Joachim Frizius*. Writing under this guise would have allowed Fludd to explore more sensitive theological and philosophical ideas with a greater degree of freedom. In this work, he provides a rare and direct insight into the nature and location of the Fraternity of the Rosy Cross, stating,

> *The dwelling place of the Brethren of the Rosy Cross is in the house of God, of which Christ is made the corner stone. By their lives they show themselves to be of the seed of God.... The foundation of the house is well known...It is not built, as fools imagine, by alchemy*

---

[1] *Apologia Compendiaria (1616); Tractatus Apologeticus integritatem Societatis de Rosea Cruce defendens (1617); Tractatus Theologo-Philosophicus (1617).*

or magic, but is a divine structure... It is, indeed, a house not made with hands, but has its eternity from above[2]. (Craven J. B., 1902, pp. 130-144)

Fludd's most well-known work was the ambitious *History of the Macrocosm and the Microcosm*, a trilogy of works left incomplete at the time of his death. In this unfinished trilogy, Fludd reveals a striking alignment in philosophical outlook between himself and the anonymous Rosicrucians, further cementing his place within the broader intellectual framework of the movement.

After receiving extensive criticisms that his own writings were too similar to those of the Fraternity of the Rosy Cross to be coincidence, Fludd disclosed that his writings in question were written four-five years before he had even heard of the Rosicrucians. He sums up this confession by stating that his own works are, "*...as far from the works of the Fraternity of the Rosy Cross as Earth is from Heaven or Light is from Darkness*" and that he has "*...never seen, known or conferred with any of the Fraternity...much to his grief*". (Huffman, 2001, p. 106)

On the surface, this would seem to indicate and admission, just like Maier who came before him, that he was not a member of the Rosicrucian brotherhood.

It is also worth noting that Helena Petrovna Blavatsky, co-founder of The Theosophical Society, considered Robert Fludd to have been *Grand Master of the Rosicrucians in England* (Blavatsky H. P., 1878) a point that is also repeated by some contemporary Rosicrucian organisations.

---

[2] See also, *Acts 17:24-34*

Johannes Valentinus Andreae

Pick up any commentary on Rosicrucian history and you will likely find the author proposing that the Rosicrucian trilogy was, in whole or in part, the product of Lutheran Theologian Johannes Valentinus Andreae and not without supporting evidence.

Lutheran theologian, Johannes Valentinus Andreae claimed to have written a work called Nuptiae Chymicae in his youth and was shocked to see how much it was analysed and valued by other readers.

Johannes Valentinus Andreae was a prominent Lutheran Theologian and was descended from a notable Lutheran family. Andreae's grandfather, Jakob Andreae was primarily responsible for drafting the *Formula of Concord*, the authoritative Lutheran statement of faith. Jakob's support for the Lutheran cause earned him the nickname, the *Luther of Württemberg*. Andreae's family crest contained a cross surrounded by four red roses. And perhaps most revealing, Andreae claimed to have authored a text in his youth known as *The Chemical Wedding* (Latin: *Nuptiae Chymicae*). As such, Rosicrucian commentators, even if they do not claim Andreae to have authored the complete trilogy of source works, will state that Andreae at least was responsible for The Chemical Wedding of Christian Rosenkreuz in the Year 1459. But is this really the admission of authorship that many claim it to be?

The source of this claim is sourced from Andreae's autobiography.

Early on in his autobiography, Andreae is reciting various creative works he composed in his youth and his feelings about these works now in his mature age.

Of relevance to us, Andreae states,

> *Superfuerunt e contra Nuptiae Chymicae, cum monstrorum foecundo foetu, ludibrium, quod mireris a nonnullis aestimatum et subtili indagine explicatum, plane futile et quod inanitatem curiosorum prodat.*
> (Schultze, 1849, p. 10)

Here, Andreae is acknowledging that (unlike some other works written in his youth) *The Chymical Wedding* (Latin: *Nuptiae Chymicae*) survived alongside a host of other *monstrous* creations (Latin: *monstrorum foecundo foetu*). However, he dismisses it as a *joke* (Latin: *ludibrium*) and deems it a *futile work* (Latin: *plane futile*), intended to expose the vanity of the overly *curious* (Latin: *inanitatem curiosorum prodat*).

Nevertheless, despite his low opinion of its worth, he notes with some surprise that it was valued and analysed in depth by some other readers (Latin: *a nonnullis aestimatum et subtili indagine explicatum*).

So it would seem that even in Andreae's lifetime, discussions were already being had regarding the authority and value of The Chemical Wedding of Christian Rosenkreuz in the Year 1459. Andreae makes this declaration in the chapter of his autobiography which covers the years of his life between 1586-1614 and makes reference to the writing of several fictional works, including *The Chemical Wedding*, in 1601-1602, making him at most, sixteen years old when it was first conceived. This might seem precocious, however, we must also keep in mind that Andreae was admitted into university at the young age of thirteen, so we are not dealing with a dullard by any means.

Most unfortunately, this 1601-1602 version of *The Chemical Wedding* is now extant, so we are at a loss as to whether this proto-manuscript was similar to the later The Chemical Wedding of Christian Rosenkreuz in the Year 1459 (published in 1616) or whether it was something rather different.

Nevertheless, we still manage to learn Andreae's thoughts regarding the Rosicrucian movement itself in a lengthy passage,

I dedicated it to Besold, through whom I expressed both Tobias Hess, whom it was not permitted to praise openly, and genuine Christianity, using veiled language. 'Hercules' also brought pleasure to the learned, among whom the theologian Eilhard Lubinus gave it great applause. Encouraged by their invitations and with youthful boldness, I ventured to send 'Turbo' out into the public, a work that had long been hidden with me, born and named in the house of Hafenreffer under his own guidance.

At the same time appeared Besold's 'Theological Axioms', dedicated to me, along with 'The Sheath of the Sword of the Spirit', attributed to Hess but entirely my own. These were followed by one or two 'Invitations to the Fraternity of Christ', set in contrast to that Rosicrucian mockery.

Then came 'Menippus', full of sharp wit and envy, a product of a free but harmless tongue. It pleased the wise while stinging the foolish, and was received with very mixed reactions: the good welcomed a sincere confession of our errors, while the wicked, troubled by their own guilt, took it as a personal insult.

Those who poured out their bile against it were, in truth, good and innocent men, ridiculous only in that they had been stirred up by others, whose trembling consciences or envy prompted them to lend their voices and pens. Nonetheless, I held them all in respectful regard throughout my life, except for one scoundrel who, under a false identity, attacked someone who had only ever deserved well of him[3]. (Schultze, 1849, p. 46)

---

3 Latin: *Besoldo inscriptum, quo Tobiam Hessum quem palam laudare non licebat, per involucra expressi et Christianismum genuinum. Fuit et Hercules eruditis vo luptati, e quibus Eilhardi Lubini theologi magnus plausus fuit, qui cum me certatim invitarent, juvenili confidentia majora ausus Turbonem in forum abire passus sum, qui pridem in aedibus Hafenrefferi ipsoque manuductore natus et nominatus, hactenus mecum latitaverat. Prodiere*

To understand this passage, it is worth providing a brief overview of the mentioned *Menippus*, which Andreae states he wrote as a satirical work in response to the mockery surrounding the Rosicrucians. This work, he notes, was both appreciated by discerning readers and offensive to those lacking understanding.

Menippus: Dialogues Satyriques (1617) draws inspiration from the Cynic philosopher Menippus of Gadara. Andreae's Menippus takes a humorous, satirical, and allegorical approach to critique various aspects of society and religion, often exposing human folly and ignorance. Andreae uses Menippus as a platform to advocate for a genuine, heartfelt Christianity rooted in humility, love, and spiritual truth, contrasting it with the more performative religiosity he critiques elsewhere. In Menippus, Andreae distances himself from the sensationalism surrounding the Rosicrucian movement, instead using satire to highlight the movement's philosophical and spiritual ideals whilst mocking its misinterpretation and exploitation by opportunists.

As can be seen, there is a lot that can be unpacked from such a small passage.

Firstly, Andreae states that he dedicated something to Christoph Besold, using it as a way to express a *genuine Christianity* and praise Tobias Hess indirectly. Tobias Hess, a friend and mentor of Andreae, was a controversial figure whose public endorsement could have brought Andreae criticism. We will see shortly that these two characters may have played an important role in igniting the spark, or at least fanning the flames, of the Rosicrucian movement.

---

simul Axiomata Besoldi theologica, mihi inscripta, cum Theca gladii Spiritus, Hesso imputata, plane mea. Successit demum post unam alteramque ad fraternitatem Christi Invitationem ludibrio illi Rosencruciano oppositam, ille plenus invidia Menippus, liberae sed innoxiae linguae foetus, qui cum tam cordatis allubesceret, quam pungeret vecordes, diversa admodum sorte exceptus est, cum boni ingenuam errorum nostrorum confessionem admitterent mali male sibi conscii ad suam injuriam revocarent. Qui bilem suam contra effuderunt, viri optimi et innocentissimi, ridicule fuerunt, sed ii profecto ab aliis instincti, quibus conscientia trepidabat, aut livebant Invidia, os et calamum commodarunt, quos nihilominus omni posthac vita reverenter habui, uno scurra except, qui sub alio tegmina laceravit optime de se meritum.

Secondly, we learn that another less popular Rosicrucian manuscript, *The Sheath of the Sword of the Spirit* (Latin: *Theca gladii Spiritus*), had been incorrectly attributed to Tobias Hess but was actually entirely Andreae's creation!

And thirdly, and most importantly, we learn that Andreae admired the spirit of the Rosicrucian movement but had become disillusioned with the way it had been reduced to a materialistic, pseudo-spiritual movement, perhaps not unlike his disillusionment he perceived in organised religion. As such, he desired a return to a *true Christianity*, much like the values held by the anonymous authors of the Fama Fraternitatis and Confessio Fraternitatis.

So it is not unusual therefore that later Rosicrucian commentators have looked at Andreae, with his history of misattributed authorship of spiritual allegories, and incorrectly attributed to him authorship or even ownership of the Rosicrucian movement.

Nevertheless, as we can rightly discern, Andreae was not the initial impulse behind the movement, even if he can be ascribed authorship of The Chemical Wedding of Christian Rosenkreuz in the Year 1459 and/or its extant proto-manuscript.

Princess Antonia's role in the Rosicrucian furore has often been neglected.

Antonia of Württemberg

Princess Antonia of Württemberg (1613-1679) is also worthy of consideration at this point. While her age automatically discounts her as a candidate for authorship of the early Rosicrucian source works, she is nevertheless relevant of consideration to the broader Rosicrucian movement that was taking place around her. Antonia was a Hebrew scholar, Christian mystic, and a patron responsible for the commissioning of mystical art, some of which are rich in Rosicrucian and esoteric Christian themes. Her work and interests place her side-by-side with many of the other notable Rosicrucian inspired figures of this era, including Johannes Valentinus Andreae and Philip Jacob Spener, the founder of the Pietism movement.

Antonia's most notable commissioning was a large triptych painting named *The Kabbalistic Teaching Painting of Princess Antonia of Württemberg* (German: *Die Kabbalistische Lehrtafel der Prinzessin Antonia zu Württemberg*). This painting was installed in the *Church of the Holy Trinity* at Bad Teinach-Zavelstein, Germany. This painting is a richly symbolic triptych altarpiece. Once opened, the central painting is quite impressive and detailed. The painting contains a large Temple at its centre. The entrance to the Temple is behind two massive pillars. The bases of the pillars are inscribed with the Hebrew names *Jachin* and *Boaz* and decorated accordingly. Behind the pillars stands an arched entrance to the Temple. At the top of the arch is hung a shield with a Pelican feeding its young with blood from its breast. Inside the Temple, we find the High Priest of Israel, recognisable by his breast plate, standing in front of the Ark of the Covenant identifying the room as the Holy of Holies. The ceiling of the room is adorned with a sun at the center. The Temple has a domed roof surmounted by a crown. Emanating away from the crown and into the sky beyond are concentric circles of angels representing the Celestial Hierarchy. In the foreground in front of the Temple is a large garden. In the center of the garden stands the figure of Christ. From the wound in his side springs forth blood which collects into a pool and flows out to irrigate the garden. The garden is made of three concentric rings. Around the innermost ring stands the twelve sons of Jacob who are surrounded by corresponding elements. The whole garden is enclosed by a hedge of red and white roses. The entrance to the garden is placed at the bottom center of the painting, and at the entrance stands Antonia herself facing the entire scene.

This painting operates as a contemplative device, similar to a Masonic tracing board and stands as a testament to its designer.

The role of an unknown, wealthy patron from the Württemberg court remains a critical but underexplored dimension in our understanding of how the Rosicrucian movement gained traction and visibility. And in this respect, Antonia's reputation has escaped attention from Rosicrucian commentators for far too long.

Tobias Hess

Tobias Hess, a physician and theologian, was an enigmatic figure whose influence radiated throughout the Tübingen intellectual community. Hess had a number of esoteric interests and was a mentor to Johannes Valentinus Andreae. He was also involved in discussions of Christian mysticism and reform. Aside from his medical expertise, Hess was a visionary who championed the integration of faith, science, and mysticism. He sought to reconcile spiritual truths with empirical observation, advocating for a holistic understanding of the divine in both the macrocosm and the microcosm. Hess's influence on Andreae did extend beyond theological discussions. In fact, he likely inspired in Andreae an interest in alchemy, numerology, and apocalyptic thought, all of which would later surface in Andreae's writings.

Christoph Besold

Christoph Besold was a jurist and scholar who had a keen interest in Neoplatonism and theology. Throughout his correspondence with Hess and Andreae, we learn that Besold held similar ideas regarding societal and religious reform.

Besold was perhaps less of a visionary than Hess, but Besold was a pragmatist whose keen intellect allowed him to synthesise complex ideas into coherent frameworks, which may have influenced the philosophical underpinnings of the Rosicrucian source works.

The Tübingen Circle

The University of Tübingen was a hub of intellectual and spiritual activity in late sixteenth and early seventeenth centuries Germany and was home to several figures whose ideas and interactions appear to align closely with the themes and ideals of the Rosicrucian movement. These individuals include the aforementioned Tobias Hess, Christoph Besold, Johannes Valentinus Andreae, as well as others who were bound by shared interests in theology, mysticism, and religious and societal reform.

Much of what we know of The Tübingen Circle first appeared in the landmark work, The Rosy Cross Unveiled (1980) by Christopher McIntosh. This would later be republished under the name, The Rosicrucians: The History, Mythology, and Rituals of an Esoteric Order (1997).

This confluence of minds has led to the proposal that perhaps the Rosicrucian source works were a collaborative effort. Given the geographical centre being Tübingen University, this collaborative authorship model has often been referred to as *The Tübingen Circle*. Much of the information we have today relating to The Tübingen Circle we owe to Christopher McIntosh who dedicates a chapter to the subject in his work *The Rosicrucians: The History, Mythology, and Rituals of an Esoteric Order*[4].

In this model, each member brings a unique perspective:

- Hess likely contributed the visionary and mystical framework, with his own specialisation in alchemy and theology;
- Besold may have shaped the philosophical and theological arguments, grounding the source works in a coherent intellectual tradition; and,
- Andreae provided the literary flair and allegorical structure, crafting narratives that captured the imagination of readers while conveying a hidden allegorical meaning.

---

4 Sometimes printed under the alternative title, *Rosy Cross Unveiled*.

Couple to this information that there were also some initiatic proto-Rosicrucian societies operating from within the University of Tübingen (McIntosh, 1998), such as *The Fruit-bringing Society* (German: *Fruchtbringende Gesellschaft*) and *The Order of the Inseparables* (German: *Orden der Indissolubilisten*) and you have a compelling case for The Tübingen Circle theory of Rosicrucian authorship.

Authorship according to Rosicrucian organisations

It would be remiss of us to not consider the authorship question without considering the proposals put forth from existing Rosicrucian organisations. Afterall, these organisations have dedicated their livelihoods towards the subject. However, as organisations are traditional in nature, they do tend to be rather slow in adopting new information, especially if they have an already established mythos.

This adherence to tradition can make them somewhat resistant to incorporating new findings or alternative theories that challenge their foundational stories. For instance, some Rosicrucian groups maintain a strong esoteric or mystical interpretation of the Rosicrucian source works which helps to emphasise their spiritual significance over historical context. For these organisations, the historicity is of lesser importance than the import that can be gained from the study by initiates within their traditions.

Furthermore, these organisations often seek to establish continuity between the Rosicrucian ideals espoused in the source work era and their modern practices, in an effort to legitimise their own tradition. For example, a contemporary Rosicrucian body might assert that the Rosicrucian trilogy was the work of a single visionary figure, such as Johannes Valentinus Andreae, or maybe they might propose that a secret initiatic brotherhood was operating in the shadows of European intellectual society, the secrecy of which prevents the general public from knowing that the contemporary organisation represents an unbroken chain of lineal descent. While such claims might have symbolic resonance, they often lack robust historical substantiation.

Nonetheless, the contributions of Rosicrucian organisations cannot be dismissed. Their custodianship of Rosicrucian texts and traditions has preserved valuable insights and interpretations that might otherwise have been lost. Their symbolic readings of the Rosicrucian source works have inspired generations of seekers to explore the philosophical and spiritual dimensions of the movement. While their narratives may not always align with historical evidence, they offer a vital perspective that complements academic approaches, reminding us that the Rosicrucian legacy is as much about inspiring inner transformation as it is about uncovering historical truths. Additionally, I can assure you from experience that some traditional organisations actually do have some items in their archives that may be surprising to many, as such, I would recommend keeping an open mind as we consider the authorship suggestions proposed by contemporary Rosicrucian organisations.

Authorship according to The Ancient Mystical Order Rosae Crucis (A.M.O.R.C.)

The Ancient and Mystical Order Rosae Crucis (A.M.O.R.C.) maintains a theory that was first proposed by their founder H. Spencer Lewis.

This can be found in several places. In the book *Rosicrucian Questions and Answers with a Complete History of the Order*, H. Spencer Lewis denies that Andreae was responsible for the Rosicrucian source works, instead stating that,

> *The real author of the pamphlets that brought about the revival in Germany was none other than Sir Francis Bacon, who was Imperator for the Order in England and various parts of Europe at the time. And his other Rosicrucian writings, and especially his book the "New Atlantis," admittedly his own work, clearly indicate the connection between Bacon and the publications issued in Germany between 1610 and 1616.* (Lewis, 1929, p. 101)

Additionally, a biography appears in some editions of A.M.O.R.C.'s *Rosicrucian Manual*, which states,

> As a pioneer in the revolution of methods of education he stands without a peer, and the effect of his "secret society" upon mankind in Europe was ever a puzzle to the multitude until it was discovered that the secret society to which much of his correspondence seemed to refer, was the Rosicrucian Order. Then it was found that some of his literary co-workers were his official emissaries or deputies of the Rosicrucian Order, making periodical journeys to foreign jurisdictions. It was Bacon who, as Imperator of the Rosicrucian Order, wrote the now internationally famous book called the Fama Fraternitatis, and to which the fictitious name of Christian Rosenkreutz was signed—meaning Rosy Cross. Through the discovery of the secret code in this manuscript, and the several acknowledged writings on secret codes, it was further discovered that Bacon wrote the famous plays attributed to the one who produced them, Shakespeare. An examination of the pages of the original plays shows not only the names and titles of Bacon concealed in the strangely arranged lines of text, but the Rosicrucian and Bacon symbols are found as water-marks in the paper. (Lewis, 1927, p. 126)

Lewis's remarks that Sir Francis Bacon was the author of the Fama Fraternitatis and was the hidden author behind Shakespeare are ideas which have continued to be maintained by A.M.O.R.C.

Today, as at the turn of the twentieth century, there were many promoters of the Baconian Theory of Shakespearian works. This is not something unique to A.M.O.R.C. But what about the idea that Bacon wrote the Fama Fraternitatis? Is there any evidence available to prove such a bold claim?

Sir Francis Bacon (1561-1626) was quite an enigmatic personality. The mystery of Sir Francis Bacon has led to all sorts of unusual proposals, especially by Rosicrucian students and Baconian Theorists. Even during his lifetime, we find his name being attributed to seemingly unrelated works.

One of these works was *The Anatomy of Melancholy* by Robert Burton (writing as a fictional character, Democritus Junior) written in 1621.

The Anatomy of Melancholy is an impressive work, which aims to address the causes, symptoms, and remedies for melancholy, a condition broadly understood at the time to encompass everything from sadness and depression to philosophical reflection and scholarly introspection. The book is both a medical treatise and an exploration of human nature. Additionally, in this work Burton demonstrates a familiarity with a wide array of occult, mystical, and esoteric traditions, including alchemy and astrology.

In this work, we find an unusual footnote, which some have pointed out as suggesting a connection between Andreae and Bacon.

It reads,

> *Joh.Valent.Andreas, Lord Verulam.*
> (Democritus Junior, 1883, p. 64)

This curious footnote has caught the attention of multiple Rosicrucian commentators. Perhaps most notably was Manly P. Hall in his *Secret Teaching of All Ages*, who would relate this correspondence to be proof of a connection between Andreae and Bacon, perhaps even evidence that Andreae had authorised Bacon to use his name as a pen-name,

> *Johann Valentin Andreæ is generally reputed to be the author of the Confessio. It is a much-mooted question, however, whether Andreæ did not permit his name to be used as a pseudonym by Sir Francis Bacon. Apropos of this subject are two extremely significant references occurring in the introduction to that remarkable potpourri, The*

> *Anatomy of Melancholy. This volume first appeared in 1621 from the pen of Democritus junior, who was afterwards identified as Robert Burton, who, in turn, was a suspected intimate of Sir Francis Bacon. One reference archly suggests that at the time of publishing The Anatomy of Melancholy in 1621 the founder of the Fraternity of R.C. was still alive. This statement – concealed from general recognition by its textual involvement – has escaped the notice of most students of Rosicrucianism. In the same work there also appears a short footnote of stupendous import. It contains merely the words: "Joh. Valent. Andreas, Lord Verulam." This single line definitely relates Johann Valentin Andreæ to Sir Francis Bacon, who was Lord Verulam, and by its punctuation intimates that they are one and the same individual.* (Hall, 1928, pp. 440-441)

However, if we were to read the section that accompanies this footnote in its entirety, then we would be able to see that this is not as unusual as some would make out,

> *Utopian parity is a kind of government, to be wished for, rather than effected, Respub. Christianopolitana, Campanellas city of the Sun, and that new Atlantis witty fictions, but mere chimeras; and Plato's community in many things is impious, absurd and ridiculous, it takes away all splendour and magnificence.* (Democritus Junior, 1883, p. 64)

When taken in context, we can see that the author is not suggesting a link between the two names, as Hall's interpretation would imply, but is simply stating that both authors have written works which describe a societal utopia; specifically, Andreae's *Christianopolis* and Bacon's *New Atlantis*. Hall also states that, "*A crucified rose within a heart is watermarked into the dedication page of the 1628 edition of Robert Burton's Anatomy of Melancholy*" (Hall, 1928, p. 447), however, I've not found this watermark in any of the editions I've had the opportunity to peruse.

While no direct evidence links Bacon with Burton or Andreae in terms of collaboration or direct influence, all were products of a late-Renaissance intellectual climate that valued the synthesis of ancient wisdom with emerging modern perspectives. It is possible that Burton's work, with its detailed observation of human nature and emphasis on reform, was simply inspired by the same cultural and intellectual currents that shaped Bacon's thought. All three individuals likewise shared similar values of societal reformation and shared a desire to improve society through the advancement of knowledge and individual well-being.

It is also worth mentioning that Bacon's New Atlantis includes references to a secretive group dedicated to the advancement of knowledge, which, given the Rosicrucian buzz of the era, could easily be interpreted as a veiled allusion to the Rosicrucians. Add into account that the Baconian Theory, seemingly demonstrating that Bacon was keen on using ciphers and pseudonyms, was being popularised during the same era that A.M.O.R.C. was being founded and you have fertile ground for proposing a connection between the two. However, as it stands, there is not enough evidence to prove that Bacon ever had a hand in authoring any of the known Rosicrucian source works. Nevertheless, given the stylistic and thematic parallels between Bacon's works and the pioneering Rosicrucian works, I would not rule out a connection entirely.

Romæ.   ¹² Hic segetes, illic veniunt fælicius uvæ, Arborei fætus alibi, atq; injussa virescunt Gramina Virg. 1. Georg.   ¹³ Lucanus, l. 6.   ¹⁴ Vi~g
¹⁵ Joh. Valent Andreas, Lord Verulam

The curious footnote that has led many to incorrectly attribute a connection between Andreae and Bacon.

Authorship according to Societas Rosicruciana (S.R.I.A./S.R.I.S./S.R.I.C.F.)

The *Societas Rosicruciana* as a Rosicrucian tradition is focused upon study, personal growth, and the pursuit of spiritual wisdom; or as the society tends to frame it, dedicated to the *Investigation of the Hidden Mysteries of Nature and Science*.

As such, Societas Rosicruciana tends to place a greater emphasis on the study of the history, principles, and doctrines presented in the Rosicrucian source works, rather than any practical application. Certainly, the subject of authorship has been discussed by many of its influential members, and there have been multiple papers presented on this subject at the *Metropolitan Study Group* (and no doubt at individual *Colleges*), but it is done more so in the spirit of inquiry, rather than authorship attribution.

As for the Societas Rosicruciana rituals, they tend to focus on the mystical, symbolic, and allegorical aspects of the Rosicrucian tradition, such as the exploration of numbers, colours, alchemy, comparative religion, etc. However, there are quotes that can be found within the rituals that are sourced directly from the Rosicrucian source works themselves (although, not explicitly identified as being as such).

In the 1920s, Right Worthy Frater Richard Hopper Holme 8°, authored a paper titled *Who was C.R.? An Essay to Commence Discussion*. This essay gained considerable popularity and was later included in a series of study booklets compiled by Supreme Magus A.B. Stephenson. In the preface to this booklet, Stephenson comments rather aptly on the essay, stating,

> *The only certainty is that the Fama Fraternitatis WAS published at Cassel in 1614 and has prompted argument ever since. Many consider this its outstanding achievement – that in 1988 we cannot be certain of anything except its ability to stimulate our thought and our study.* (Stephenson, 1988)

Holme would make some comments as to authorship of the Rosicrucian trilogy. In this text, Holme would state,

> There was also a ROSICRUCIAN FRATERNITY among the members of which occured [sic] the names of Elias Ashmole, Sir Francis Bacon and other eminent men. A MORAL ORDER. This idea let to the adoption of a small RED CROSS worn on the front of the headgear, as specially referred to in a pamphlet called the "Journey of the Rosicrucians to Atlantis."
> (Holme, 1988)

Such a statement must at first appear odd and I'm not certain what pamphlet he read with the title *"Journey of the Rosicrucians to Atlantis"*, but it is no doubt referring to Sir Francis Bacon's New Atlantis, which includes the following confirming statement,

> The morrow after our three days were past, there came to us a new man, that we had not seen before, clothed in blue as the former was, save that his turban was white, with a small red cross on top. (Bacon, 2020)

In any case, whilst this essay was written by a senior member of the society, it should not be seen as in any way an official statement or endorsement from the society. As such, it is perhaps better to state that the Societas Rosicruciana in Anglia has no official stance as to authorship of the Rosicrucian source works; even if prominent individuals within the society have proposed their own suggestions.

Authorship according to The Rosicrucian Fellowship (T.R.F.)

The Rosicrucian Fellowship, founded in 1909 in the U.S.A. by Max Heindel, was another Rosicrucian organisation which arose at the turn of the twentieth century. The Rosicrucian Fellowship is overtly Christian; however, it is anything but orthodox. It blends Christian mysticism with esoteric teachings rooted in astrology, alchemy, and the western mystery tradition.

Leaders from across the diverse Rosicrucian spectrum have repeatedly pointed to the enigmatic Sir Francis Bacon as being a hidden architect behind the movement. Although evidence for this attribution is still outstanding, it's difficult to deny his influence upon the tradition.

The cornerstone text of the Fellowship is *The Rosicrucian Cosmo-Conception* written by Max Heindel. This text describes humanity's spiritual journey through cycles of existence, emphasising reincarnation and the law of cause and effect (karma). It presents seven distinct planes of existence, governed by spiritual hierarchies, and explains the creation and evolution of humanity through successive epochs, each epoch corresponding to stages of spiritual and physical development; the ultimate goal of humanity being to achieve divine consciousness.

The organisation remains active today and is headquartered in Oceanside, California.

Heindel claimed that the Fellowship was inspired by the teachings of an invisible Rosicrucian Order, which he presented as guiding humanity's spiritual evolution.

Max Heindel preferred to view the Rosicrucian phenomenon as being a brotherhood being led by elder brothers.

Heindel claims that Christian Rosenkreuz's birth in the thirteenth century[5] marked the start of a new spiritual era for the Western world and asserts that this figure has continuously reincarnated in different bodies and across multiple generations throughout Europe to guide humanity's spiritual evolution, inspiring the great thinkers, including Francis Bacon, working as an unseen but pivotal force in the intellectual and spiritual development of the West.

From his work, The Rosicrucian Cosmo-Conception,

> *In the thirteenth century a high spiritual teacher, having the symbolical name Christian Rosenkreuz - Christian: Rose: Cross - appeared in Europe to commence that work. He founded the mysterious Order of Rosicrucians with the object of throwing occult light upon the misunderstood Christian Religion and to explain the mystery of Life and Being from the scientific standpoint in harmony with Religion.*
>
> *Many centuries have rolled by since the birth, as Christian Rosenkreuz, of the Founder of the Rosicrucian Mystery School, and by many his existence is even regarded as a myth. But his birth as Christian Rosenkreuz marked the beginning of a new epoch in*

---

5 The thirteenth century is significantly earlier than what can be inferred from the original Rosicrucian source works. It is possible that Heindel chose to place Rosenkreuz's birth at the dawn of the Renaissance to suggest formative Rosicrucian influence on that era. This, of course, is my own speculation, though it is consistent with his broader Rosicrucian philosophy. Heindel may also have been influenced by Rudolf Steiner, who likewise attributed Christian Rosenkreuz's life to the thirteenth century.

spiritual life of the Western World. That particular Ego has also been in continuous physical existence ever since, in one or another of the European Countries. He has taken a new body when his successive vehicles have outlived their usefulness, or circumstances rendered it expedient that he changes the scene of his activities. Moreover, he is embodied today - an Initiate of high degree, an active or potent factor in all affairs of the West - although unknown to the World.

He labored with the Alchemists centuries before the advent of modern science. He, through, an intermediary, inspired the now mutilated works of Bacon, Jacob Boehme and others received through him the inspiration which makes their works so spiritually illuminating. (Heindel M., 1911, p. 518)

As such, it may be fair to state that the Rosicrucian Fellowship does not necessarily have an opinion upon the authorship question, rather, it sees the source work era as being an outward public proclamation coming from a pre-existent movement.

Authorship according to Builders of the Adytum (B.O.T.A.)

The *Builders of the Adytum* (B.O.T.A.) is an educational mystery school founded in 1911 by Paul Foster Case. Case himself had been an initiate of the Hermetic Order of the Golden Dawn.

Case was a voluminous writer, developing a series of lessons for his organisation. These lessons, particularly on Tarot, are still valued by many Rosicrucian students today. However, perhaps his best-known work is, *The True and Invisible Rosicrucian Order* written in 1927.

In The True and Invisible Rosicrucian Order Case rejects Andreae as being an author of the Fama Fraternitatis or Confessio Fraternitatis; but accepts that he was the author of The Chemical

Wedding of Christian Rosenkreuz in the Year 1459. Christian Rosenkreuz according to Case was a literary device utilised by Andreae but was completely separate to the *CR/CRC/Father Christian* character of the Fama Fraternitatis and Confessio Fraternitatis. Furthermore, Case asserts that Andreae may have deliberately chosen to circulate his alchemical romance at this time,

> *...in the hope of profiting by the excitement stirred up by the two manifestoes.* (Case, 1989, p. 3)

Case states that the Rosicrucian fraternity is described as being invisible, not because its members are discarnate or supernatural beings, but because it lacks a formal external organisation, stating,

> *The Order is invisible because it has no external organization. It is not composed of invisible beings. Its members are men and women incarnate on earth in physical bodies. They are invisible to ordinary eyes because the minds behind those eyes cannot recognize the marks of a true Rosicrucian.* (Case, 1989)

Case event went so far as to argue that any society claiming to be a direct historical successor to the authors of the original manifestoes should be,

> *...judged as invalid.* (Case, 1989, p. 5)

Naturally, this put him at odds with the views of A.M.O.R.C. the latter organisation maintaining that there was a physical body behind the Rosicrucian source works and which A.M.O.R.C. was the modern representative. Nevertheless, Lewis maintained a level of respect for the work of Case as illustrated by communications written to Case in 1935 (more about this in a later section of this book, see *War of the Roses*).

HALLMARKS OF THE R+C

*S*o far we have looked at potential authors for the Rosicrucian source works. In every case, the outcome has either been a lack of evidence, or the suggested author themselves expressly denied being a member of the Rosicrucian fraternity. However, there is perhaps another reason why we cannot find the existence of Rosicrucians during the era that the Rosicrucian source works were penned.

The initial Rosicrucian writings contain a rather holistic, albeit, often inexplicit, doctrinal framework for man to *Know Thyself* and study the relationships that exist between *Man*, *Nature*, and *God*. A careful reading of the Fama Fraternitatis and Confessio Fraternitatis suggests that the cryptic statements and peculiar elements within them are best understood if the Rosicrucians are viewed as an ideal; not as a group of people. From this perspective, it would certainly be possible to be responsible for drafting and publishing the Rosicrucian publications whilst simultaneously denying membership in the Fraternity of the Rosy Cross.

Every person sees and understands historical events differently depending upon our own preconceptions (naturally, shaped by our age, culture, education, etc) which can influence our understanding of history. It is natural that our twenty-first century viewpoint addresses the question of Rosicrucian membership by seeking a physical filiation between members in a common meeting place. But it would appear that the Rosicrucian writers of this era were keen on using metaphors and allegories to describe their cause. The Rosicrucian writings of this period were more akin to spiritual allegories and utopian aspirations than historical narratives. With this outlook in mind, being a Rosicrucian would entail having already achieved an enlightened state, akin to *Christhood*. By viewing the Rosicrucian source works as representing an allegorical or mystical ideal, we can reach the conclusion that the desire to meet the true Rosicrucians, a primary theme throughout these works, is analogous to the desire for reunion with that source from which we are all emanated, and that the purpose of the fraternity was to assist man to come to know the relationship that exists between Man, Nature, and God; and heal that *division* that exists between them. From this perspective, the enigmatic and cryptic phrases contained within the Rosicrucian source works start to make a lot more sense, such as the closing line from the Fama Fraternitatis,

> *And our building, even if a hundred thousand people had seen it from close to, shall forever remain untouched, undestroyed, unseen, and completely hidden from the godless world.* (Godwin, McIntosh, & McIntosh, 2016, p. 33)

This is not to say that the Rosicrucian source works should *only* be regarded as a spiritual allegory. Certainly, these texts do contain political, religious, and historical concepts that are especially relevant to their time. However, these notions are of less importance and are not their primary motivation nor the reason why Rosicrucianism is still spoken about today.

The authors of the source works were quite clear that Rosicrucianism was not anything new, but rather it was a contemporary expression of a primordial wisdom,

> *Our Philosophia is nothing new but is the same which Adam received after his fall and which Moses and Solomon applied.* (Godwin, McIntosh, & McIntosh, 2016, p. 31)

Hallmarks of the R+C

The *timelessness* of the Rosicrucian philosophy as described during this period does make it increasingly challenging to define what makes Rosicrucianism unique. This budding Rosicrucian tradition shares so many similarities with other unique traditions, such as Gnosticism, Hermeticism, and Neoplatonism, often blending elements of these traditions into its own composition. However, as Rosicrucianism begins to take shape, distinct features do begin to emerge that help define its unique identity.

In this section, I wish to explore some of the features that help to identify the Rosicrucian tradition and distinguish it from adjacent philosophies.

These *hallmarks*, or distinguishing characteristics, are recurring elements that seem to arise consistently across the tradition's diverse manifestations. Whether in the ancient wisdom that inspired the early-Rosicrucian writers, the alchemical renaissance of the fifteenth-to-seventeenth centuries, the occult revival of the nineteenth century, or in modern expressions, these hallmarks provide continuity and identity to the Rosicrucian tradition.

Whilst I have opted for the term hallmark, partially to distinguish it from the similar term, landmark, which is so heavily associated with the Masonic tradition, the meaning is conceptually similar. These hallmarks serve as signposts, pointing to the essential themes that identify Rosicrucianism through its various historical incarnations. The difference however is, unlike landmarks, these devices cannot and should not be used for attempting a quantitative analysis to attempt to categorise any tradition as being *more* or *less* Rosicrucian. This is not a point-keeping system. Rather, these are simply a recurring theme that help us to recognise the *true* Rosicrucian current by the fruit it produces.

HALLMARK ONE: *Service*

The first governing rule of the Fraternity of the Rosy Cross, as outlined in the Fama Fraternitatis, states,

> *That none of them should profess any other thing than to cure the sick, and that gratis.* (Godwin, McIntosh, & McIntosh, 2016, p. 23)

The above decree became a defining mark of the Rosicrucian tradition. According to the earliest Rosicrucian writings, members of the fraternity were said to travel the world, adopting the customs, language, and attire of the local communities they chose to *serve*. They participated in healing work, blending into their surroundings while aiding humanity.

This emphasis on healing is often interpreted quite literally by Rosicrucian commentators. Indeed, many contributors to the Rosicrucian tradition have been medical physicians and healers.

Among them we find,

Tobias Hess (1568-1614)

Michael Maier (1568-1622)

Robert Fludd (1574-1637)

Louis Charles Édouard de Lapasse (1792-1867)

Adrien Péladan (1815-1890)

Gérard Encausse (1865-1916)

Franz Anton Mesmer (1734-1815)

William Wynn Westcott (1848-1925)

William Robert Woodman (1828-1891)

Nizier Anthelme Philippe (1849-1905)

Franz Hartmann (1838-1912)

Given the explicit references to healing in the Rosicrucian source works and the notable contributions of physicians to the tradition, it is no surprise that many Rosicrucian commentators regard *healing* as a cornerstone of the Rosicrucian path.

Certainly, a healthy body is of vital importance. In Rosicrucian thought, the human body is a sacred vessel by which man may become aware of the Word of God. In our body we can see reflected the glories of nature and the universe. It is also this distinction which sets Rosicrucianism apart from Gnostic philosophy. To the Rosicrucian, nature, far from being a prison for the Divine, is a revealer thereof. Nature therefore is highly regarded by the Rosicrucian philosopher.

Let us look upon the early Rosicrucian writings with the eyes of a Rosicrucian. From this perspective, Rosicrucian healing can be looked upon more holistically than purely *physical* pursuits and the relief of disease. Rosicrucian healing should not be considered only in the literal physical sense but should be broadened to encompass healing that divide which *seemingly* exists between who we appear to *be*, and who we *truly are*.

Many have taken the First Law of the Rosicrucian Fraternity to allude to literal healing. Although, it may be better illustrated by the word *Service*.

This is a holistic rectification of Man that addresses the physical, moral, and spiritual dimensions. Healing in this context extends to reconciling Man with his divine purpose and fostering harmony in all spheres of life.

Therefore, it may be more fitting to reframe the commonly understood Rosicrucian principle of healing as one of *Service*.

Whether through advancements in the arts, sciences, or spirituality, the work of Rosicrucianism has been defined by its contribution to uplifting and transforming humanity. *Service* has been at the heart of this mission, making it truly a Hallmark of the Rosicrucian ideal.

Joséphin Péladan (1858-1918), a French Rosicrucian of Toulouse lineage, had famously established the *Salons de la Rose + Croix* for artists who shared his mystical ideals. He laid great emphasis on the transformative power of art, which he postulated was capable of manifesting the highest of ideals on the earthly plane. He conceived artists as initiates; individuals who are capable of bringing a small part of the divine into the mundane world.

His vision was encapsulated in the following exhortation he made to artists,

> *Artist, you are a priest: Art is the great mystery, and when your effort results in a masterpiece, a ray of the divine descends as on an altar. O real presence of the resplendent divinity under these supreme names: Vinci, Raphael, Michelangelo, Beethoven and Wagner.*
>
> *Artist, you are king: Art is the true empire; When your hand writes a perfect line, the cherubim themselves descend to delight in it as in a mirror.*
>
> *Spiritual drawing, line of soul, form of understanding, you give body to our dreams, Samothrace and Saint John, Sistine and Cenacolo, Saint Ouen, Parsifal, Ninth, Symphony, Notre-Dame.*
>
> *Artist, you are a magician: Art is the great miracle and proves our immortality.*[1] (Péladan, 1892)

---

1   French: *Artiste, tu es prêtre: l'Art est le grand mystère, et lorsque ton effort*

Whilst the efforts of Péladan to use art as an instrument to inspire and ennoble humanity was to some extent a response to the social decadence he perceived in French society at that time, the same pioneering spirit can be seen expressed by Rosicrucian philosophers throughout history.

This is not just true for the arts, but can be equally applied to the sciences, especially during periods of Rosicrucian revival.

It is no wonder then that so many later Rosicrucian organisations throughout time have wished to include Sir Francis Bacon, a pioneer of scientific methodology, as one of their own; and as we have seen in our discussion on authorship, many Rosicrucian groups often portrayed him as a secret member of the Fraternity of the Rosy Cross or even as the author of the Fama Fraternitatis. Bacon advocated for systematic observation and experimentation to uncover nature's secrets, a methodology that challenged the Aristotelian scholasticism dominating medieval thought. In his *Novum Organum* and *The Advancement of Learning*, Bacon sought to advance human understanding and alleviate human suffering through the systematic exploration of nature's laws. Couple this with his story of a utopian society being guided by a secret brotherhood, as seen in his *New Atlantis*, and you must admit, despite the lack evidence, Bacon really does make a compelling Rosicrucian!

When it comes to contemporary Rosicrucian organisations, service is achieved in multiple ways, but most notably through education and metaphysical aid.

---

aboutit au chef-d'oeuvre, un rayon du divin descend comme sur un autel. O présence réelle de la divinité resplendissante sous ces noms suprêmes: Vinci, Raphael, Michel-Ange, Beethoven et Wagner. Artiste, tu es roi: l'Art est l'empire véritable; Lorsque ta main écrit une ligne parfaite, les chérubins eux-mêmes descendent s'y complaire comme dans an miroir. Spirituel dessin, ligne d'âme, forme d'entendement, tu donnes le corps à nos rêves, Samothrace et saint Jean, Sixtine et Cenacolo, saint Ouen, Parsifal, Neuvième, Symphonie, Notre-Dame. Artiste, tu es mage: l'Art est le grand miracle et prouve notre immortalité.

A large print from 1892 advertising Joséphin Péladan's (1858-1918) Salon de la Rose + Croix. The artist who designed it was a fellow Symbolist, Carlos Schwabe (1866-1926).

For example, education is a cornerstone of the work of the Societas Rosicruciana tradition. Active participation in educational pursuits is not merely encouraged but is an integral part of membership. Members are expected to contribute meaningfully to discussions and often prepare educational material to share with their fellow Fratres. This tradition of mutual learning fosters an environment of exploration and enlightenment, where ideas are exchanged, and personal insights are celebrated. This also contributes to an academic culture which distinguishes Societas Rosicruciana from other Rosicrucian traditions. There are no formal requirements which members must adhere to, but historically, these contributions have taken the form of small research papers, personal reflections of their journey in the society, or even a book review. However, these papers should not be thought of as simply scholarly exercises; they serve as a means for members to explore more fully their chosen subject. This not only provides an opportunity for the individual member to better understand the topic at hand but also contributes insights that uplift the society as a whole.

Hallmarks of the R+C

Since its inception, a presentation of a paper has been customary at nearly every meeting of the Societas Rosicruciana in Anglia's (S.R.I.A.) *Metropolitan College No. 1*. Some of these papers would make their way into printed Transactions. This enthusiasm for esoteric education would eventually lead to the establishment of a study group, in part, designed to be an esoteric counterpart to the Freemasonic *Quatuor Coronati Lodge of Research*. This study group was first chaired by Frater R. Palmer Thomas who would state:

> ...a small band of M. Ms [Master Masons] who, in their wish for more Masonic knowledge, had gravitated into the ranks of the Soc. Ros. In Anglia, wished to meet together more often than at the quarterly convocations of the Met. College. They accordingly obtained the consent of the M.W.S.M. [Most Worthy Supreme Magus] to their so doing. Their object in the first instance was to exchange views, discuss questions, and study those liberal arts and sciences that are so frequently referred to in the Craft rituals. (SRIA Province of Greater London, 2023)

In the modern era, the methods of presentation have evolved significantly, embracing the tools of the digital age. Today, Fratres present their work through various formats, including PowerPoint slides, multimedia presentations, and even video content. In 2024, an online session hosted by S.R.I.A. London even had a paper written and presented live using Artificial Intelligence! Naturally, you can imagine that this historical event stimulated a vibrant and colourful discussion.

The S.R.I.A. has also established a prestigious recognition to honour exceptional contributions to its educational endeavours: the *Companion of Christian Rosenkreuz* (C.C.R.) *Award*. This esteemed accolade represents one of the highest distinctions within the society, granted only to members whose papers are deemed of exceptional value to the Rosicrucian community. The selection process for this honour is rigorous and impartial, overseen by an anonymous body known as the *Panel of Eight*. These judges evaluate submissions with the utmost discretion and fairness.

Acts of Service can also be found in other Rosicrucian organisations that conform to the more traditional concept of healing. For example, A.M.O.R.C. members across the world regularly contribute to metaphysical aid. This aid is often extended informally and privately, carried out by individual members within the sanctity of their personal Sanctum. In this space, members focus their thoughts, prayers, and meditations on offering healing energy, comfort, or strength to those in need.

On a larger scale, A.M.O.R.C. Grand Lodges around the world institutionalise these principles through a daily *Council of Solace* ceremony. Conducted at midday, this ritual is a collective effort where members focus their intentions on assisting individuals who have requested aid, promoting healing, and fostering peace. The ceremony not only serves those in need but would surely also serve to strengthen the fraternal bond between members, uniting them in a shared purpose, and a collective act of compassion.

In addition to the Council of Solace, individual A.M.O.R.C. affiliated bodies often organise Metaphysical Aid Committees dedicated to providing assistance to both members and non-members. These committees often extend their support to a wide range of circumstances. They provide metaphysical support to individuals who are dying, recently deceased, or even in the process of being born, providing spiritual comfort and support during these most crucial initiatory events.

In a similar manner to A.M.O.R.C., The Rosicrucian Fellowship also conducts a metaphysical method of healing, taking inspiration from the Gospel of Luke: *Preach the Gospel and Heal the Sick*. The method of healing is by prayer and directing concentrated thoughts to the petitioner. The healing is further amplified by taking advantage of certain astrological periods which are most conducive to healing work. Whilst the healing efforts are carried out by *Invisible Helpers* (Rosicrucian

Fellowship members and those who wish to assist the cause) the work itself is overseen by the *Elder Brothers* (transcendent and invisible Masters. For more information, see *Hallmark Four: Rosicrucian Masters*).

Across the globe and spanning centuries, Rosicrucian students have consistently engaged in acts of quiet, unseen service. These selfless efforts are not motivated by profit, recognition, or glamour. Instead, they stem from a commitment to the betterment of humanity and the realisation of more noble spiritual ideals.

Historically, this tradition of quiet service has been a defining feature of Rosicrucian communities. From aiding individuals in need through metaphysical means to supporting global causes through unified spiritual efforts, these acts of service reflect a universal commitment to alleviating suffering and promoting societal progress. And whilst only several organisations have been mentioned here, such work should not be assumed to be limited to these societies alone.

The unassuming nature of these contributions is deliberate. By remaining unseen and unacknowledged, Rosicrucians ensure that their work is pure, driven solely by the intention to aid and uplift, free from any desire for personal validation. It is through this quiet, selfless work that Rosicrucians fulfill their mission.

HALLMARK TWO: *The Rosicrucian Pulse*

As the Rosicrucian identity has evolved over the centuries, we find that it has managed to intertwine an ancient, universal wisdom with a new body, creating a tradition that is both rooted in the past, but also contemporary to the time in which it presides; one which incorporates a primordial wisdom, but also has its own contemporary *personality*. Far from being a relic of the past, Rosicrucianism is a living tradition, continuously reborn and renewed across the ages.

From this process, we can start to see a recurring motif emerge. A pattern so repetitive that it can be safely regarded as a *hallmark* of the tradition.

This has become one of the most striking features of Rosicrucianism; its cyclical nature, alternating between periods of outward public activity and inward private introspection.

During its public phases, Rosicrucianism emerges in visible forms, engaging with broader society and influencing culture, philosophy, and spirituality. These periods are marked by the publication of manifestoes, philosophical treatises, or the establishment of schools and orders, making its presence felt in the intellectual and spiritual spheres of the time.

Conversely, during its inward phases, Rosicrucianism retreats from public view, safeguarding the tradition from those forces in society that inevitably seek to imitate, commercialise, and exploit its identity for selfish means. To protect it from those who would work to the detriment of humanity and against the ideals that the Rosicrucian tradition seeks to express.

These cycles of activity and dormancy help to ensure that the tradition remains dynamic and capable of responding to the needs of humanity in different historical contexts. This ebb and flow between visibility and invisibility is a defining characteristic of Rosicrucianism, ensuring its continual evolution and relevance.

Naturally, Rosicrucianism being a holistic philosophy, we should be able to see evidence of this hallmark within ourselves as well as within the world around us.

Duality is an inherent principle that pervades all aspects of manifestation and has been recognised by humanity since ancient times. It is evident in the rhythms of nature and the cycles of existence. The sun rises in the morning, bringing light and life to the world, only to set in the evening, giving way to the stillness and rest of night.

Our own lives mirror this pattern; we experience periods of wakefulness and activity, balanced by moments of sleep and restoration.

This duality is not merely oppositional but complementary. It can be seen in the dance of creation and destruction, expansion and contraction, order and chaos. Ancient traditions often symbolised this duality through archetypes such as light and darkness, masculine and feminine, or Yin and Yang, highlighting their interconnected and interdependent nature. Far from being in conflict, these dual-forces work together to sustain the equilibrium and harmony of existence, reminding us that one cannot exist without the other.

This same cyclical nature is evident in the rise and fall of empires, a pattern as ancient as civilisation itself. History reveals that societies, much like individuals and natural phenomena, experience periods of ascendancy and decline, creation and destruction. Empires emerge with vitality, driven by innovation, vision, and collective purpose. During their rise, they expand territories, build monumental achievements, and cultivate flourishing cultures that leave indelible marks on humanity.

Yet, just as the sun must set after its zenith, these civilisations inevitably reach a point where their momentum slows. Internal divisions, complacency, or overextension often erode their foundations. External pressures, such as invasions, economic shifts, or environmental changes, further destabilise them. In time, the once-mighty empire wanes, leaving behind only ruins and lessons for future generations. This phenomenon was illustrated remarkably by the English-born American painter, Thomas Cole (1801-1848) in his series of paintings entitled, *The Course of Empire*, which illustrates beautifully the transitory and cyclical nature of human achievements.

This is the third painting in *The Course of Empire*, a five-part series by American artist Thomas Cole (1801-1848). It depicts the empire at its zenith. Yet when viewed in the context of the full cycle, one can see both the elements that gave rise to the empire as well as the seeds which shall lead to its downfall.

Societal progress and decline are part of a larger rhythm, akin to the ebb and flow of tides or the changing of seasons. It is perhaps not surprising then the fascination humanity has had with prognosticating arts like astrology which seek to understand and predict these cycles. Nevertheless, out of the decline of one civilisation often arises the seeds of another, which learns from the past while charting a new path forward. This enduring cycle serves as both a cautionary tale as well as a source of hope, reminding us that no fall is final and that renewal is always possible.

These hallmarks of cyclical activity are not Rosicrucian. They are natural. However, if Rosicrucianism is a holistic philosophy, then we must see this pervasive tenet reflected in its tradition as well.

Reformation as the Pulsebeat

Each recurrence of the Rosicrucian impulse is marked by emergence and reformation. This is a fundamental resetting and recasting of the tradition's outer form to meet the inner needs of a *new age*. In this way, reformation is not simply one attribute of Rosicrucianism; it is the very pulsebeat of its lifecycle.

Even the earliest Rosicrucian source works called for a *universal and general reformation* of all systems of human civilisation, be they science, the arts, religion, or government. But we should be clear here, this is presented as a restoration, not as a revolution. It was an intended return to a more pure and divine image of a world better suited to the current needs of humanity. It was no coincidence that the Rosicrucian announcements arose at a time of upheaval, almost as if summoned by the crisis itself. This theme has continued through each reappearance of the Rosicrucian current. And if you happen to be more of an idealist, you might even start to recognise this same theme at play even prior to the seventeenth century; perhaps even into antiquity.

Many Rosicrucian commentators would recognise the Rosicrucian impulse being present at many major advancements of human civilisation, even those that we would not ordinarily associate with initiatory orders. Each reinvention was not meant as an attempt to return to a fossilised perceived golden age, but to foster the expression of the Rosicrucian impulse with the consciousness of its time. This also explains why I have chosen to refer to these repeating characteristics of the Rosicrucian tradition as hallmarks rather than landmarks. Any attempt to degrade a modern expression of the Rosicrucian impulse by its lack of adoption to any set of perceived historical standard or criteria would be folly. We cannot say with any certainty what form the expression of a Rosicrucian impulse in society will take in the future, other than that it will adopt the language and customs of the time in which it appears.

From this perspective, reformation is never merely cosmetic. It is a structural rectification. It is an initiatory passage each cycle *must* undergo. Without it, the Rosicrucian tradition would stagnate. But with it, the Rosicrucian tradition continually renews itself, ever seeking its most valuable expression.

The Rosicrucian Pulse as presented in Rosicrucian groups

We have already seen in the story presented in the Fama Fraternitatis how the successors of a previous Rosicrucian generation inherited the Rosicrucian wisdom by finding the tomb of their founder, Father Christian. This tomb was described as a *compendium* of Rosicrucian knowledge, furnishing the new generation with all that they needed to accomplish the task at hand, of restoring Rosicrucianism, and reforming humanity. And all of this started with the opening of the tomb.

Perhaps then it should not be surprising that Rosicrucian groups have often incorporated such symbolism into their own traditional histories.

In the case of A.M.O.R.C. this was done in quite a curious (if mostly now forgotten) way.

An early A.M.O.R.C. document, entitled *The Light of Egypt*, discusses how the opening of the tomb, as recounted in the Fama Fraternitatis, was not the only time that such an event had occurred. It describes how this was only one of many occasions that the tomb of C.R.C. had been opened.

Under the pseudonym Sri Ramatherio, H. Spencer Lewis would recount of the 1604 opening of the Tomb of C.R.C.,

> *Upon opening the tomb with due reverence and with magical rites transmitted to them through many generations of initiated forbears, they found the silent resting place of the former founder of their secret*

> *fraternity. Here they saw by the mystic light that had remained undiminished for one hundred and twenty years, the well-preserved body of that most mysterious of all beings, C. R. C.* (Sri Ramatherio, 1927)

This document would go on to describe how the soul of C.R.C. reincarnates periodically to bring about a renaissance-like period of advancement in human civilisation. During the life of each of these incarnations, the reincarnated C.R.C. would locate the tomb from his previous incarnation and find within it the secrets that had been left from the previous generation. With these secrets in hand, the incarnated C.R.C. would then have the tools necessary to proceed with the next revival period.

These secrets were referred to as being contained within a *Brown Casket*,

> *Near him in this old cave, which had been a study, laboratory and sanctum, were treasures of knowledge in manuscript form and marvels of devices for the demonstration of nature's most profound and secret laws. Performing their long-practiced processes, the Brethren restored the invisible writings to perfect legibility, removed from the hands of C. R. C. the sacred key and seal ring, and opened the ancient Brown Casket that bore the cartouche of a former Pharaoh of Egypt.* (Sri Ramatherio, 1927)

This Brown Casket that had been deposited with the body of C.R.C. would wait with the body to be found upon the next incarnation. The knowledge in this Brown Casket would then be carried by and added to over the centuries and was described as being integral to the revival of the Rosicrucian fraternity (what H. Spencer Lewis would simply refer to as *The Order* or *The Brotherhood*) in each incarnation.

The opening of the Tomb of C.R.C. in 1604 was simply one of the more recent revival events of this tradition.

This is a stylised version of H. Spencer Lewis's Brown Casket. This image was taken from an A.M.O.R.C. document called The Little Brown Casket (1920).

It is possible to see here an elaboration upon the Fama Fraternitatis narrative. So whilst the Fama Fraternitatis narrative states that Father Christian was to be found in a *Tomb* which contained all the secrets necessary to reconstitute the Fraternity of the Rosy Cross, Lewis's narrative would state that the *Body of C.R.C.* would be found near to a *Brown Casket* that contained all of the knowledge necessary to provide a physical vehicle for the *Brotherhood*.

Naturally, for Lewis to announce A.M.O.R.C. as a current vehicle for the Brotherhood, he must (allegorically) find the body of *Father Christian/C.R.C.* and be in possession of the knowledge contained in the *Brown Casket*.

Lewis would relate how he did encounter such a *tomb* in a series of private writings prepared for senior Officers and members. Between 1917-1918 in these writings Lewis would express that he was anticipating a significant spiritual transformation. After this transformation he expected that he would need to step back from the day-to-day operations of the organisation. Lewis would eventually undergo the spiritual transformation which he had anticipated on 21 April 1918. In private writings, titled *Confessio R.C. Fraternitatis,* a document originally intended only for select high ranking members, Lewis would recount a series of events which began when he was giving a lecture in the East of a Temple in southern California. During an address to the members he states that there appeared in front of him a beautiful figure with a perfect violet aura. At this time, the building began to shake so much that some members left the building in fright. Over the course of twelve days, he recalled how his body and mind were undergoing a transitory process that would see him drift in and out of a trance-like state. This would culminate in him finding an old Rosicrucian Temple founded by a previous Rosicrucian settlement,

> *It was to this cave and the ruined temple that Dr. Lewis journeyed in 1918, performed the rituals and rites, followed the formulas, and brought to light the well-preserved "body" of C. R. C. again.* (Sri Ramatherio, 1927)

From this event onwards, Lewis would adopt *Alden* as his *nomen mysticum*[2], named after a mystic from this previous settlement. Curiously, it would appear that there was an earthquake during the time Lewis was giving his Temple address in southern California (Southern California Earthquake Data Center, 2023) and so this event constitutes an example of Lewis developing a legend out of real and symbolic information.

It should be noted that Lewis would soon afterwards solidify this concept in the A.M.O.R.C. teachings and refer to this as *The Rosicrucian Cycle* which he would ascribe a specific time-period of 108 years. Ergo, a complete cycle of Rosicrucian activity from activity-to-dormancy-to-activity would span 216 years. Each cycle however would be geographically determined. So whilst one area of the world might be in a period of activity, another may be in a period of dormancy. He further asserted that A.M.O.R.C. was the current vehicle for the Rosicrucian tradition in the U.S.A. and predicted its period of activity would conclude approximately 108 years after his initiation in Toulouse, coinciding with the year 2017. At this point, the tradition would become dormant, preserved only by a few individuals, who would assist in safeguarding the spark until the time came to reactivate the cycle. Some high ranking A.M.O.R.C. members even went so far as to pledge to reincarnate in a later life within the U.S.A. to assist with the reactivation of this cycle, such as disclosed in the following document received by select senior A.M.O.R.C. members,

2 *Mystical Name.* It is quite common for senior Rosicrucian initiates to incorporate such names.

> *The "body" of C.R-C is nothing more or less than the body of reincarnated individuals who will come together and form the body of the first lodge of Rosicrucians to start the new cycle, and the manuscripts and secret teachings found with the body will be the intelligence and understanding that will be found in the schools and psychic minds of each one of the persons constituting this new body. In other words, when the year 2125 comes, the tomb of silence and long sleep will be opened and out of that tomb will come the body of C.R-C. That body will consist of a group or lodge or Supreme Council of several hundred men and women who are ready to be the Supreme Body of the new Rosicrucian cycle. And each one of these will contribute from his past knowledge in the Order, certain teachings and knowledge to aid in the re-establishment of the Order. This is the secret of the allegory of the "body" of C.R-C and the tomb.* (From a private manuscript prepared by H. Spencer Lewis)

Sometime after Lewis's era however, for reasons that remain unclear A.M.O.R.C. adjusted the cycle's starting point to 1915, the year the first constitution was signed. With this amendment, the period of activity would then conclude around 2023. In acknowledgment of this significant milestone, A.M.O.R.C. held a special convention in April 2023. During this convention, the Imperator of the organisation declared that A.M.O.R.C. would not enter a period of dormancy. The reasoning provided was that A.M.O.R.C., unlike in earlier historical cycles, was no longer limited to activity in specific jurisdictions but had evolved into a global movement.

The recognition of a Rosicrucian pulse was in no way limited to just one Rosicrucian organisation. In September 1913 William Wynn Westcott, the Supreme Magus of the Societas Rosicruciana in Anglia would provide an address to members entitled, *Rosicrucians Past and Present, at Home and Abroad*. He would repeat this paper for Woodman

College in October 1915, the same year A.M.O.R.C. was established. The paper was later published in the S.R.I.A.'s 1915 Transactions.

William Wynn Westcott (1848-1925) pictured here in the S.R.I.A. ceremonial attire of a Supreme Magus, also observed the Rosicrucian pulse.

Diverging from the approaches of other Rosicrucian-thought leaders of the day, Westcott avoids casting the personalities associated with the Rosicrucian tradition as exclusive members of a singular initiatory body. Likewise, he refrains from advocating that the S.R.I.A. represents the culmination of a lineal transmission of an ancient initiatory authority. Instead, Westcott assembles an overview of various Rosicrucian apologists from the source work period onwards. In so doing, he portrays Rosicrucianism as an expression of a philosophy represented by various esoteric principles and not by an exclusive organisation.

This is perhaps more in line with the desires of the original source work writers who, as we have discussed, proclaimed that their philosophy was not necessarily new, but was the modern expression of an ancient primordial wisdom. This did not escape Westcott's attention who repeats these same sentiments in the opening paragraphs of his paper.

Throughout the text, Westcott cites various authors as authorities on the topic of Rosicrucianism. This includes Robert Fludd, Michael Maier, Eliphas Levi, Kenneth R.H. Mackenzie, Robert Wentworth Little, Edward Bulwer-Lytton, Rudolf Steiner, and Franz Hartmann.

However, no explicit influence of note from any of these commentators can be read in Westcott's paper, and so it would be reasonable to suggest that this paper represents Westcott's appreciation for the broader mystical and occult landscape of Rosicrucianism whilst incorporating elements from different historical periods and geographical locations.

Westcott does acknowledge that, whilst the S.R.I.A. represents an expression of the Rosicrucian tradition, that it is not the only Rosicrucian group; stating that there are in fact other Rosicrucian groups from Austria and Germany who preserve a form of the Rosicrucian tradition,

> ...which are not fettered by any of the limitations which Freemasonry has imposed upon us. (Westcott W. W., 1915)

The identity of these other Rosicrucian groups remains shrouded in mystery. One plausible connection could be the German branch of The Theosophical Society which was led by Rudolf Steiner and whom Westcott states shortly thereafter was responsible for renewing interest in the German Rosicrucian tradition. In 1904, Steiner was also appointed by Annie Besant to be the head of the Theosophical Esoteric Society.

Another intriguing and mysterious possibility can be inferred from a handwritten note of Westcott preserved in the S.R.I.A. archives titled, *Origins of the SRIA*. It contains the heading, *Communicated by the Supreme Magus Dr. W.W. Westcott March 1908*. In this note, Westcott makes mention of an old German Rosicrucian lineage that was still active in Germany called, *Fratres Rosae Crucis, Rosae Rubeae et Aureae Crucis*[3] (Westcott W. W., 1908). Westcott goes on to mention that he has several of their rituals.

---

3 This is likely referring to the *Ordo Rosae Rubeae et Aureae Crucis* which was the name of the Second Order of the H.O.G.D. established in 1892. Curiously, H. Spencer Lewis would also claim A.M.O.R.C. had descended from *Antiquus Arcanus Ordo Rosae Rubeae et Aureae Crucis* (the latinised variation of the name A.M.O.R.C.), potentially showing that both the S.R.I.A., H.O.G.D., and A.M.O.R.C. share a grandfathered lineage.

The more likely and simple explanation however is that Westcott was referring to the semi-historical legendary narrative involving Kenneth R.H. Mackenzie's initiation into an existing circle of the Orden des Gold- und Rosenkreuzer; a historical lineage that Westcott had proposed as a foundational history for the S.R.I.A. and which first appeared in 1894 in a paper entitled, *Rosicrucians, their History and Aims* (Westcott W. W., 1894) and was expanded upon in Westcott's, *History of the Societas Rosicruciana in Anglia* (Westcott W. W., 1900, p. 9).

But what is important to us at this time to recognise was Westcott's appreciation of the periodicity of Rosicrucian activity.

Westcott would state,

> *The Star of Rosicrucianism is now once more in the ascendant and our Society has made rapid strides in the past ten years. It is curious to note that waves of interest in occult and mystical subjects seem to sweep over a nation at intervals; periods of Rosicrucian enlightenment alternate with other periods of materialistic dogmatism. We must remember that Rosicrucianism itself was "no new thing" but only a revival of still earlier forms of Initiation, and was a lineal descendant of the Philosophies of the Chaldean Magi, of the Egyptian priests, of the Neo-Platonists, of the Hermetists of Alexandria of the Jewish Kabalists and of Christian Kabalists such as Raymond Lully and Pic de Mirandola.* (Westcott W. W., 1915)

Westcott has faced scrutiny in some modern commentaries on the S.R.I.A. and the Hermetic Order of the Golden Dawn, particularly regarding the history of the S.R.I.A. Despite potential inaccuracies, Westcott's work contains valuable insights, and his claims, especially those related to lineage, suggest he was engaged with Rosicrucian ideals; even if we have to look to the *spirit* of his message, rather than to the *letter*.

Westcott's appreciation for the broader mystical and occult landscape of Rosicrucianism is evident and in his work, especially the aforementioned paper, he acknowledges other Rosicrucian groups beyond the S.R.I.A., perhaps even hinting at a mysterious connection with an older Rosicrucian organisation via a semi-historical narrative involving Kenneth R.H. Mackenzie (see *Appendix One* section on the history of Societas Rosicruciana).

HALLMARK THREE: *The Invisible College of the Rosicrucians*

> *For where two or three are gathered together in my name, there am I in the midst of them.*
> Matthew 18:20

In 1622, several years after the publication of the Fama Fraternitatis, anonymously printed posters would appear in Paris, claiming to be authored by the Rosicrucian brotherhood.

One summer morning the citizens of Paris would awake to find these posters plastered at the major intersections of their town. Upon these posters were written a curious message from an enigmatic group calling themselves *The Brotherhood of the Rosy Cross*.

Translated, these posters read as follows,

> *We, Deputies of the Principal College of the Brothers of the Rose-Croix, are making a visible and invisible sojourn in this town, by the grace of the Most High to Whom the hearts of the just are turned. We shall show and teach without books or signs to speak all kinds of languages of the countries where we wish to go, to save our fellow-men from the mirror of death.*

> *If he causes trouble to one of us by finding out about us for curiosity alone, he will never communicate with us, but, if desire truly drives him to have his name inscribed on the register of our confraternity, we, who will judge thoughts, will make him see the truth of our promises, so that we will not need to divulge the place of our residence, since the thoughts, joined to the true will of the reader, shall be capable of making us known to him and him of us.* (Sédir, 2006)

These posters really amplify the messages that were contained within the Confessio Fraternitatis. Just as with authorship of the other Rosicrucian source works, the author of these posters remains anonymous.

These messages appeared over the course of two separate days. The first poster contained the writing in the first paragraph. The second paragraph appeared several days later in similar circumstances. The events leading up to and after their posting is recounted in the *Mercure François* of 1623 and shows that the Parisian newsagents of Pont Neuf were quite infatuated with these *Invisible Rosicrucians*.

The Fraternity of the Rosy Cross in the Fama Fraternitatis obligated their members to work hiddenly, and adopt the customs, clothing, and language of the land in which they chose to reside.

If these posters were not authored by the same individuals as the original source works, then it would appear that some other unnamed persons had taken these messages seriously and were working in their spirit.

Whether the Fraternity of the Rosy Cross ever truly existed in 1614 remains unknown. As we have discussed in an earlier section of the book, the texts appear to reflect that the Rosicrucian brotherhood, The Fraternity of the Rosy Cross, existed more as an allegorical ideal, rather than a physical brotherhood.

Nevertheless, it is becoming increasingly clear that Rosicrucianism was beginning to exert an influence that would sooner or later express itself through other individuals and eventually, even organised groups.

These groups exhibited, and continue to exhibit, incredible diversity. It is no wonder that so many Rosicrucian students have looked across the fence into neighbouring Rosicrucian territories and stated, "*That is not real Rosicrucianism*". And yet, across nearly all varieties of Rosicrucian expression, one theme has remained consistent: *The Invisible Rosicrucians*.

But to what does this invisibility entail? At its simplest, it can mean merely not being seen. At its most fantastical, it conjures up notions of magical cloaks of invisibility, reminiscent of *Harry Potter*. Interestingly, both interpretations, and everything in between, have found their way into the lore and practices of various Rosicrucian groups.

This representation of the Fraternity of the Rosy Cross appeared in a Rosicrucian source work of 1618 titled, The Mirror of the Wisdom of the Rosy Cross, published by Theophilus Schweighardt Constantiens. This was a pseudonym for the German alchemist Daniel Mögling (1596-1635).

In the era of the Rosicrucian source works, this idea of invisibility was initially understood more as an act of remaining unseen in plain sight. The authors of these texts, as well as the Paris posters, claimed that the Rosicrucian brotherhood was dispersed across Europe, speaking any language, and blending seamlessly into society. They could be anyone: your family doctor, your teacher, or perhaps even a labourer. However, the historical evidence suggests that Rosicrucians in this period were far more likely to be among the first two categories than the latter.

Certainly, there were practical reasons for remaining anonymous.

The response to the Rosicrucian pamphlets was not universally positive. The authors were being accused of necromancy, sorcery, and blasphemy. Such allegations were not merely idle words; during the early seventeenth century, charges of heresy or witchcraft could lead to persecution or even execution. This makes anonymity a strategic choice necessary for survival.

In addition, the societal critiques contained in the Rosicrucian source works posed a direct challenge to powerful interests. Not just religious interests, but also those of the medical and pharmaceutical establishments of the time. Corrupt apothecaries were losing business as customers began turning away from their exotic alchemical remedies, which often resembled fantastical potions more suited to a fantasy novel than effective medicine. And that was if the remedies actually contained the expensive ingredients the curator claimed it contained. As a result of the Rosicrucian movement, public trust in this institution was being eroded and customers were turning away. Even today, whistleblowers challenging pharmaceutical companies would need to have considerable resources, wealth, and legal protection to withstand any potential retaliation.

Moreover, the Rosicrucian source works were not shy about criticising established religious authorities, an especially perilous stance in an era dominated by religious conflict. The Protestant reformation, still unfolding, was criticised by the Rosicrucians as a failed movement that had not delivered on its promises of a meaningful reform.

The religion of Islam, which during the early seventeenth century was advancing under the Ottoman Empire, was dismissed in the Rosicrucian texts as blasphemous. Yet it was the Catholic Church and its head, the Pope, who bore the brunt of their critique. The Confessio Fraternitatis described the Pope as the Antichrist and envisioned a future where the Rosicrucians would lead the world into a utopian Christian society. In this prophesied new order, the Catholic Church would fall, giving way to a purer, truer Christian faith, guided by the principles of the Rosicrucian brotherhood. Such bold and incendiary claims ensured that any identified author would attract powerful adversaries from all corners of society.

Remaining anonymous was certainly an advantageous safeguard to protect the wellbeing of the authors! But this anonymity had a secondary consequence. Whether this consequence was ever anticipated by the authors may never be known with certainty. But by remaining anonymous, the messages took on an air of mystique which only served to amplify their message and make it even more compelling to those who were similarly disillusioned with the established order.

We might consider therefore that this secrecy was not only practical but perhaps served a symbolic purpose as well. It aligned with the Rosicrucian ethos of quiet service to humanity. The invisibility they claimed was less about literal concealment and more about embodying a spiritual ideal that was characterised by such traits as humility, discretion, and ultimately service (see *Hallmark One*). Over time however, this concept of invisibility evolved, branching into more *esoteric* interpretations that linked it to spiritual states, metaphysical capabilities, and the idea of transcendence beyond ordinary perception.

One such esoteric interpretation involves that of an invisible fraternity of enlightened souls, as would be explored in great detail by the Bavarian mystic Karl von Eckartshausen (1752-1803), who sought to unite faith and reason at a time when he believed science was beginning to eclipse the spiritual. Written at the end of his life, *The Cloud upon the Sanctuary* (1795) was Eckartshausen's Swan Song. It describes an invisible church of illuminated souls whose existence mirrored the ideals perpetuated by the Rosicrucian source work authors nearly two centuries earlier. The work is arranged as six mystical letters, preceded by *A Short Method of Reflection*.

Eckartshausen presents it as an extract from a treatise on chemistry, no doubt a deliberate and symbolic gesture aimed at linking the terrestrial with the celestial. Within this work, Eckartshausen presents the mystery of an *Invisible* or *Inner Church*. This hidden inner church, he taught, is composed of souls united by divine illumination rather than by name, dogma, or form. And while he never names the Rosicrucians, later esotericists saw in his, *Society of the Elect* a reflection of the hidden Fraternity of the Rose Cross.

> *This community of light has been called from all time the invisible and interior Church, or the most ancient of all communities...This illuminated community has been through time the true school of God's spirit, and considered as school, it has its Chair, its Doctor, it possesses a rule for students, it has forms and objects for study, and, in short, a method by which they study.*
> (Eckartshausen, 2003, pp. 24-25)

Like the mystics before him, Eckartshausen taught that the path to this invisible sanctuary begins from within (Osborne, M. R., 2025 p. 93). Rather than a ritual, true initiation was a process of Regeneration, an *entire change, a complete and absolute overturning and upsetting of our being.*

Throughout The Cloud upon the Sanctuary, Eckartshausen reaffirms the ideals espoused by the Rosicrucians. It is unknown just how familiar Eckartshausen was with Rosicrucianism as an initiatory order. He was briefly affiliated with the Order of the Illuminati (discussed further in, *War of the Roses*) and one does have to wonder whether he ever affiliated with the German Order of the Gold and Rosy Cross (German: *Gold- und Rosenkreuzer*).

In 1896, an English translation was published by A.E. Waite, and The Cloud upon the Sanctuary quickly became a popular text of the twentieth century occult revival.

When it comes to more contemporary viewpoints on the nature of the *invisible* brotherhood, Paul Foster Case, author of *The True and Invisible Rosicrucian Order* and founder of the modern mystery school Builders of the Adytum (B.O.T.A.), argued that the Rosicrucian brotherhood was considered *invisible* not because its members were supernatural or discarnate beings, but because it lacked a formal external organisation.

He explains,

> *The Order is designated as being invisible by the manifestoes themselves. It does not come in corporate form before the world, because by its very nature it cannot. True Rosicrucians know one another, nevertheless. Their means of recognition cannot be counterfeited nor betrayed, for these tokens are more subtle than the signs and passwords of ordinary secret societies.*
>
> *Let none suppose that because the Rosicrucian Order is invisible it is composed of discarnate human intelligences. Neither are its members supermen inhabiting a region vaguely designated by the term "higher planes." The Order is invisible because it has no external organization. It is not composed of invisible beings. Its members are men and women incarnate on earth in physical bodies. They are invisible to ordinary eyes because the minds behind those eyes cannot recognize the marks of a true Rosicrucian.* (Case, 1989)

Case further maintained that the Fama Fraternitatis and Confessio Fraternitatis were *written by members of an actual fraternity that conceals itself from all who are incompetent to share its aims and participate in its work* (Case, 1989, p. 5). He also stressed that Rosicrucianism, as an occult philosophy, is deliberately kept hidden by those who understand the true nature of its principles, and that any attempt to disclose its true nature to those that were not ready would be, at best futile, and at worst, dangerous,

> *Those who ask it forget that the essence of anything truly occult is that it is hidden -hidden not only by the ignorance that keeps men from seeing but hidden also by those who are custodians of certain kinds of knowledge. It is hidden primarily out of compassion for those persons whose minds are unprepared to grasp the real meaning of occult doctrines. These are doctrines that are susceptible to misconstruction if their true import is not fully apprehended. To give them to the unprepared is to violate the old alchemical maxim that before one uses the Philosophers' Stone to transmute metals, the metals must first be purified. He who rashly communicates to another what that other is almost certain to misunderstand, and consequently misapply, is responsible for the consequences.*
> (Case, 1989, pp. 94-95)

Whilst Case took on a philosophical, yet rather rational approach, Max Heindel from The Rosicrucian Fellowship would opt for a more mystical Christian stance on the nature of the Rosicrucians invisibility, often citing passages from the Bible for support.

Max Heindel believed he inherited his Rosicrucian knowledge from a group of *Elder Brothers*; highly advanced spiritual beings who remained *invisible* to the general public. It was these Elder Brothers (who we will discuss further in the next section) who instructed Heindel in the *Etheric Temple of the Rose Cross*. This temple could be likened to the *temple not made with hands* mentioned by Christ in Mark 14:58 and referenced again in Acts 17:24.

Hallmarks of the R+C

Perhaps no organisation has been more misunderstood in relation to the concept of Rosicrucian invisibility than A.M.O.R.C.

H. Spencer Lewis received a great deal of criticism from his contemporaries for stating that A.M.O.R.C. was a *real* Rosicrucian organisation. However, had his critics taken the time to read his writings carefully, they might have discovered that his perspective was not as materialistic or elitist as they often claimed.

In one address given to A.M.O.R.C. members, Lewis addressed this topic directly,

> *Now I want to say to you definitely that the true Rosicrucian Brotherhood or, in other words, the true fraternity or secret assembly of Rosicrucians is an invisible organization, just as thousands of books have referred to it. Why this is so and how it is so will be discussed in detail in later lectures.*
>
> *Secondly, I want to say to you definitely that the AMORC in all of its outer, objective, material operations is a part of that invisible brotherhood.*

To clarify his position, Lewis offered an analogy,

> *Now we can compare this statement with some others. Let us say that someone was to claim that a little child of one year old is not a human being because all human beings are grown up and strong, and able to read and write and talk, and carry on great work, and support themselves, etc. You would say to such a person that the average conception of a human being is an adult but a child can also be a human being in process of developing into an adult.*

In other words, Lewis viewed A.M.O.R.C. as a preparatory school, a vehicle (though not the only one) through which students could ready themselves for entry into the invisible Rosicrucian brotherhood.

In another address, he would expand,

> ...the real or highest, or most advanced Rosicrucians, constituting the inner, secret group, do not have temples or lodges in which to pursue their studies.

And that the most advanced members of A.M.O.R.C....

> ...will have no lodge or temple where you come together to study that is visible, but meet in the invisible psychic sanctuary. Yet it is possible for you to meet others in the same sanctuary and come in personal touch with them.

A.M.O.R.C. also took a more literal approach to the idea of invisibility, incorporating practical experiments on the subject into their higher-degree teachings. One advanced exercise involved the formation of a *cloud* which could be used for (among many other things) obscuring visibility.

An early instruction from H. Spencer Lewis describes this method,

> You hear reports to the effect that in a far off land, called the land of the Hindu, they perform seeming miracles by disappearing from the sight of many assembled in one place to watch them. You will realize how easily many of their demonstrations of occult power are possible through the use of these laws of creating, building, and increasing a cloud between them and the spectators, through which others cannot see. Then add to this the additional principle whereby the misty cloud can be pulled into one's aura and make the aura around one's body so misty that one cannot be seen -- being really enveloped in a misty cloud. It is also possible to make the misty cloud take on the shape and color of anything near it; so that a person could stand against a brown wall and with a brown colored mist in the aura make one's self really invisible against the brown wall.

The H.O.G.D. tradition also provided instructions to its members for practical methods of invisibility, involving the formulation of a shroud that has the appearance of a cloud.

These experiments might seem quite new-age and to be quite a departure from traditional Rosicrucian teachings, but actually, such techniques were already discussed in relation to the Rosicrucian tradition as early as the seventeenth century.

In the preface to *The Fame and Confession of the Fraternity of R.C. commonly, of the Rosie Cross,* Thomas Vaughan (writing as Eugenius Philalethes) references an ancient practice of invisibility utilised by the Rosicrucians that had previously been utilised by the Brahman of India,

> *The Wise-men (saith Apollonius) dwelt on a little Hill, or Mount, and on the Hill there rested always a Cloud, in which the Indians hous'd themselves (for so the word signifies,) and here did they render themselves visible or invisible, at their own will and discretion. This secret of Invisibility was not known to the Dutch Boor, nor to his Plagiary, the author of the Manna: but the Fraternity of R.C. can move in this white Mist. Ut nobiscum autem convenias (say they) necesse est hanc lucem cernas, sine enim hace luce, Impossibile est nos videre, nisi quando volumus*[4]. *But Tyaneus tells us something more; namely, that the Brachmans themselves did not know whether this Hill was compassed about with Walls, or had any Gates that did not lead to it, or no; for the Mist obstructed all Discoveries. Consider what you read, for thus some body writes concerning the Habitation of R.C. Vidi aliquando Olympicas domos, non procul a Fluviolo & Civitate nota, Quas S. Spiritus vocari imaginamur. Helicon est de quo loquor, aut biceps Parnassus, in quo Equus Pegasus fontem aperuit perennis aquae adhuc stillantem, in quo*

---

4   English: *But in order that you may meet with us (say they) it is necessary that you see this light, for without this light it is impossible to see us, except when we will.*

*Diana se lavat. Cui Venus ut Pedissequa, & Saturnus ut Anteambulo, conjunguntur. Intelligenti nimium, Inexperto minimum hoc erit dictum.*⁵ (Philalethes, 1658)

Whilst practical methods of invisibility can be found in more contemporary Rosicrucian groups it would be an error to think that this practical experimentation is a departure from the tradition of the Rosicrucian source work-era.

The notion of invisibility within Rosicrucianism, whether interpreted as literal concealment, symbolic anonymity, or esoteric transformation, remains a persistent and evolving theme within the Rosicrucian tradition. From the anonymous posters in seventeenth century Paris, and the writings of Philalethes, to the teachings of contemporary Rosicrucian leaders such as Paul Foster Case, Max Heindel, H. Spencer Lewis, and Israel Regardie, we can see that invisibility has played a crucial role in shaping both the identity and the mystique of the Rosicrucian movement.

Perhaps it serves also as a reminder that true knowledge is not always meant for open display but is meant for those who have cultivated the inner sight to perceive it. And so, the Rosicrucians remain, unseen, but ever present, watching, guiding, and waiting for those who seek the light beyond the veil.

---

5   English: *I once saw the Olympic houses, not far from the river and the well-known city, which we imagine to be called St. Spiritus. It is the Helicon of which I am speaking, or the biceps of Parnassus, in which the horse Pegasus opened a spring of perpetual water still dripping, in which Diana bathed. To which Venus as Pedissequa, and Saturn as Anteambulus, are conjoined. To the intelligent too much, to the inexperienced the least this will be said.*

HALLMARK FOUR: *Rosicrucian Masters*

Perhaps the most misunderstood aspect of initiatic systems is that in all cases the initiation is conferred upon the candidate by an external initiator. Whilst there have been and do exist individuals who appear to have some unique ability to elicit a transmutative initiatory experience upon a candidate, these circumstances are exceptionally rare and have nearly always provided the impetus that would eventually give rise to something of significance, such as the establishment of a physical, or outer, order of the Rosicrucian tradition, or else of the transference of an initiatory authority. In most cases, the initiation provided in initiatic groups is more symbolic and it is the hope that the sincerity of the candidate will lead them to the true initiation which takes place within. That is certainly not to belittle the act of fraternal initiations; but simply to distinguish between the initiation that is common and the initiation that is uncommon. I'll leave it to the esoteric readers to conclude whether these two types of initiation truly arise from different sources.

Perhaps then it is no surprise that initiatic fraternities have cautioned students away from an over-reliance upon exterior Masters who can bestow some special initiatic lineage. For instance, A.M.O.R.C. explicitly posits to its students that the only *Master* that the student should seek with their most ardent desire is what they term, the *Master Within*. Similarly, many magical groups have as their ultimate goal for their students to come to a personal relationship with their own *Holy Guardian Angel*.

And yet, we find this curious hallmark throughout the Rosicrucian tradition; this all-pervasive concept of the *Rosicrucian Masters*.

Every student needs a teacher. Did Frodo Baggins not have the age-old Gandalf as his guide? Did Harry Potter not have his inquisitive Dumbledore hiddenly watching over him? And perhaps Anakin Skywalker would not have gone so far astray if it were not for the untimely and premature passing of Master Qui Gon Jinn.

Perhaps then it is not so surprising to see a tradition like Rosicrucianism, a tradition that perfectly encapsulates the initiatic journey from *Aspirant-to-Initiate* and *Initiate-to-Adept*, naturally incorporating the idea of hidden Masters watching over the tradition like unseen Guardians.

However, there is very little suggestion in the three foundational Rosicrucian source works, the Fama Fraternitatis, Confessio Fraternitatis, and Chemical Wedding of Christian Rosenkreuz in the Year 1459, to indicate the existence of any hidden Masters. Certainly, they do suggest a hidden brotherhood, as discussed in *Hallmark Three: The Invisible Rosicrucians*. No, to find references to the hidden Rosicrucian Masters during this era, we may have to expand our search to encompass some of the Rosicrucian source works beyond the Rosicrucian Trilogy.

Alternatively, maybe you could consider that we have already hinted at the existence of Rosicrucian Masters when discussing authorship. No, I don't mean Andreae, Fludd, Maier, and the like. But if you cast your mind back to this section, you might recall that many of these potential authors, despite the evidence suggesting their active role in the Rosicrucian tradition, all explicitly denied being a Rosicrucian. If you were an idealist (and it just so happens that I am) you might say that the true Rosicrucian Masters were guiding their hand all along. Naturally, however, this explanation will leave many wanting, and so it is worthwhile expanding upon this subject a little further, if only to satisfy our intellect and curiosity.

It has to be said that the characteristics often ascribed to the Rosicrucian Masters is somewhat in variance to the various fictional characters recently alluded: Harry Potter, Frodo Baggins, and Anakin Skywalker. Unlike the fictional Masters who guided these heroes, Rosicrucian Masters often do not work side-by-side with those with whom they guide. They are not a human-shaped magic-8 ball that initiates can consult to help answer their every question. It would seem that they remain almost uncaring about the woes of our daily lives. In fact, it would appear that they do not even care to communicate with most people, even those in senior positions of authority in Rosicrucian organisations.

And in those exceptionally rare occasions that a Rosicrucian Master has decided to pay a visit to somebody, it has never been for a minor event or trivial matter. They don't seem to care about the myriad of ritualistic styles to be found across countless Rosicrucian groups. We don't see them cc'd in emails nor being consulted about upcoming events. And they certainly don't appear to care about the order of business being discussed in a Lodge-room or Temple.

Rosicrucian Masters, on the rare occasions that they can be sensed to have involved themselves in some matter, have often been rather selective about the time, circumstances, and individuals to whom they have chosen to make contact. This contact itself often takes the form of an initiatory event which is soon after followed by a new expression of the Rosicrucian tradition; perhaps a new artwork, group, or philosophy.

And when the Rosicrucian Masters have chosen an initiate, their relationship is quite one-sided. To the outsider, they might even appear to be remarkably critical. Their demands are challenging and the consequences they place upon their students for failure are often severe. They will not hesitate to sever connection with their chosen contact for a perceived failure or if the initiate's service is no longer of value.

Those initiates who have been contacted will occasionally attempt to identify the Master either by name or by description. Whether this identification is correct is not always certain. It would appear that in some cases these communications deny clear cognitive interpretation. At other times, it appears that the contact is deliberately veiled in symbolism; either to obscure the facts from unintended audiences, or to assist in revealing information only to those *with eyes to see.*

Masters during the Rosicrucian source work period

As mentioned, during the source work era we find very few references to Rosicrucian Masters in any literal sense, and no explicit mentions within the Rosicrucian trilogy itself. And the references we do find tend to be more symbolic in meaning and take the form of symbolic fictional narratives. We will discuss esoteric, or didactic fiction in detail in a later chapter.

But a good example of a symbolic reference to Rosicrucian Masters from this period can be found in a book appearing in 1651 called *Lumen de Lumine* written by Eugenius Philalethes (pseudonym, Thomas Vaughan),

> *There is a Mountain situated in the Midst of the Earth, or Center of the world, which is both small, and Great. It is soft, also above measure Hard and Stonie. It is far off, and near at hand, but by the providence of God, invisible. In it are hidden the most ample Treasures, which the world is not able to value. This Mountain by Envie of the Devill, who alwaies opposes the Glory of God, and the Happinesse of Man, is compassed about with very cruell Beasts and Ravenous Birds, which make the way thither both difficult, and dangerous. And therefore hitherto, because the Time is not yet come, the way thither could not be sought after, nor found out. But now at last the way is to be found by those that are worthy, but not withstanding by every man's self-labour, and endeavours.*
>
> *To this Mountain you shall goe in a certaine Night (when it comes) most long, and most dark, and see that you prepare your selves by Prayer. Insist upon the way that leads to the Mountaine, but aske not of any man where the way lyes: only follow your Guide, who will offer himself to you, and will meet you in the way, but you shal not know him. This Guide will bring you to the Mountain at Midnight, when all things are Silent and Dark. It is necessary that you arme your selves with a resolute, heroic courage, least you feare those things that will happen, and so fall back. You need no Sword, nor any other Bodily weapons, only call upon God sincerely, and heartily.*

Hallmarks of the R+C

This Renaissance masterpiece called *The Annunciation* by Fra Angelico (c. 1426), depicts a moment of divine transmission. Just as the angel brings a message from the celestial hierarchy, so too do some Rosicrucian philosophers consider there to be hidden Rosicrucian Masters silently guiding the soul's awakening from somewhere unseen.

> *When you have discovered the Mountaine, the first Miracle that will appeare, is this. A most vehement and very great wind, that will shake the Mountaine, and shatter the Rocks to pieces. You will be incounter'd also by Lions and Dragons, and other Terrible Beasts, but fear not any of these things. Be resolute, and take heed that you returne not, for your Guide who brought you thither, will not suffer any Evil to befall you. As for the Treasure, it is not yet discovered, but is very neer. After this the wind will come an Earthquake, that will overthrow those things, which the wind had left, and make all Flat. But be Sure, that you fall not off. The Earthquake being past, there shall follow a Fire, that will consume the Earthly Rubbish, and discover the Treasure, but as yet you cannot see it. After all these things and neer Day-break, there shall be a great*

Calm, and you shall see the Day-star arise, and Dawning will appear, and you shall perceive a great Treasure. The Chiefest thing in and the most perfect, is a certain exalted Tincture with which the world (if it served God, and were worthy of such Gifts) might be touched, and turn'd into most pure Gold.

This Tincture being used, as your Guide will teach you, will make you young when you are old, and you shall perceive no Disease in any part of you Bodies. By means of this Tincture also, you shall find pearls of the Excellency, which cannot be imagined. But doe not arrogate any thing to your selves because of your present power, but be contented with that which your Guide shall communicat to you. Praise God perpetually for this

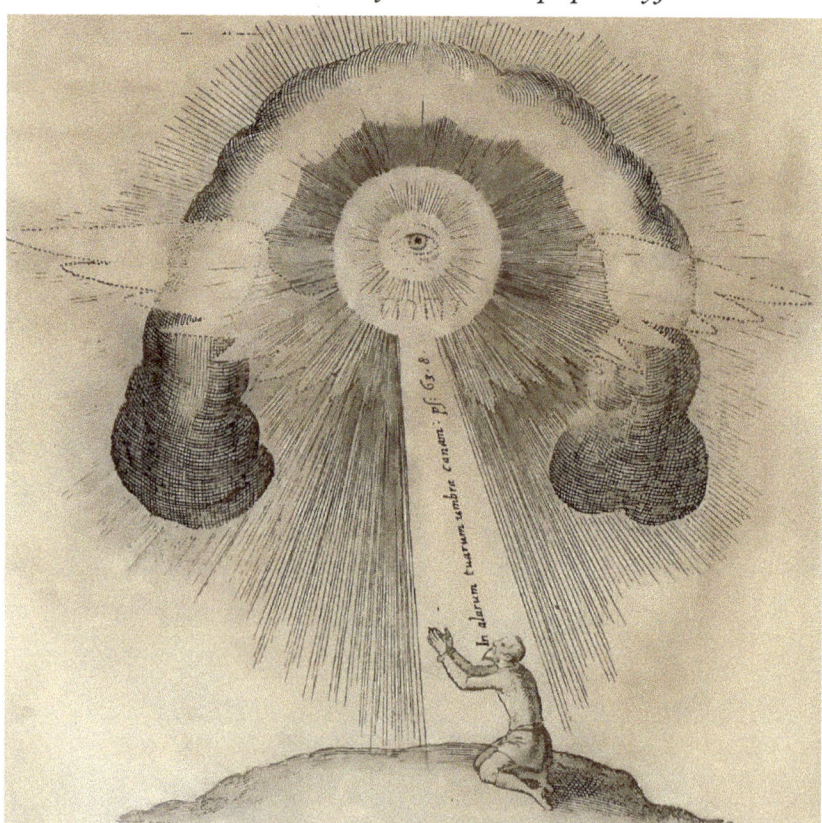

This image is taken from the second tractate of Robert Fludd's *Utriusque Cosmi maioris scilicet et minoris metaphysica, physica, atque technica Historia.*

his Gift, and have a special care that you use it not for worldly pride, but imploy it is such works, which are contrary to the world. Use it rightly and injoy it so, as if you had it not. Live a temperat life, and beware of all sin, otherwise your Guide will forsake you, and you shall be deprived of Happinesse. For know this of a Truth, whosoever abuseth this Tincture, and does not exemplarly, purely, and devoutly before men, he shall lose this Benefit, and scarce hope will there be left, ever to recover it afterwards. (Philalethes, 1651, pp. 35-37)[6]

As we can see from the above, Philalethes' reference to the hidden Guide is not to be taken as a literal person. Rather, it would be more appropriate to view the Guide or Master in this passage as referring to an inner wisdom, Divine providence, or, more likely, an intuitive force, who can direct the seeker through this alchemical journey. I would even narrow the definition represented in this fragment even further and state that it represents *Conscience*, which can be inferred by how the Guide may be *lost* should the seeker choose to lead life devoid of virtue.

This approach to a hidden Master can be found throughout many of the Rosicrucian source works and using a very similar approach. In these cases, we aren't looking at a highly evolved personality who has ascended beyond the need for a physical body, as is the case with some of the latter Rosicrucian traditions. These Masters represent something more symbolic; something the initiate may seek out and find. Nevertheless, the role these *Masters* play is very similar. They are difficult to seek out, they speak in curious cryptic phrases, they offer words of warning, and they impart secret knowledge. So whilst they do not represent literal people, they do offer the voice of authority as would be expected from a Master.

However, this theme would evolve and take on new dimensions. Soon *whispers* of true Master personalities begin to emerge like shadows in the twilight. Their presence, no longer just a symbolic echo, but reaching out a hand to guide those seekers whom they deemed worthy.

---

6 Thank you to Rev Fred Shade for providing me with a copy of this work.

Rite of Strict Observance

Perhaps the first Masonic society to incorporate the concept of hidden Masters occurred in 1743, when Baron Von Hund, a German Freemason, claimed to have been initiated into the Knights Templar in Paris by Scottish Knights led by an individual referred to as the *Knight of the Red Feather*. Although Von Hund was bound by secrecy and could not disclose the name of his initiator, he strongly inferred that it was Prince Charles Stuart. Following this initiation, Von Hund claimed he was granted the authority to introduce *Masonic Templarism* to Germany and he established the *Rite of the Strict Observance* in 1751 to fulfill this purpose.

Baron Karl Gotthelf von Hund, founder of the *Rite of Strict Observance*, whose claimed contact with *Unknown Superiors* introduced the hidden Master concept into European Masonic circles.

According to Von Hund, the Rite was being guided by hidden, *Unknown Superiors,* and members were expected to be obedient to them. The Rite enjoyed a rapid expansion throughout Europe, particularly in German speaking regions, for several decades. After the death of Baron Von Hund in 1776 and the decline of the Jacobite cause, the Rite of the Strict Observance faced significant challenges that even their mysterious Unknown Superiors could not overcome. The fate of the Rite was sealed at the Wilhelmsbad congress in 1782, where it was unanimously agreed that Freemasons were not the successors of the Knights Templar. This declaration marked the effective end of the Rite of the Strict Observance (Gould, 1951, p. 241) as well as the Templar continuation myth (Clausen, n.d.). Although, the convent maintained that there existed a symbolical link between Freemasonry and the Knights Templar, the outcome being a promotion of the French-inspired Rite, the *Knights Beneficent of the Holy City* (French: *Chevaliers Bienfaisant de La Cite Sainte*) (Noel, 1995).

Although the Rite of the Strict Observance was to disappear, it would not mark the end of the belief of hidden Masters guiding an initiatory society. And whilst we would not classify this Rite as explicitly Rosicrucian, it is possible to see a continuation of this concept in later initiatory organisations, including those which we would now consider to be Rosicrucian.

The Martinist Voice

At the same time the Rite of the Strict Observance was active we find another curious esoteric Masonic system being developed in France. This was *The Order of Knight-Masons Elect Priests of the Universe* (French: *Ordre des Chevaliers Maçons Élus Coëns de l'Univers*) usually referred to simply as, the *Élus Coëns*.

Founded in 1767, the Élus Coëns sought to restore humanity's lost unity with the Divine through the practice of theurgy. Its teachings were rooted in the Judeo-Christian tradition, yet infused with Kabbalistic, Hermetic, and Gnostic influences. While some have drawn parallels to Valentinian Gnosticism, its doctrines also bear traces of Manichaean and Mandaean thought, particularly in the writings, rituals, and catechisms of its founder, Martinez de Pasqually.

At the heart of the order's philosophy was the concept of *Reintegration*: the belief that humankind, fragmented since the fall of Adam, could be reconciled with the Divine through spiritual purification and direct communion with God. This process was not merely symbolic but could actually be enacted via elaborate ceremonial rites. Theurgy, as practiced by the Élus Coëns, involved invoking angelic hierarchies and intermediary spirits, seeking their guidance and intervention to overcome malicious spiritual influences and hasten an individual's or humanity's return to divine perfection.

Unlike traditional ecclesiastical institutions, the Élus Coëns envisioned an invisible Church, existing beyond the material realm, unbound by earthly structures. It was a spiritual sanctuary for those dedicated to uncovering the hidden knowledge of nature and preparing for the inevitable decline of the physical Church.

Within this framework, Freemasonry provided a suitable structure for transmitting its esoteric wisdom and methods. Pasqually was himself a Freemason and structured the order using Masonic frameworks that required initiates to be Master Masons before advancing into its higher degrees.

It is important to acknowledge, that not all hidden forces in esoteric traditions can be equated with a Rosicrucian Master. Such is the case with the Élus Coëns.

In the tradition of the Élus Coëns, *The Thing* (French: *La Chose*) was a cryptic term used to refer to a mysterious spiritual force or divine presence occasionally, albeit rarely, to be encountered in their theurgical practices. It was believed to occasionally manifest during advanced ritual operations, particularly in the invocation of celestial intelligences.

Pasqually described The Thing as an ineffable and powerful presence that could be perceived but not fully understood. Some interpretations suggest it was an emanation of divine energy, a spiritual intermediary, or even a purified state of consciousness achieved in the course of the initiate's rigorous theurgical work.

This seal is attributed to Martinez de Pasqually, founder of the *Élus Coëns*. Pasqually and some of his contemporaries would report the presence of *La Chose* that would arise during their theurgical work. However, this would be better described as a psychic phenomenon rather than a Master.

In some respects, The Thing shares some similarities to a hidden Rosicrucian Master, in the sense that both represent an unseen guiding force within an esoteric tradition, yet the comparison is not entirely precise. Within the Rosicrucian tradition, hidden Masters (whether real or symbolic) serve as enlightened initiates who guide seekers toward wisdom, often operating from behind the scenes in secrecy. The Thing, however, was not described as a human or even an embodied intelligence but rather as an impersonal spiritual manifestation encountered through theurgical practice. Whereas a Rosicrucian Master might impart knowledge and direction, The Thing was more of an ephemeral presence, a sign of *successful* ritual engagement with the Divine; a manifestation of higher spiritual forces at work during the order's rituals. The Thing therefore is more akin to a psychic phenomenon than an individual master transmitting secret teachings.

Pasqually had two principal students who would carry forward his teachings, albeit in markedly different ways: Louis-Claude de Saint-Martin and Jean-Baptiste Willermoz.

Saint-Martin, initially devoted to the Élus Coëns and its elaborate theurgical rites, gradually distanced himself from ceremonial magic, believing that true spiritual enlightenment could be attained through inner contemplation and direct communion with God rather than external ritual. He developed a mystical path focused on what he described as the *Inner Way*. These ideas were further refined and imparted among a small circle of intimate associates. The methods preferred by Saint-Martin emphasised quiet meditation and prayer over the complex theurgical operations prescribed by Pasqually and the Élus Coëns. His shift in focus led to a divergence from his master's methods, favouring a more introspective and mystical approach to spiritual reintegration.

Willermoz, on the other hand, remained engaged with the ritualistic and hierarchical structure of Freemasonry and sought to further integrate Pasqually's esoteric teachings into the Masonic framework. He played a crucial role in shaping the *Rectified Scottish Rite* (French: *Rite Écossais Rectifié*) which, while incorporating some doctrinal elements of the Élus Coëns, abandoned the complex theurgical processes whilst also placing them within a system of chivalric Christian-Freemasonry.

In the late nineteenth century, Gérard Encausse, better known by his pseudonym, Papus, founded the *Martinist Order* (French: *Ordre Martiniste*), an esoteric society that sought to revive and unify the teachings of Martinez de Pasqually, Jean-Baptiste Willermoz, and Louis-Claude de Saint-Martin, although it would be fair to say that Papus' Martinist movement was primarily influenced by Saint-Martin and his doctrine of the Inner Way.

Unlike Saint-Martin, who had distanced himself from formal initiatory structures, Papus reintroduced a system of initiation, borrowing heavily from Masonic and occult initiatory traditions of his time, and whilst his Martinism preserved Saint-Martin's emphasis on mystical introspection, it also drew upon Willermoz's structured Masonic approach and Pasqually's idea of spiritual reintegration, albeit without the elaborate theurgical rituals that defined the Élus Coëns.

In Papus's Martinist Order, he suggested that advanced adepts, acting as unseen spiritual guides, oversaw the progression of humanity toward enlightenment, an idea reminiscent of both the Rosicrucian tradition and the concept of the *Great White Brotherhood*, later popularised by The Theosophical Society. Papus portrayed these hidden adepts as intermediaries between the Divine and the initiated, transmitting sacred wisdom through a lineage of esoteric societies, and via these societies, towards individual initiates.

This approach became quite standard with the work of Papus, who often brought together multiple seemingly disparate traditions in an effort to demonstrate an evolution of a timeless esoteric current that could re-express itself in contemporary movements. This not only revitalised the doctrines of Saint-Martin, Pasqually, and Willermoz, but also had a tremendous influence on contributing to a broader occult renaissance.

However, this synthesis came at a cost. By merging these traditions through superficial correspondences, their distinct identities became blurred. As a result, disciplines and traditions such as alchemy, hermeticism, tarot, Kabbalah, hypnotism, and astrology were now being conflated, diluting what once made these traditions distinct.

Today, there continue various Masonic obediences and Rosicrucian traditions that have maintained a doctrine of hidden Masters, guiding their respective traditions.

'Mahatma' or 'Mahatmas'?

A common misconception is that the idea of advanced hidden Masters originated with The Theosophical Society. And whilst, as we have seen, earlier inspirations for this concept certainly exist, the publication of *The Secret Doctrine* by the Society's co-founder, Helena Petrovna Blavatsky, helped to bring this concept widespread attention and popular appeal.

In The Secret Doctrine, Blavatsky discusses hidden Masters, either referring to them as *Adepts*, *Masters of Wisdom*, or, most notably, *Mahatmas*. And it is this last name which might give us a clue as to one of Blavatsky's inspirations.

Between 1870 and 1880, the French visionary thinker and mystic Saint-Yves d'Alveydre[7] developed a universal philosophy that he believed could guide not only individuals but all aspects of human life, including family, society, politics, and government. He called this philosophy *Synarchy*.

Although Saint-Yves' writings would go on to influence much of the avant-garde Parisian occult world, he himself was more reserved. His reclusive and conservative nature contrasted sharply with the many charismatic personalities he would go on to influence.

In 1886, Saint-Yves penned a work called, *The Mission of India in Europe* (French: *Mission de l'Inde en Europe*). In this work, Saint-Yves describes a hidden subterranean world that exists side-by-side

---

7   His real full-name was, *Joseph-Alexandre Saint-Yves.*

with us called, *Agartha*. Many of mankind's greatest achievements had been assisted by the Agarthan residents. Not only did it maintain a living primordial tradition, and ready access to secret esoteric knowledge, but it also had various connections to ancient pre-diluvian civilisations, notably, *The Ancient Southern Continent* (French: *L'antique Continent Austral*), a land that had been engulfed in the sea, the remnants of which include vast libraries that can still be located off the coast of America.

According to Saint-Yves, Agartha was already being governed by the complex social and political Synarchic philosophy that he expounded. In fact, this was the source of Synarchy. Saint-Yves describes the complex hierarchical administration of Agartha, including its military, its judiciary, healthcare, and governance. And whilst this underground realm may not exactly be deemed a utopia, it was certainly described as being far superior to any existing government on Earth's surface. Indeed, according to Saint-Yves,

> *The entire Agartha is a faithful image of the eternal Word throughout all creation.* (d'Alveydre, 1910, p. 34)

Presiding over the whole realm of Agartha is a trio of offices.

At the top of this triangular administration sits, *The Sovereign Pontiff*, the ultimate central authority of Agartha.

The second point of the triangle is assumed by, *The Brâhatmah*.

And the third point of the triangle is assumed by two *assessors*: *The Mahatma* and *The Mahânga*.

Together, this triune leadership support the *Universal Soul* (French: *Âme universelle*).

Interestingly, there is mysterious legend surrounding this book. Reportedly, Saint-Yves had been warned by the Masters of Agartha that the knowledge in the book would be too dangerous for humanity to acquire. As such, these Masters allegedly instructed Saint-Yves to destroy all manuscript copies of the work; a command

The French philosopher Saint-Yves d'Alveydre (1842-1909) introduced the term *Mahatma* into French occult discourse in his work on Agartha. As there was a delay in the publication of this work, it is uncertain whether he introduced the concept prior to or independently from Helena Blavatsky's usage in *The Secret Doctrine*.

which he promptly obeyed. All copies of The Mission of India in Europe were believed lost. That was until a single surviving copy was discovered.

In 1910, it was posthumously published by *Dorbon Aîné*, a prominent occult bookseller in Paris. The publication was organised by a group of Saint-Yves' followers under the collective pseudonym, *The Friends of Saint-Yves* (French: *Les amis de Saint-Yves*). While the exact individuals behind this group remain unknown, it is widely speculated that Papus played a key role in the effort.

Later commentators on Synarchy would inject various noxious themes into the philosophy, such as racial hierarchy and antisemitism. This would then go on to influence Nazi ideology. However, it should be noted that Saint-Yves did not appear to hold these viewpoints, instead arguing for the need of alliances and federations across the Earth's differing races and nations, even stating of the leadership of Agartha that,

> *All the Epopts[8] of Humanity are there, all its benefactors, all its revealers, without any distinction of Cult or Race.* (d'Alveydre, 1910, pp. 94-95)

---

8   The *Epoptae* was a name given to the highest initiates of the Eleusinian mysteries. However, it is likely that Saint-Yves uses this term to refer to those that are advanced in any secret or mystery tradition.

What is most important for our current discussion however was that Saint-Yves had included a Master that used the title, *Mahatma*. And for some reason, this title had struck a chord with the unknown Friends of Saint-Yves, who seemed to neglect that Saint-Yves had included Mahatma as only one part of the leadership triangle of Agartha.

There is a critical point of note in the front-matter[9] of, The Mission of India in Europe, where The Friends of Saint-Yves (who were responsible for locating and publishing the lost copy after Saint-Yves death) state,

> ...the question, not "of" but "of the" Mahatma is restored to its proper place[10]. (d'Alveydre, 1910, p. 1)

It would appear that there was a pre-existing concern regarding the current understanding surrounding this concept of the Mahatma, and that this book intended to re-establish the true place of this concept. Whatever this current understanding was, it was considered flawed, by referring to *Mahatmas* in a plural or general sense (French: *des*) rather than focusing on a specific *Mahatma* (French: *du*).

So what was the pluralistic understanding of Mahatmas and why was it so concerning for The Friends of Saint-Ayves? No doubt, the pluralistic understanding of Mahatmas that The Friends of Saint-Ayves were trying to counter was the doctrine of the Mahatmas that had recently been popularised by The Theosophical Society and its founder, Helena Petrovna Blavatsky. Whilst Saint-Yves had written about the Mahatma contemporaneously with Blavatsky, it is not known who preceded who or if either individual had influenced the other. But it would seem probable that some cross-pollination had occurred.

If Papus did have a hand in resurrecting this book, then this warning would not be difficult to understand. Papus's relationship with The Theosophical Society by this stage had become strained. He had initially joined The Theosophical Society in the 1880's but

---

9   See the *AVERTISSEMENT* section in the opening pages of *The Mission of India in Europe*.

10 French: "...la question, non pas « des » mais « du » Mahatma est rétablie à sa véritable place".

had become disenchanted with their focus on Eastern mysticism. It was perhaps this opposition that influenced his decision to establish the *Martinist Order* which was primarily focused upon Western esotericism and Christian mysticism and which directly challenged many of the doctrines expounded by The Theosophical Society.

The Theosophical Mahatmas

There are many ways in which to approach the history of The Theosophical Society. But rather than bombard the reader with an avalanche of dates and names, I wish to narrow our discussion down to the relevance that the history of The Theosophical Society has on the Rosicrucian tradition, and more especially to the doctrine of hidden Masters. To achieve this, we must turn to the background of one of its founders, Helena Petrovna Blavatsky. This will also allow us to expand upon some interesting points about this curious mystic that are often neglected by many researchers who tend to focus their attention upon the society she would go on to form.

Biographies on Blavatsky differ dramatically between authors. Apologetic biographers have presented her as psychically gifted and a profound mystic with a dramatic and commanding presence. Whilst those that are more critical present her as a chain-smoking charlatan who engaged in hoodwinking the gullible with her social and racial narratives that were manipulated by deceitful people and subsequently utilised to justify harmful value systems that have led to great violence and suffering in the world.

There is no doubt that the varied biographies of Helena Petrovna Blavatsky can be attributed to her undeniably influential character and the aura of mystery that surrounds her. This was in large part due to her background. She was born Helena Petrovna Hahn von Rottenstern and of noble parents in the Russian Empire (in what is now Dnipro, Ukraine) in 1831. At the time of her birth, her town was in the midst of a cholera epidemic, of which her mother barely survived whilst pregnant with Helena.

Blavatsky recalls her memorable night. In French, "Nuit mémorable! Certaine nuit, par au clair—de lune qui se couchait a Ramsgate 12 Aout: 1851 lorsque je rencontrais M ∴ le Maître—de mes rêves!! Le 12 Aout c'est Juillet 31 style russe jour de ma naissance—Vingt ans!"

Helena's mother was the daughter of a Russian princess, and a highly intelligent woman. When Helena was only a young girl, her mother had worked on Russian translations of the works of Edward Bulwer-Lytton. Bulwer-Lytton's influence on the Rosicrucian tradition cannot be understated and will be discussed in a later chapter (see *Off with the Fairies: Rosicrucian didactic literature*). Helena's father was a noble of German and Russian descent and at the time of Helena's birth, he was a Captain in the Russian army. Due to her father's work, Helena and her family had the opportunity to travel to various military garrisons throughout the Russian Empire furnishing Helena with many opportunities that were not afforded to other Russian girls; including learning English, and residing for a short time with the Kalmuck Buddhist tribes who resided in a small town called Astrakhan which was located near the mouth of the Volga River (Cranston & Williams, 1993, pp. 13-14).

Her aunt Nadya recalled that in her childhood, Blavatsky showed great sympathy and attraction towards people of the lower class, preferring to play with servants' children rather than her social equals. In fact, she had to be constantly watched over in order to prevent her from befriending *ragged street boys* (Cranston & Williams, 1993, p. 18). This sympathy for those in a humbler station continued throughout her life, as she maintained a noticeable indifference to the nobility of her birth.

Despite being a divisive personality, Helena Petrovna Blavatsky (1831-1891) commanded a presence that helped shape esoteric thought in the twentieth century.

Though best known for co-founding The Theosophical Society, Blavatsky often referred to herself as a Rosicrucian and saw her mission as the revival of a hidden initiatic current guided by unseen Masters.

But her compassion was not the only thing that separated Blavatsky from other children. From a young age, Blavatsky was considered by those close to her to be gifted with remarkable psychic powers. She appeared to sense things other people could not. She was often in the company of invisible beings whom nobody else could see. And whilst some of these invisible beings appear to have had no physical existence, this would not remain the case forever. Amongst the incorporeal beings that visited upon Blavatsky, one stood out. This person she referred to as her *mature protector* (Sinnett, 1886, p. 49) and it would not be until her adult life that she would meet this Master in the flesh.

Of this meeting which occurred in 1851, she would state privately,

> *Memorable night! On a certain night by the light of the moon that was setting at Ramsgate on August 12, 1851 when I met M∴ the Master of my dreams!!* (Blavatsky H. P., 1981)

Blavatsky had planned to keep the details of this meeting private, choosing only to share it with a small amount of close friends. However, her chance meeting with *Master M∴* was eventually revealed by her longtime friend and confidante Countess Constance Wachtmeister in her book *Reminiscences of H. P. Blavatsky and The Secret Doctrine* which was published after Blavatsky's death.

Between 1866-1873, Helena travelled extensively throughout the Balkans, Russia, Egypt, Syria, Italy, Palestine, Lebanon, and Paris, before finally settling down in a small apartment in New York in July 1873. During her travels, she would make some important acquaintances that would later help her in establishing The Theosophical Society.

Helena would elicit strong reactions from those she met. Those she became close to made similar remarks about this strange woman. She was cultured and talented. Powerful and gifted. One individual, Charles Johnson, would simultaneously remark that being in her presence was like being among *the primal forces of Nature* and yet she possessed a *subtle sense of great gentleness and kindliness* and an *unfailing readiness to forget herself entirely and to throw herself heartily into the life of others*. Those with whom she was especially close to would remark how it felt like they had known each other for many centuries and how they felt like this was simply commencing the work they had previously left off some centuries ago.

Two men she would soon work very closely with were Colonel Henry Steel Olcott and William Quan Judge. Olcott recalled his striking first impression with Helena, that her,

> ...*massive Calmuck[11] face, contrasting in its suggestion of power, culture, and imperiousness, as strangely with the commonplace visages about the room as her red garment did with the grey and white tones of the walls and woodwork and the dull costumes of the rest of the guests.* (Olcott, 1895, p. 4)

Judge's first impression was even more striking, stating,

> *It was her eye that attracted me, the eye of one whom I must have known in lives long passed away. She looked at me in recognition at that first hour, and never since has that look changed. Not as a questioner of philosophies did I come before her, not as one groping in the dark for lights that schools and fanciful theories had obscured, but as one who wandering many periods through the corridors of life, was seeking the friends who could show where the designs for the work had been hidden. And true to the call she responded, revealing the plans once again, and speaking no words to explain, simply pointed them out and went on with the task.* (Cranston & Williams, 1993, p. 142)

These two reports are fairly typical of the initial impression Blavatsky made on others.

At a later unknown date, although speculated to have been in early-1875 (Algeo, 1996, p. 25), Blavatsky would pen in her notebook a curious passage pertinent to our current investigations. It would seem that her Master $M\therefore$ was beginning to exert a greater influence upon her,

> *O poor, foolish, credulous, wicked world! $M\therefore$ brings orders to form a Society- a secret Society like the Rosicrucian Lodge. He promises to help.*
> *H.P.B.* (Blavatsky H. P., n.d.)

---

11 The *Kalmyks* (or *Calmucks*) are a Mongolic ethnic group who reside in the easternmost part of the European Plain.

Blavatsky's use of the term *Rosicrucian* was not uncommon as she would often refer to herself as a *Rosicrucian* in her intimate associations with colleagues.

Shortly after this passage was written, Blavatsky, Olcott, and Judge were attending a lecture on the secrets of ancient Egyptian rites given by an Egyptologist George H. Felt. It was during this meeting that Olcott handed Blavatsky a piece of paper, upon which was written,

> *Would it not be a good thing to form a society for this kind of study?* (Cranston & Williams, 1993, p. 143).

Blavatsky would agree. The rest of how The Theosophical Society came to be has been amply discussed in many other works, suffice it to say, after several meetings to discuss by-laws, constitution, and names (one name suggested including the word, *Rosicrucian* (Olcott, 1895, p. 132), finally on November 17 1875, The Theosophical Society was officially founded in New York City, with Olcott as its first President and Blavatsky as its Corresponding Secretary.

The Society's stated objectives[12] were (and remain):

- To form a nucleus of the Universal Brotherhood of Humanity, without distinction of race, creed, sex, caste, or color;

- To encourage the study of comparative religion, philosophy, and science;

- To investigate the unexplained laws of nature and the powers latent in man.

As it was Master M who Blavatsky claimed was responsible for guiding her to establish The Theosophical Society, his presence and advice would be shared to students by his disciple. And in time, other Masters would also make their presence known to Blavatsky.

---

12 Introduced in 1896.

It was from these Masters, whom Blavatsky described as her teachers, that she would receive the Theosophical teachings; Blavatsky would then impart these teachings to the society. Whilst it is not known exactly how many Masters Blavatsky was ever in contact with, details regarding two notable Masters would be made available in a collection of letters purportedly written between two Masters, Mahatma *Koot Hoomi* (K.H.) and Mahatma *Morya* (M.), and a British journalist and Theosophist, Alfred Percy Sinnett between 1880 and 1884. This collection of letters would be published in 1923 under the name, *The Mahatma Letters to A. P. Sinnett*. Whilst these Masters were physically incarnated beings residing in Tibet, Blavatsky claimed to be in contact with these individuals via telepathic and astral methods. The letters were supposedly transmitted through unusual means, sometimes appearing out of thin air or allegedly materialising in other mysterious ways.

In The Theosophical Society, these Masters, or Mahatmas (a Sanskrit word meaning, *Great-Souls*), are presented as highly evolved spiritual beings who have attained wisdom and mastery over nature through lifetimes of self-discipline and service to humanity. These enlightened adepts often reside in remote regions like Tibet and guide humanity's spiritual evolution by transmitting esoteric knowledge to worthy disciples, and while they remain largely hidden from the public eye, they choose to communicate through selected intermediaries, influencing philosophical and occult teachings. Theosophists believe the Masters uphold an ancient wisdom tradition, and that they can assist seekers in advancing toward enlightenment. However, their aid is conditional upon the seeker's sincerity, ethical purity, and dedication to selfless service.

Blavatsky would occasionally refer to these Masters collectively as the *Masters of Wisdom* or *Brotherhood of Adepts*. However, she did not use the phrase *Great White Brotherhood*, a term that was coined well after her death.

A year before her death, she was elected president of the European branches. She also held the unique position of Head of the *Esoteric Section* (E.S.) of The Theosophical Society, a body dedicated to the deeper study of esoteric philosophy. The constitution and sole direction of the E.S. were vested in her, and she was solely responsible to its members. In the years immediately following Blavatsky's death on May 8 1891, The Theosophical Society continued to operate and, in some ways, experience further growth and influence.

Another close admirer and supporter of Blavatsky was Annie Besant. After discovering Theosophy through *The Secret Doctrine*, Besant would meet Blavatsky and become one of her most devoted followers. Besant is also well-known for her pioneering efforts in establishing the *International Order of Freemasonry for Men and Women LE DROIT HUMAIN,* in Great Britain. However, what is less well-known is that she was also responsible for founding a short-lived and obscure Rosicrucian organisation called the *Temple of the Rosy Cross.*

The suspension of the Temple of the Rosy Cross in 1915, the same year A.M.O.R.C. was officially established, has led to speculation about a possible connection between the two groups. This theory is further fuelled by the involvement of Mary Henrietta Banks (also known as May Banks Stacey), who was both a member of the E.S. and also played a key role in the founding of A.M.O.R.C. However, despite these coincidences, the available evidence disproves any direct relationship between the Temple of the Rosy Cross and A.M.O.R.C., let alone any shared lineage.

A major factor in dismissing this connection comes from the words of Curuppumullage Jinarājadāsa, a prominent Theosophist and leader of the Temple of the Rosy Cross. Under the direction of Annie Besant, Jinarājadāsa was tasked with modifying the Temple's ritual and incorporating it into a new order known as the *Ritual of the Mystic Star.*

Of the original ritual of the Temple of the Rosy Cross, he would state,

> *In the ritual of the Temple of the Rosy Cross the ceremonial action consisted of offering a candle to each of the Great Teachers of the past, preceded by a description of His work. There was one candle taller than all the others which was dedicated to the Great Teacher who was to come. This candle was not lit as were the other candles, for the idea was that it would be lit by the Great Teacher Himself when He came. Since this ceremony of offering candles was very beautiful, I determined to keep that part of it in the ritual which I was to construct. In the Ritual of the Mystic Star, there is the offering of a candle to each of the Great Teachers,*

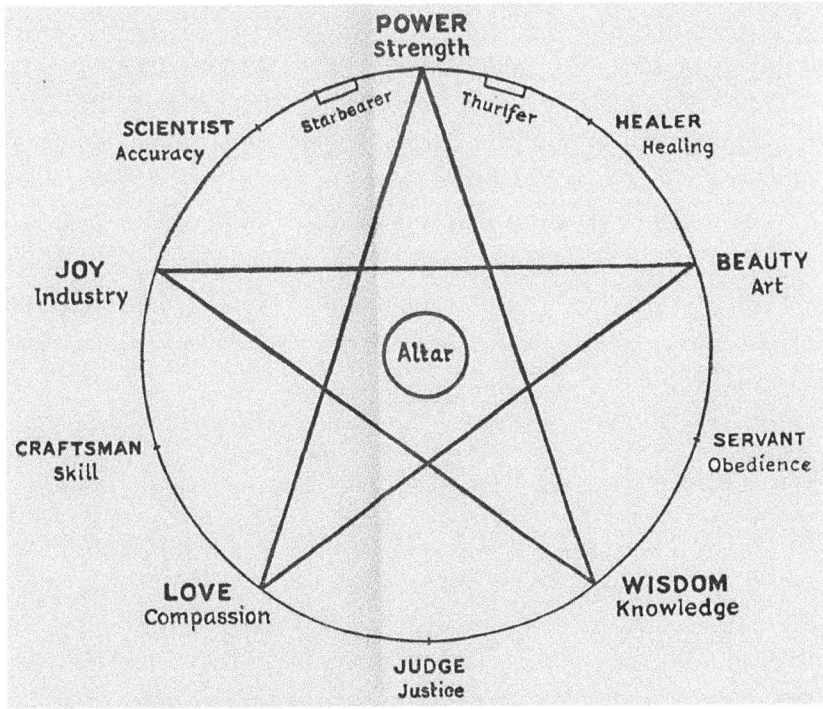

Temple layout diagram for the Ritual of the Mystic Star taken from Ritual of the Mystic Star (4th edition) by C. Jinarajadasa (Theosophical Publishing House, Adyar, 1951).

> *as in the old ritual, though the message of each Teacher is given in more precise words. There is, however, one special difference; it is that the candle dedicated to the Great Teacher who is to come is lit in the course of the ceremony of the Mystic Star, as a symbol that the Great Teacher is present in mystic ways in the world today, and is working through various channels.* (Jinarajadasa, 1939, pp. 4-5)

Anyone familiar with the ritual work of A.M.O.R.C. would immediately recognise that, while the ritual described above may sound elegant, it bears no reference, connection, thematic resemblance, or ritualistic similarity to any A.M.O.R.C. rituals, neither in 1915 nor today. Nor does it appear to share any similarity with any other known Rosicrucian organisation at the time.

Nevertheless, the idea of hidden, guiding intelligences working behind the scenes to advance humanity's spiritual evolution has remained a persistent theme across the Western esoteric tradition. The Theosophical Society, under the influence of Helena Petrovna Blavatsky, expanded upon this concept through the doctrine of the Mahatmas, or Masters of Wisdom, spiritual adepts who guided specially chosen and devoted disciples. Blavatsky's accounts of her encounters with these Masters provided a modern articulation of an older idea: that esoteric knowledge is preserved and transmitted by an enlightened hierarchy working in secret.

Masters as a Mask: The case of Alois Mailänder

While much discourse around Rosicrucian Masters revolves around metaphysical or symbolic interpretations, history also presents cases where the figure of a *Master* has been used to conceal a more physical human being operating under the veil of anonymity. One prominent example is the case of Alois Mailänder (1843-1905), a German mystic whose name was deliberately obscured within the esoteric circles whom he influenced. After experiencing a spiritual awakening in 1877, Mailänder would lead a small group of students from his homestead in Kempten, Germany. This group was called the *Covenant of Promise* (German: *Bund der Verheißung*) (Robinson, 2021, p. 2). Mailänder's spiritual gifts led him to attract many Theosophists as students. These students would eventually purchase Mailänder a house near Frankfurt, bringing the community out from Kempten. Some of Mailänder's students would go on to refer to the mystic as an adept of the Rosicrucian tradition, such as one student, Gustav Meyrink who would refer to his teacher as a *true Rosicrucian* (Robinson, 2021, p. 52).

Mailänder himself never sought fame or public acknowledgement of any kind and his wish for anonymity was respected by his students, who veiled his identity in most of their published references to him. As such, his students would refer to Mailänder in their communications by the letter *M* or *J,* or by the name *Johannes*. This deliberate concealment was so effective that for a long time, only limited or veiled mentions of his activities existed. These would usually appear in private correspondence or were published in periodicals of The Theosophical Society

One of these publications was contributed by Franz Hartmann, who would refer to Mailänder only as the *German Adept* (Robinson, 2021, p. 4) and go on to describe Mailänder's appearance and abilities (Robinson, 2021, pp. 129-133).

Another common title used by Mailänder's students was simply *M*, a reference, that would be more explicitly linked to Mailänder via Karl Weinfurter's book, *Der Königsweg*, where the editor would add in his name for clarity (Robinson, 2021, p. 57). This recurring reference to a *Master M* has led to suggestions that mentions of such a figure in occult literature of this era, at least in some cases, might actually refer to Mailänder, prompting a need for re-examination of some historical accounts.

Mailänder's guidance was considered so valuable that even Hartmann would credit the mystic, albeit anonymously, within his own works. For instance, a reading of Hartmann's Rosicrucian didactic novel, *An Adventure Among the Rosicrucians* reveals that some of the locations and events described in this text are not entirely fictional but rather elaborate upon the community led by Mailänder[13].

This anonymity likely served a dual-function. Firstly, it helped maintain the sanctity of the mystical work carried out in Mailänder's community, preserving it from the more mundane and social pressures that co-exist with such communities. However, more subtly, it also echoes the Rosicrucian ideal of an invisible *Master*.

Ex Deo nascimur. In Jesu morimur. Reviviscimus per Spiritum Sanctum.

Franz Hartmann (1838-1912) incorporated events and people surrounding Covenant of Promise into his fictional literature, most notably his Adventure among the Rosicrucians. The following image is taken from In the Pronaos of the Temple of Wisdom which later formed a part of the same series. The writing on top says, We are strengthened by his presence in our death. Below it says, We are born of God. We die in Jesus. We live again through the Holy Spirit.

---

13 See *An Adventure Among the Rosicrucians: Annotated Edition*, published by *Temple & Vault Press* to explore this further.

While some Masters may be more symbolic existing as metaphysical ideals or otherwise super-human-like beings, Mailänder's case illustrates how the figure of a Master can blur the lines between the metaphysical and the historical. Although, it is worth mentioning that Mailänder himself preferred the word *guide* over *Master*.

Though he was but a mere man, his followers believed his message to be divine. By choosing obscurity, Mailänder helped to ensure that the focus remained on the teaching rather than the teacher, allowing the message to shine untainted by the interference of any cultural pressures, such as those associated with social rank or status.

The Elder Brothers of The Rosicrucian Fellowship

Max Heindel (1865-1919), founder of The Rosicrucian Fellowship, presented a complete spiritual philosophy based on teachings he claimed to have received from hidden Masters he referred to as, *Elder Brothers*. These Masters, according to Heindel, act as hidden guides for humanity's spiritual evolution. The doctrine of these Elder Brothers is discussed throughout many of Heindel's works but covered perhaps most comprehensively in his most well-known work, *The Rosicrucian Cosmo-Conception*.

According to Heindel, the Elder Brothers, although not infallible (Heindel M., 1911, p. 8), are advanced human beings who have reached a stage of spiritual development that allows them to operate beyond ordinary human perception.

Unlike ordinary initiates, the Elder Brothers have attained a level of enlightenment that enables them to work in the spiritual realms while subtly influencing world events and guiding humanity's progress.

According to Heindel, in the thirteenth century, there existed a spiritual teacher by the name of Christian Rosenkreuz. Christian Rosenkreuz would select twelve Elder Brothers to assist him in forming the first Rosicrucian Order (Heindel M., 2011, pp. 142-143).

Rosenkreuz would reincarnate from time-to-time (although, not always with the same name) as the needs of the world necessitated; each time reforming the Rosicrucian Order.

At the time Heindel was establishing his organisation, these wise Masters had expressed grave concerns about the direction of humanity and the *fate of the Western World* (Heindel M. , 1911, p. 113), which was facing increased materialism. As such, they were looking to develop a new vehicle for the Rosicrucian Order.

Max Heindel (1865–1919), founder of The Rosicrucian Fellowship, claimed to receive his teachings from *Elder Brothers*. His writings were presented as transmissions of their higher wisdom.

In 1907, Heindel claimed to have met an Elder Brother in Germany who would charge him to establish The Rosicrucian Fellowship as a vehicle to promote the mission of the *Aquarian Age* and conduct a renewed *campaign of education and enlightenment* (Heindel M. , 2011, p. 58). Although Heindel did not know this at the time, the Elder Brother, who appeared in his *vital body*[14], belonged to the Rosicrucian Order. The Elder Brothers were looking for a suitable person to carry on their occult knowledge. Allegedly, they had evaluated several candidates, including Rudolf Steiner, who was considered unsuitable in 1905; the Elder Brothers thinking it unsuitable to have a Rosicrucian leader who was promoting both Western and Eastern occultism (Westenberg, 2014, p. 63). Steiner would eventually go on to establish The Anthroposophical Society in 1913[15].

14 Within the teachings of The Rosicrucian Fellowship, the *Vital Body* is the second of the human being's seven bodies. The Physical Body is the first body. As such, the Vital Body is very closely associated with the physical body and can appear as an etheric double of it.

15 For anybody wishing to investigate further the relationship between

Eventually, Heindel was put through a test, and after having passed, he was given permission to share occult knowledge with humanity. This occult knowledge could only be communicated by reaching the *Temple of the Rose Cross*, which resided *between the border of Bohemia and Germany* (Heindel M., 2011, p. 9) where Heindel was instructed by the same Elder Brother who had previously tested him, only this time he appeared in his regular physical form (Westenberg, 2014, p. 68).

The teachings imparted to him there became the foundation of The Rosicrucian Cosmo-Conception; the cornerstone text of The Rosicrucian Fellowship. Consequently, members of The Rosicrucian Fellowship do not necessarily view its teachings as the personal philosophy of Heindel but rather as an extension of the wisdom of the Elder Brothers. Furthermore, the members of the Fellowship are considered servants of the Elder Brothers.

According to Heindel, these Elder Brothers are the same as the Blavatsky's Mahatmas. However, Heindel does point out that his own descriptions of these Masters do contradict the descriptions used by Blavatsky and Sinnett, not because of any fundamental distinction between these beings, but due to the challenge in attempting to convey such nuanced doctrines. And whilst Blavatsky had made mistakes in her descriptions, Heindel also notes that he himself may err in such a challenging endeavour (Heindel M. , 1911, p. 270). It should also be pointed out that Heindel had served as vice-President of a branch of The Theosophical Society in Los Angeles in 1904-1905 (Heindel A. F., 2012, p. 6). This prior association with The Theosophical Society may further explain the thematic parallels between his teachings and those of The Theosophical Society.

Nevertheless, despite Heindel's assertion that these beings are fundamentally the same, their actions within The Rosicrucian Fellowship suggest notable differences in approach between the

Steiner and Heindel, I would recommend the work, *Max Heindel and The Rosicrucian Fellowship* by Ger Wesenberg.

two organisations. The Elder Brothers appear far more accessible compared to the Mahatmas of The Theosophical Society. Whilst the Mahatmas focused their communications to a few notable high-ranking officers of The Theosophical Society, the Elder Brothers may communicate with any Brother or Sister of The Rosicrucian Fellowship. The Elder Brothers do not ever impose their will but act as *friends and [...] Teachers* (Heindel M., 2011, p. 151) offering inspiration and advice to all Brothers and Sisters. As Heindel emphasises, they,

> *never under any condition demand obedience to any mandate of theirs nor command us to do this or that. At most, they advise, leaving us free to follow or not.* (Heindel M., 2011, p. 151)

According to Heindel, The Rosicrucian Fellowship is not the sole interest of these Masters, but they also support other mystery schools across the Earth. In each of these mystery schools, there are twelve Elder Brothers. Seven of them remain incarnated and support the physical work of the school whilst five remain at the temple working as missionaries. Behind these twelve Elder Brothers resides a hidden Thirteenth Elder Brother. The Thirteenth Elder Brother of each school then participate in the *White Lodge* which acts as a,

> *...supreme conclave of the Eldest among our Brothers, who are now in full charge of human evolution and plan the steps we are to follow in order to advance.* (Heindel M., 1922, p. 361)

This lodge is not a singular physical location but rather a collective of highly evolved individuals operating on higher spiritual planes.

According to Heindel, the esoteric teachings of the West had advanced beyond their counterparts in the East who are,

> *... bound hand and foot, figuratively speaking, to that Master. He must blindly follow the instructions of his Master, without the least hesitancy or exhibition of*

> *curiosity concerning the purpose of whatever directions are given him. He must render the Master personal service of whatever kind required and at whatever cost or inconvenience to himself, and thus, in short, he becomes virtually the slave of an often very exacting taskmaster.* (Heindel M., 1922, p. 361)

Conversely, initiates in the West,

> *...have advanced to such a stage of individuality that we can only progress by action from within, and if we make any promises or take any vows we ought not to obligate ourselves to anyone else, but make our promises and vows to ourselves; for if we cannot keep our vows to ourselves, we certainly cannot keep promises made to others.* (Heindel M., 1922, p. 362)

Whilst this section has certainly not aged well from the perspective of political correctness, it nevertheless demonstrates that Heindel was, like his A.M.O.R.C. Rosicrucian peers, satisfied with initiates seeking out an *internal* Master.

The Cosmic Masters of A.M.O.R.C.

The doctrine of Rosicrucian Masters also played a significant role during the formative period of the Ancient and Mystical Order Rosae Crucis (A.M.O.R.C.). These Masters, often referred to as *Cosmic Masters,* were not just understood from an abstract or philosophical perspective, but they were also integral to the understanding of A.M.O.R.C.'s organisational structure and purpose. However, as we have seen during our discussions of A.M.O.R.C. in the previous chapter, the organisation of A.M.O.R.C. was often understood as being more than the physical administrative body. As such, it would be more accurate to state that the early A.M.O.R.C. doctrine of Cosmic Masters was seen as something central to the Rosicrucian tradition as a whole and not just to the physical institution of A.M.O.R.C. itself.

These Masters were not understood as deities or gods. Rather, they were highly advanced human personalities who had attained a high degree of spiritual and intellectual development. This state of *mastership* was believed to be the result of sustained personal growth across multiple lifetimes, eventually reaching a level where physical incarnation was no longer a necessity (Lewis, 1990, p. 185).

A.M.O.R.C.'s founder, H. Spencer Lewis, would state that these Masters collectively formed a *wonderful union or assembly of Master Minds* known as the *Holy Assembly of the Cosmic* (Lewis, 1927, p. 135). They were also perceived as being intrinsically linked to the *Great White Brotherhood* and its inner council, the *Great White Lodge*. The Great White Lodge's primary function is to assist humanity. To carry out this mission, the Great White Lodge was understood to operate through various organisations, each serving as a vehicle for its greater aims. Some of these were initiatic and traditional in nature, such as A.M.O.R.C., though this was by no means always the case (Lewis, 1927, p. 136). In this way, we can see an evolution of the concept of an *Invisible College* of the Rosicrucians.

The Cosmic Masters were seen as playing a crucial role in guiding the work of A.M.O.R.C. and ensuring that its teachings evolved in concert with human progress and civilisation. They also prepared high-level initiates for further spiritual work. Similar to the *Elder Brothers* of The Rosicrucian Fellowship (a phrase also used occasionally by H. Spencer Lewis) the Cosmic Masters could actually be contacted to provide direct and personal instruction to qualified students via *Cosmic* (or non-physical) means. As such, even though the doctrine of Cosmic Masters allowed for the possibility of physical incarnation and meeting, communication was usually expected to be facilitated by more subtle means, relying upon psychic faculties that had been developed and cultivated via A.M.O.R.C.'s curriculum.

Ultimately, A.M.O.R.C. viewed these Masters as embodying the supreme goal of Rosicrucian studies: the attainment of personal Mastership and psychic illumination (Lewis, 1927, pp. 133-148).

Through consistent study and application of A.M.O.R.C. teachings, members could be prepared to gain admission into the *Great White Brotherhood,* joining a group of personalities that work collectively to assist humanity.

In the early days of A.M.O.R.C., H. Spencer Lewis would work closely with a select group of high-ranking members. During these intimate meetings, this circle of initiates would participate together in advanced esoteric pursuits. It was often during this work, that the Masters were believed to transmit specific requests or instructions and sometimes express their concerns over perceived shortcomings in the work or direction of the organisation.

H. Spencer Lewis (1883-1939), founder of **A.M.O.R.C.**, taught that advanced initiates known as *Cosmic Masters* guided the spiritual evolution of humanity. To carry out their mission, the Cosmic Masters work with select advanced initiates and organisations.

Nevertheless, A.M.O.R.C. explicitly states that the only Master that A.M.O.R.C. students should seek with their most ardent desire is what they term, the *Master Within,* defined as the Inner Self, or the Divine Intelligence resident in each individual, whose voice is that of conscience.

The Celestial Hierarchy

> *"There is, then, as I think, nothing absurd, if the Word of God calls our Hierarch, Angel, since he participates, according to his own capacity, in the messenger characteristic of the Angels, and elevates himself, as far as attainable to men, to the likeness of their revealing office."*
> **Pseudo-Dionysius the Areopagite**

Sometime in the late fifth or early sixth century, a series of mystical writings emerged in Syria. These works, later known collectively as the *Corpus Dionysiacum*, included the influential treatise *De Coelesti Hierarchia* (English: *The Celestial Hierarchy*).

Their author identified himself as *Dionysius the Areopagite*, the Athenian convert of St. Paul mentioned in Acts 17:34. In reality, he was an unknown writer of a later age, now referred to as *Pseudo-Dionysius the Areopagite*.

The impact of The Celestial Hierarchy upon the Roman Catholic tradition, is well understood. As is its influence upon the apophatic and mystical theology of the Eastern Orthodox Church. Less known, however, is its impact upon the Rosicrucian tradition.

As has been amply described throughout this book already, the Rosicrucian tradition is a holistic one. It would not be surprising, therefore, to find the tenets presented in an inspired mystical work being reflected in the Rosicrucian tradition. However, this influence goes beyond independent expressions of a primordial wisdom, as we will soon see that there have been Rosicrucian leaders who were well aware of the mystical theology of The Celestial Hierarchy and sought to incorporate many of its ideas into their own traditions. This discussion will also lead us to perhaps the most esoteric and sublime understanding of Rosicrucian Masters. But to get to this point, we must first outline the doctrine of the Celestial Hierarchy as presented by Pseudo-Dionysius.

The Celestial Hierarchy of Pseudo-Dionysius presents a vision of the cosmos governed by spiritual intelligences who act as intermediaries between God and humanity, transmitting divine illumination and wisdom. These intelligences are presented in nine divisions arranged as a hierarchy, with the most superior division being closest to God and the most inferior division being closest to humanity. The author states that this arrangement was made known to him by the *Divine Initiator*.

These divisions are arranged in three three-fold Orders. The first and most superior of the three divisions form the *First Order,* the second three divisions form the *Middle Order*, and the third and most inferior of the three divisions form the *Final Order*, thus:

First Order
1. Seraphim
2. Cherubim
3. Thrones

Middle Order
4. Dominions
5. Virtues
6. Powers

Final Order
7. Principalities
8. Archangels
9. Angels

Pseudo-Dionysius describes how the light and providence of God are transmitted outwards via the Celestial Hierarchy, with those divisions that are superior transmitting this wisdom to those divisions that are inferior. Each of these divisions has a specific function and duty in regards to transmitting the divine wisdom of the Godhead. As a hierarchy, those divisions that are inferior are not familiar with the tasks of those that are superior, but those that are superior are aware of the functions and duties of those that are inferior. For example, the Seraphim contain the wisdom of the Angels, but the same cannot be said of the Angels regarding the Seraphim.

The Celestial Hierarchy is ultimately manifested symbolically *for our instruction*, and intended to lead us *through the sensible to the intelligible, and from inspired symbols to the simple sublimities of the Heavenly Hierarchies.*

Unsurprisingly, the function of the Celestial Hierarchy is threefold. That of Purification, Illumination, and Perfection[16].

---
16 *"For it is an Hierarchical regulation that some are purified and that others*

1. Purification (Cleansing)

The function of purification involves the removal of taint and the separation from lower, dissimilar elements. Those who purify *should impart, from their own abundance of purity, their own proper holiness.*

2. Illumination (Enlightenment)

The function of illumination involves receiving and imparting the Divine Light, leading to contemplation. Those who are being illuminated should be *filled with the Divine Light,* and be *conducted to the habit and faculty of contemplation in all purity of mind.* Those who illuminate are *more luminous intelligences* whose function is *to receive and to impart light,* and they *overflow, in proportion to their own overflowing light, towards those who are worthy of enlightenment.*

3. Perfection

The function of perfection involves reaching the intended purpose or end of initiation, gaining scientific knowledge of sacred things. Those who are being initiated (or perfected) should be *separated from the imperfect, and become recipients of that perfecting science of the sacred things contemplated.* Those who make perfect, *as being skilled in the impartation of perfection, should perfect those being perfected, through the holy instruction, in the science of the holy things contemplated.*

In summary, these three functions describe the sequential process of deification (assimilation and union with God). Starting with Purification, leading to Illumination, and culminating in Perfection.

Naturally then, one has to ask, *Whom is doing the purifying, illuminating, and perfecting, and who is being purified, illuminated, and perfected?*

This question is both simple and challenging to answer. The simple answer is that the ultimate authority and cause of all

---

purify; that some are enlightened and others enlighten; that some are perfected and others perfect." (Dionysius the Areopagite. 1899)

purification, illumination, and perfection is the Godhead, who is the *self-perfect source and cause of every Hierarchy* and described as being *above purification, above light, [and] preeminently perfect*. The Godhead is the essence of light and the *Cause of Being, and Vision itself* and as the *Author of initiation*, ministers the highest purification, light, and perfection directly to the First Order.

The First Order then proceeds to purify, illuminate, and perfect the divisions of the Celestial Hierarchy, beginning with the Middle Order, who in turn minister to the Final Order.

The purifying, illuminating, and perfecting flow that began from the Godhead, moves through the Celestial Hierarchy from higher to lower Orders, and finally passes on, via the intermediary of angels, to the Terrestrial Hierarchy and its members. The Terrestrial Hierarchy is the earthly expression of the Celestial Hierarchy and is represented by the prophets and faithful. The Terrestrial Hierarchy then continues the same process through its own ministers outwards to all humanity.

Therefore, according to the text, the Celestial Hierarchy serves as an intermediary structure for the transmission of God's goodness and light, which remains *simplex* but is revealed *under various forms*.

The text also cites several passages from scripture (often referred to by the author as the *Oracles*) that allude to the Celestial Hierarchy. These include the visionary accounts of prophets such as Isaiah, Daniel, Zechariah, and Ezekiel, in which the celestial orders are revealed in mystical visions.

Angels as Divine Messengers

In this system of theology then, Angels, being the most inferior of the Celestial Hierarchy and that division immediately superior to Man, play a very important role in the transmission of Divine Light and Mysteries (also referred to in the text as *Mediation*).

The Angels, comprising the *last Order of the Heavenly Beings*, occupy the crucial mediating position immediately superior to the terrestrial realm, as their Hierarchy is *occupied with the more manifest, and is more particularly concerned with the things of the world*. The Angels make known the supermundane mysteries to *Hierarchs,* who are the prophets and spiritual leaders on earth. They also participate in directing nations and preside over *hierarchies* amongst men[17].

Additionally, contrasted to the angelology expressed in some other Christian traditions, which might view Angels as residing in an intermediary plane independent from and unattainable by man, the doctrines contained in The Celestial Hierarchy express the view that man may not only attain to the virtues of the Angels, but may eventually become an Angel himself. In fact, as per the three-fold function of the Celestial Hierarchy expressed above, it is precisely their role to ensure that mankind may reach this esteemed point. This is why the author states that the Hierarchs among men are sometimes called Angels,

> *There is, then, as I think, nothing absurd, if the Word of God calls our Hierarch, Angel, since he participates, according to his own capacity, in the messenger characteristic of the Angels, and elevates himself, as far as attainable to men, to the likeness of their revealing office.* (Dionysius the Areopagite. 1899)

As can be appreciated, in this system of angelology, there is very little that separates Pseudo-Dionysius's definition of a human Hierarch and that of a Rosicrucian Master. In fact, the two are synonymous.

---

[17] The division of Principalities, Archangels and Angels, "...*presides one through the other over the human hierarchies so that their elevation and turning to God and their communion and union with Him may be in order.*" (Dionysius the Areopagite. 1899)

Rosicrucian Groups as a Terrestrial Hierarchy

The very first Rosicrucian organisation that we know of was the Order of the Gold and Rosy Cross (German: *Gold- und Rosenkreuzer*), or G.u.R.C., which emerged as one of the most influential esoteric societies of the eighteenth century.

G.u.R.C. employed an initiatic system of nine degrees. While the reason for this structure remains uncertain, many scholars and Rosicrucian commentators have suggested a Kabbalistic origin based on numerical correspondences. However, I have not found this confirmed in any surviving G.u.R.C. source texts.

One possible alternative is to consider that the nine-grade system was intended to be modelled after the nine divisions of the Celestial Hierarchy. Whether this hypothesis turns out to be the case or not cannot be confirmed without further research into G.u.R.C. history.

What is clear, however, is that following G.u.R.C., numerous Rosicrucian organisations have appeared and disappeared, many adopting the same nine-grade initiatic framework and naming convention first established (and likely formulated) by G.u.R.C.

Within these later groups, both interpretations can be found. Some Rosicrucian organisations align their grades with the Sephiroth of the Kabbalistic Tree of Life, whilst others relate them to the nine divisions of the Celestial Hierarchy as described by Pseudo-Dionysius.

And whilst there do exist overlaps in the doctrinal framework of the Celestial Hierarchy of Pseudo-Dionysius and the Tree of Life of the Kabbalah, it would be incorrect to assume a direct correlation. Each system contains its own identity and tradition, which has been further elaborated upon by the individual initiatic streams that later adopted these systems for their own initiatory frameworks.

Naturally, despite the contrasts between these systems, the underlying principles they express are often universal. These are human attempts to describe an order of existence that lies beyond ordinary comprehension. For this reason, it is possible to find similar cosmogonies across cultures, portraying supramundane intelligences that participate in the creation and governance of the universe and, at times, intervening in the affairs of human leaders. In some cases, these parallels reflect a cross-pollination between traditions, whilst in others they appear to have emerged independently from a shared human experience.

The existence of these heavenly intelligences was not unknown to the pioneers of Rosicrucian organisations who incorporated some of these ideas into their own traditions. Thus we can find examples of prayers and invocations referencing various heavenly intelligences across the vast array of Rosicrucian organisations.

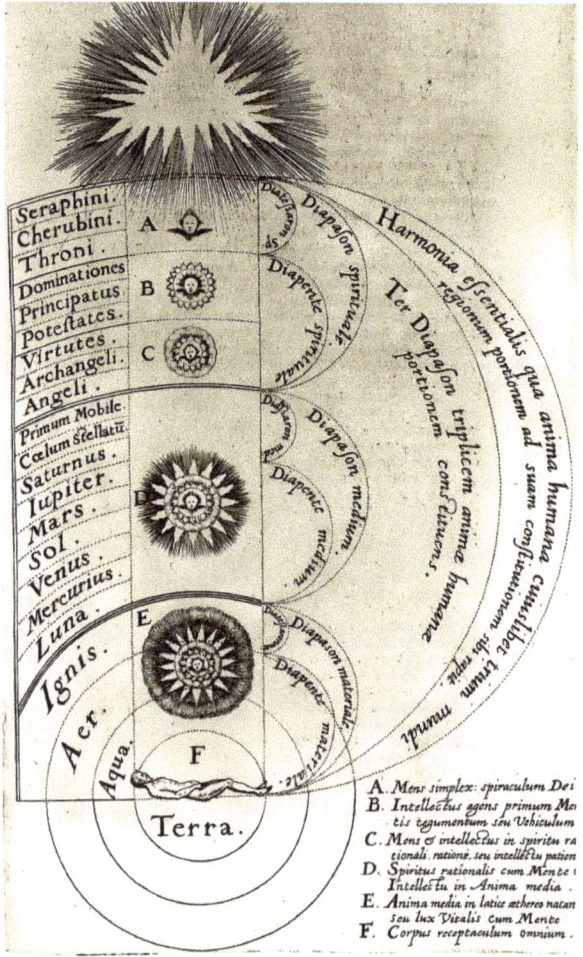

This illustration by Robert Fludd (1574-1637) depicts the harmony between the Celestial and Terrestrial Hierarchies.

For example, in the Societas Rosicruciana tradition, we find the following prayer,

> *Fountain of Light and Glory of the Universe, we humbly adore Thee. Bless the Union of our hearts, symbolized by the joining of our hands, and illuminate our spirits with the brightness of Thy perfection. Sanctify our desires and purify our thoughts, so that we may become worthy to commune with the Holy Ones whom Thou hast created; and finally grant us an everlasting inheritance in the dominions illuminated by the rays of wisdom from Thine unapproachable Throne. AMEN*

And it is not uncommon to find references to heavenly intelligences or even specific angels or archangels being invoked in the ritual work of many Rosicrucian organisations.

The Rosicrucian Master

You might now expect me to give you an index of the various personalities said to guide any number of Rosicrucian traditions. But I will not do this. On several occasions throughout this book I have reiterated that the purpose of this book is not to be an exposé.

The effects brought about by claimed contact with these hidden Masters has had powerful transcendent outcomes upon the individuals who claim to have been contacted. This has led to significant advances to the Rosicrucian tradition and to human civilisation. Nevertheless, these influences are still rather subtle. Not subtle in regard to efficacy, but subtle in regards to the ability to perceive. It naturally follows that to be cognisant of these influences requires the adoption of faculties that transcend what can be written (well, at least my ability to describe them). So I would rather not delineate names as such would most certainly not be helpful and would nearly always lead to misidentification anyway. But perhaps just maybe, if I have achieved my desired result as a writer, some of you might come to recognise the fruit produced by the Rosicrucian Masters.

While the concept of Rosicrucian Masters has played a significant role in the mystical worldview of many Rosicrucian organisations, these external masters should always be subordinated to the primacy of seeking out a more valuable internal source of wisdom.

We should aim to awaken and attune ourselves to the divine spark within, a spark which, through discipline, contemplation, and ethical living, can become a guiding light on our Rosicrucian path.

The ultimate Rosicrucian guide, the Invisible Master, speaks to us through the quiet voice of conscience and the enlightenment of our intuition. It leads us inward toward the sanctum of the soul, where the mystical Rose unfolds from within. And in the end, is this not the very center to which all Masters have ever sought to guide their disciples?

The Light of the World (1853) by William Holman Hunt depicts Christ standing before a closed door. Note that there is no handle on the door, signifying that it can only be opened from within.

THE LOST ROSICRUCIAN SECRET

Intentionally left blank
(see conclusion)

A ROSE BY ANY OTHER NAME

Juliet

'Tis but thy name that is my enemy;
Thou art thyself, though not a Montague.
What's Montague? It is nor hand, nor foot,
Nor arm, nor face, nor any other part
Belonging to a man. O, be some other name!
What's in a name? That which we call a rose
By any other name would smell as sweet;
So Romeo would, were he not Romeo call'd,
Retain that dear perfection which he owes
Without that title. Romeo, doff thy name,
And for that name which is no part of thee
Take all myself.

Romeo

I take thee at thy word:
Call me but love, and I'll be new baptized;
Henceforth I never will be Romeo.

Romeo & Juliet Scene II:Act II

The cross is symbolic of the human body, and the two symbols together – the rose on the cross – signify that the soul of man is crucified upon the body, where it is held by three nails. (Hall, 1928)

The Secret Teaching of all Ages by Manly Palmer Hall

His very name is an embodiment of the manner and the means by which the present-day man is transformed into the Divine Superman. This symbol,

"Christian Rosen Kreuz"

[The] Christian Rose Cross,

shows the end and aim of human evolution; the road to be travelled, and the means whereby that end is gained. (Heindel M. , 1911, p. 319)

The Rosicrucian Cosmo-Conception by Max Heindel

To the Rosicrucian, the "Rose" was the symbol of Nature, of the ever prolific and virgin Earth, or Isis, the mother and nourisher of man, considered as feminine and represented as a virgin woman by the Egyptian Initiates. (Blavatsky H. P., 1918, pp. 296-297)

The Secret Doctrine Vol. 3 by Helena Petrovna Blavatsky

A Rose by any other name

Throughout the previous chapters, you will have noticed that I have provided a great deal of quotes and references from Rosicrucian organisations and commentators. However, you may have also noticed that I have also included references from organisations and individuals that do not belong to any Rosicrucian tradition; such as The Theosophical Society, Paracelsus Research Trust, and Freemasonry. This has been deliberate and is not an oversight on my behalf.

When we looked at *The Invisible Rosicrucians* we discovered that there are many Rosicrucian organisations that expounded a belief that there exists an inner, or esoteric, invisible Rosicrucian brotherhood. In fact, aside from some differences of opinion about whether a physical society could also meet the definition of Rosicrucian, all of the leaders discussed in this book have expressed a belief that there does exist an invisible Rosicrucian current that is somewhat independent of any physical society. This begs the question then, does a organisation need to have *Rosicrucian* in their name to be Rosicrucian?

For instance, could we make a reasonable case to refer to The Theosophical Society as a Rosicrucian organisation? Afterall, we have already seen in the chapter on *Rosicrucian Masters* that The Theosophical Society was partially established as a Rosicrucian organisation and that it was nearly named as a Rosicrucian society when it was being established.

What about Freemasonry? Could we make a reasonable case that Freemasonry could be referred to as a Rosicrucian organisation? Afterall, many Masonic commentators of eminence, such as Gould, de Quincy, and Buhle all assert that Freemasonry owes its existence to the Rosicrucians as the former was established in search for the latter.

It is only fair, that after considering the previous thought experiment that we proceed into hyperbole and find where we should draw the line. Would we consider Christianity to be Rosicrucian?

What about Buddhism? Naturally, we do have to draw a line somewhere, but you can see how this can become quite challenging when we get down to the details.

Perhaps we could narrow down some criteria. Afterall, the agreement upon masonic Landmarks has worked quite effectively in providing *recognition* amongst various Masonic jurisdictions. Masonic Landmarks are considered the core principles or essential elements that define Freemasonry. They are considered unchangeable features that distinguish Freemasonry from other systems or organisations. Although, there is no universal agreement on the exact number or content of these landmarks, there are many which are quite common, such as the belief in a Supreme Being, requiring an open Volume of the Sacred Law (such as the Bible) when the Lodge is opened, and modes of recognition.

What would prevent us from isolating some *Rosicrucian landmarks* to help us to narrow down *authentic* Rosicrucian organisations. Perhaps we could use the *Hallmarks* as presented earlier in this present book?

Unfortunately, I daresay that such an approach would not only be unsuccessful but would also prove a frivolous exercise. In fact, I would go even further and state that attempting to identify a group or person as *Rosicrucian* simply by measuring how well it meets some arbitrary criteria would actively prevent us from recognising something as genuinely Rosicrucian.

Sub-Rosa

Many have sought to understand the rose by resorting to the ancient myths of Greece and Rome, and whilst these stories are indeed important and should not be neglected, we must also recognise that these myths did not necessarily come to define the meaning behind the rose, but that the rose led to the development of the myth.

A Rose by any other name

The rose has long been regarded as a symbol of mystery, secrecy, sacred knowledge; a symbol intimately entwined with femininity and wisdom. Just as a woman nurtures and gestates life, transforming raw potential into an independent consciousness, so too does the rose harbor a hidden truth within its delicate petals, awaiting the moment of revelation. The unfolding of the rose bud is slow and deliberate. Each petal unfurls like layers of understanding. And as it opens, its fragrance, like wisdom itself, grows richer, becoming a silent harbinger of the deeper mystery concealed within.

The Soul of the Rose (1908) by John William Waterhouse.

Greek mythology offers us one of the earliest mythical examples of the symbolism of love and secrecy being associated with the rose. As the goddess Aphrodite (Roman: *Venus*), the goddess of feminine beauty and wisdom rushed to attend to her dying lover Adonis, she inadvertently pricked her foot on a white rosebush. Her spilled divine blood transformed the blossoms into the vibrant red roses we have come to know today (GreekMythology.com, 2025).

The element of secrecy enters the tale through Aphrodite's son, Eros (Roman: *Cupid*), who, having overheard a piece of divine knowledge, sought to ensure its silence. He gifted a rose to Harpocrates, the god of silence, as a token of discretion, thus cementing the rose's narrative role as a guardian of an unspoken truth (Harvey, 2023).

This stone is from The Temple of Jupiter in Split, Croatia. The stonemason was evidently familiar with the esoteric meaning of these symbols when designing this block.

Historically, the Latin phrase *sub rosa* (English: *under the rose*) has been employed to denote confidential discourse.

In some cases, a rose was suspended above a meeting space, or an image of a rose was carved or painted upon the ceiling, as a promise of discretion and a reminder to the participants to maintain confidential the discussions that took place below.

During the medieval period, five-petalled roses were often depicted in art so as to represent the five-wounds of Christ. Such roses can be found in the painting *The Virgin Adoring the Sleeping Christ Child* painted by Botticelli in approximately 1490. The roses in this painting have been identified as Damask roses which were carried by crusaders from the middle-east to locations as far away as Britain.

The rose's association with femininity is also intimately linked with its celestial counterpart, Venus. The planet Venus traces a near-perfect pentagram in its synodic cycle. With its five points reflecting the natural geometry found in some species of rose, it was perhaps only natural that occultists of the renaissance sought to combine both as symbols of divine order or cosmic harmony. From here, we can naturally see correspondences in other traditions. Some have even sought to align the rose with the Egyptian goddess Isis and her personification of Maat (truth, cosmic order, harmony, and justice); and whilst roses were unknown to the ancient Egyptians, it is possible to see how the symbols of Maat and the rose correspond to the same fitting description of cosmic harmony.

The Rose-Cross

Nevertheless, despite various correspondences, we find no mention of the word *Rosicrucian* prior to the early seventeenth century, during the publication of the foundational source texts. The term enters the English language from the name given to the Rosicrucian fraternity first introduced in the Fama Fraternitatis, where the group is named in German as the *Orden des Rosenkreuzes*. Their aims were further articulated in the Confessio Fraternitatis, where they are identified in Latin as the *Fraternitas Rosae Crucis*. The name also appears in the title and protagonist's name in, The Chemical Wedding of Christian Rosenkreuz in the Year 1459, where *Rosenkreuz* literally means *Rose-Cross* in German.

So why should the rose and cross be brought together in this name? Unfortunately, there is no indication from the author/s as to why they chose either the rose or the cross, let alone for their combination. But some of the Rosicrucian writings of this period do inform us as to the meaning.

We could consider then that the fraternity got its name from the symbol of the Rose-Cross. Afterall, some Rosicrucian commentators have speculated that the Rose-Cross predated the Rosicrucian source works.

Albert Pike in his commentary on the grade of *Knight of Kadosh* of the *Ancient and Accepted Scottish Rite*, speculated that the first use of the Rose-Cross occurred in The Divine Comedy of Dante Alighieri,

> *Commentaries and studies have been multiplied upon the Divine Comedy, the work of DANTE, and yet no one, so far as we know, has pointed out its especial character [...]*
>
> *His Hell is but a negative Purgatory. His Heaven is composed of a series of Kabalistic circles, divided by a cross, like the Pantacle of Ezekiel. In the centre of this cross blooms a rose, and we see the symbol of the Adepts of the Rose-Croix for the first time publicly expounded and almost categorically explained.* (Pike, 1871, p. 593)

However, it would seem that the combination of the rose and the cross in this fourteenth century text is purely circumstantial and not related to the Rose-Cross symbol as used by the pioneers of the Rosicrucian movement.

One of the more credible theories regarding the origin of the Rose-Cross is related to an important figure of the source work era whom we have already discussed, Johannes Valentinus Andreae (see the chapter *Authorship*).

This stylised Rose-Cross appears on the front page of a Rosicrucian work Summum Bonum by Robert Fludd, writing under the pseudonym Joachim Frizius.

Andreae was a prominent Lutheran Theologian and was descended from a notable Lutheran family and the Andreae family crest contained a cross surrounded by four red roses. However, as previously discussed, Andreae was unlikely the author of the Fama Fraternitatis and attributing him as author of other Rosicrucian source works (with exception of The Chemical Wedding of Christian Rosenkreuz in the Year 1459) is highly unlikely.

Without definitive evidence of authorship, we can only speculate on the intended meaning of the term Rosicrucian based on our interpretation of the source works. As for the Rose-Cross itself, we must recognise that it is an artificial symbol; mystical and profound, certainly, but distinct from natural symbols such as the Sun or Moon, whose meanings can be intuited without any prior knowledge.

Therefore, any earlier instances of a rose and cross being combined are likely to be coincidental rather than any deliberate reference to the Rosicrucian fraternity.

That said, identifying an accurate meaning is not impossible.

A Rose by any other name

Beyond the numerous interpretations given by later Rosicrucian groups, the source works themselves also provide us with some insight into the significance and meaning of the Rose-Cross. This meaning might appear at first to be superficially similar to the common *Coniunctio Oppositorum* (English: *Union of Opposites*) interpretations we see in many contemporary Rosicrucian organisations. And with some reflection, it is possible to see how little the meaning has drifted even after 400 years.

In his work, *Summum Bonum*, Robert Fludd, writing under the pseudonym Joachim Frizius, alerts us to his interpretation of the Rose-Cross by stating that access to its true meaning can only be found with diligent effort and inquiry into the self,

> *In order to reach the Rosy blood of the cross flowing in the centre of the subject, it must be understood that we can spend no small amount of work and labour on that business, since we must not act superficially with it, but dig, knock, and search for the very centre of the earth, or our work will be finished.*
>
> *[...]*
>
> *This, then, is the work of true and divine Alchemy, by means of which access is made to the paradise of worldly pleasure, so that we may gather that red rose with the lilies of the valley and eat from the tree of life*[1]. (Frizium, 1629, pp. 48-49)

For Fludd, the mystical blood of the Cross and the figure of Christ serve as parables, guiding the seeker toward the *most red Rose*, which he equates multiple times throughout the text with Divine Knowledge. He suggests that only through this inner transmutation

---

1 Latin: *Ut ad Roseum crucis sanguinem in centro subiecti delitcescentem perueniamus, intelligendum est, quod opus & laborem haud exigum in eo negotio impendere possimus, quoniam non est superficialiter cum co agendum, sed ad terrae viq; meditullium fodere, pulsare, & quaere, aut ctum erit de opere nostro. [...] Hoc ergo est verae & diuinae Alchymiae opus mediante quo in voluptatis paradisum mundanis fiat aditus, ut rosam illam rubeam cum Liliis conuallii colligamus & de arbore vitae comedamus.*

can one become truly worthy of being called a *Brother of the Rose Cross* and partake in the unity of the fraternity. He presents the Rose-Cross as both a Christian mystery and an alchemical key to spiritual enlightenment, accessible only to those who earnestly seek it,

> *Therefore, having carefully considered these things, it will be clear that this mystical blood of the cross and the cross of Christ is like a parable, and that every true Christian should investigate with the utmost care, until he finds that most red Rose or most precious blood of the cross fixed and permanent there, so that at last he can be deservedly called a Brother of the Rose Cross and be rewarded with true brotherhood, verifying the axiom of that royal Psalmist: How good and how pleasant it is for brothers to dwell together in unity*[2]. (Frizium, 1629, p. 50)

Michael Maier, another highly influential personality associated with the early Rosicrucians movement and friend of Robert Fludd, provides his own interpretation of the Rose-Cross, which emphasises its dual-nature, and perhaps makes it further aligned to more contemporary interpretations. He states that the rose, traditionally associated with beauty and enlightenment, contrasts with the cross, which signifies suffering and sacrifice. To live *amidst Roses, and under a crosse*, Maier suggests, is to endure both the pleasures and burdens of existence. But despite life's sorrow, the beauty of the rose far outweighs the sorrow of the cross.

> *Some out of proper names will make Anagrams, see what is included in R.C. the Rosy Cross γλυκόπικρος*[3], *Ha, Ha, Eheu*[4], *in the same is contain'd a laughter and*

---

[2] Latin: *His ergo bene ponderatis liquebit quá parabolicus sit, & mysticus iste crucis sanguis & Christi crux, quam omnis verus Christianus summopere inuestigare debet, quousque rubicundiffimam illam Rosam seu pretiosissimum. illum crucis sanguinem ibi fixum & permanente inueniat, ut tandem merito dici possit Roseae crucis frater & de fraternitate vera munerari, istius Psalmistae regii axioma verificando: Fratres habitare in unum quam bonum & quam iucundum.*

[3] English: *Bitter-sweet*

[4] These are likely mean to represent sounds. "*Ha, Ha*" being laughing and

> *a complaint, sweetness and bitterness, joy and sorrow, for to live amidst Roses, and under a crosse are two contrary things. Man being about to be borne partly by change of places, partly by the naval string cut, is said most commonly to shed teares, and rarely doe rejoyce;* so there whole life is but a continued sorrow, and have more of the Cross then Rose in it: But I rather take R. for the substantial part C. for the Adjective which holds not good in that interpretation of the Rosy-Crosse. (Maier, 1656, p. 114)

This wordplay is quite common in Rosicrucian texts. As Maier himself states about such word games,

> *If you look not to the letter but right interpretation; [you will] have a Key to open secrets, and attain the true knowledge thereof.* (Maier, 1656, p. 113)

While there are few explicit references to the Rose-Cross as a symbol in the source works, we do find the cross surrounded by four roses being used as a sign of recognition by the protagonist of The Chemical Wedding of Christian Rosenkreuz in the Year 1459,

> *Thereupon I prepared for my journey. I put on my white linen coat, and girded myself with a blood-red belt bound crosswise over my shoulders. In my hat I stuck four red roses, so that I could be more easily recognized in the crowd by this sign.* (McLean & Godwin, 1991, p. 21)

If Andreae had been the author of this text, then this may well be an allusion to his own family coat of arms, which featured a red coloured St. Andrew style cross adorned with four red roses (one rose in each quadrant between the arms of the cross).

So in the period immediately following the publication of the Rosicrucian source works which announced the allegorical Fraternity of the Rosy Cross, we find several interpretations as to the meaning of

---

"Eheu" crying.

the Fraternity's name and the symbol of the Rose-Cross. It has been used as a mystical Christian symbol to symbolically explain the end result of our spiritual endeavours, as a metaphor for the mystic's path which encompasses both the burdens and joys of human existence, and as a sign of recognition between Rosicrucian philosophers. This latter function may have been inspired by one of the original governing rules of the Fraternity of the Rosy Cross as stated in the Fama Fraternitatis, that,

> *The word C.R. should be their seal, password, and sign.*
> (Godwin, McIntosh, & McIntosh, 2016, p. 23)

At first glance, the Rose-Cross might seem like a dualistic symbol. But it is better understood as triadic in its character. It unites two complementary or opposing elements into a triune manifestation. Bringing together the symbol of the cross to represent hard-work, determination, sorrow, hardship, and ultimately our physicality, with the beauty of the rose, representing the blood of sacrifice, our hopes, aspirations, virtues, and ultimately that intangible part of us.

This stylised version of the Rose-Cross comes from the title page of the 1681 version of the Fama Fraternitatis.

A Rose by any other name

And just as man is formed of both the *Dust of the Earth* and the *Breath of life* to make Man a *Living Being*, so too is the Rose-Cross a *living* symbol where the rose blossoms upon the cross.

While the word Rosicrucian is commonly understood to derive from Rose and Cross, some commentators have proposed an alternative etymology. In this alternative assessment, the prefix ros- does not refer to the flower but to *ros*, the Latin word for *dew*. The assumption is that dew played a role in early modern alchemical thought as an important substance imbued with special properties necessary for some alchemical operations. In some assessments, the full import of dew has been expanded to represent an internal vital fluid that can be directed with internal alchemical practices in order to hasten spiritual or psychic development. However, whilst this spiritual alchemical assessment sounds interesting, it is likely casting too many external interpretations. Even Arthur Edward Waite, who is quite possibly the source of this original creative etymology, casts his doubt on this assessment by stating that *this opinion exaggerates the importance attributed to the dew of the alchemists* (Waite A. E., 1887, p. 6)[5].

The rose is a potent metaphor of organic life. It begins as a bud, concealing its hidden potential, the promise of maturity. Only through time and the right conditions may it bloom and open. Likewise, our initiatic journey requires inner cultivation, perseverance, and patience before our own spiritual enlightenment may be attained.

Thus, the Rose-Cross is a mystical symbol that reflects our place in the universe. It also serves as a reminder of our own spiritual journey and speaks to our purpose as active participants in the process of illumination. As H. Spencer Lewis explains,

---

5 Waite would publish two large books on the Rosicrucians. The first was *The Real History of the Rosicrucians* published in 1887. The second was *Brotherhood of the Rosy Cross* published in 1924. Of the two, the latter is far more reliable. Waite critiques the *dew* etymology in both works.

> *We now find that we have three reasons for the incarnation of the Soul in the body. First, that [...] the Soul is to have certain earthly experiences and, secondly, the physical, human body is to have the advantage of spiritual knowledge and illumination in addition to its mundane knowledge; thirdly, that the character and personality of man may be perfected.*
> (Lewis, 1930, pp. 70-71)

It is through this journey of self-perfection that we may truly become a *Brother of the Rosy Cross*; raising the definition of what constitutes a Rosicrucian from simply being a dues-paying member of a Rosicrucian organisation, to an illumined mystic. To be a Rosicrucian in the fullest sense is not a matter of organisational affiliation but of illumination; of embodying that wisdom that the Rose-Cross represents. To live as an awakened soul in harmony with the divine.

This distinction however has presented a challenge to some Rosicrucian organisations creating a conflict of identity. How can one claim membership in a Rosicrucian order without having attained the enlightenment that defines true Rosicrucianism?

To solve this dilemma, some organisations have resorted to one of the favourite Rosicrucian pastimes: *wordplay*! Members might be referred to (or refer to themselves) as Rosicrucian *students*, or *philosophers*, acknowledging that they are but humble seekers on the Rosicrucian path and not a fully realised Rosicrucian adept. Others, like The Hermetic Order of the Golden Dawn took a more definitive stance: they declared that anyone who openly identifies as a Rosicrucian has, by that very declaration, proven themselves not to be one since a true Rosicrucian is, by nature, invisible.

In some cases, a separate definition is proposed for when referring to an illumined member of the Rosicrucian brotherhood. In the A.M.O.R.C. tradition, such advanced individuals are referred to as *Rose-Croix* or having attained a particular state of development baring the same name. Whilst *The Rosicrucian Fellowship* speaks of the *Elder Brothers of the Rosicrucian Brotherhood*. These distinctions are attempts to resolve the tension between membership and true spiritual attainment.

Ultimately, however, such definitions are a matter of semantics for they represent ways in which we may best communicate upon a nuanced topic.

This ongoing debate over definitions highlights a fundamental challenge in esoteric traditions: how does one convey profound spiritual truths that are, by their nature, difficult to articulate or even ineffable? If the essence of Rosicrucianism transcends formal membership and fixed labels, how then can its wisdom be shared without diminishing its mystery?

OFF WITH THE FAIRIES:
ROSICRUCIAN DIDACTIC LITERATURE

You are going to learn how to command over Nature's Self: You'll have God alone to your Teacher, and the Sages alone to your Equals: The supreme Intelligences will be proud to obey you; the Daeomons will not dare to be present where you are; your Voice will make them tremble in the Well-Hole of your bottomless Pit; and all the invisible Nations, who inhabit the four Elements, will esteem themselves happy in being the Ministers of your Pleasure. I adore Thee, Thou great God! That though has crown'd Mankind with so much Glory, and establish'd him the Sovereign Monarch over all the Works of thine Hand! Do you feel, my son, (added he, turning to me) do you feel in yourself that Heroick Ambition, which is the assured Character of the Children of Wisdom? Have you the Courage to desire to serve God alone, and to rule over whatever is not God? Are you appriz'd what it is to be a Man? And does it not go against you to be a Slave, since you were born to be a Sovereign? (Montfaucon de Villars, 1670, p. 45)

The Comte de Gabalis

A very popular approach for revealing occult knowledge in the Rosicrucian tradition has been the employment of esoteric didactic literature. *Didactic* comes from the Greek word, *didaktikós*, meaning *skilled in teaching* (SuperSummary.com, 2025).

Didactic literature employs symbolic and allegorical language to engage the reader's intuition, guiding them toward an insight that is often more easily grasped on an emotional or intuitive level than through purely rational analysis. Esoteric didactic literature resorts to the use of narrative and metaphor rather than attempting to express mystical knowledge in a direct or expository manner. The benefit of this method is that understanding is not handed down but is rather awakened within the reader through their engagement with the narrative.

It is no coincidence that some of the most enduring Rosicrucian texts take the form of allegory rather than straightforward exposition.

Esoteric didactic literature also serves another purpose. Not only can it reveal insights to the reader, but it also has the ability to conceal information from the uninitiated.

By encoding esoteric knowledge in an often multi-layered, allegorical narrative the text can ensure that only those with the necessary inner preparation can decipher its meaning. To the uninitiated, such writings may seem like mere fiction, fanciful allegory, or even pure nonsense. But to the initiate, it can serve as a guide towards a valuable insight. Those who merely skim its surface will find little of substance, while those who approach these texts with an open and searching mind will be rewarded as they uncover layers of meaning that unfold as their understanding deepens.

Finally, authors of didactic literature may also take advantage of the unique relationship that forms between the reader and the text. By presenting their teachings through fiction, they are freed from the burden of assuming the role of a spiritual authority. This allows the wisdom in the narrative to speak for itself, without the distractions of personal reputation or hierarchical status. Many writers of esoteric didactic texts take this a step further by adopting a pseudonym or attributing their work to an anonymous or symbolic figure. This deliberate distancing removes the focus from the author and places it entirely on the message, preventing debates over personal credibility and ensures that the narrative remains the true focal point. In doing so, these works invite the reader to engage with the text on its own terms, allowing the author to foster in the reader a direct and personal encounter with the wisdom embedded within the text.

The use of esoteric didactic literature is by no means unique to the Rosicrucian tradition. Since the dawn of civilisation, humanity has conveyed wisdom through didactic narratives, often in the form of myths, legends, and folktales, where they have served as vehicles for transmitting spiritual, moral, and philosophical teachings across generations.

Some of these narratives even have ancient origins, beginning as oral traditions that have been passed down and refined over time. In some cases, some of these narratives have made their way into written religious texts which have been employed by sages and spiritual leaders. From the parables of Jesus and the allegories of Plato to the sacred myths of ancient Egypt, India, and Mesopotamia, esoteric storytelling has long been a means of preserving and transmitting hidden knowledge.

The Rosicrucian didactic literature, therefore, is part of a much older and broader lineage of wisdom literature. Nevertheless, it has been quite influential on the Rosicrucian tradition and many important Rosicrucian texts take on this important form.

We have already discussed the Fama Fraternitatis and Confessio Fraternitatis in depth in an earlier chapter. It is not necessary to re-examine these texts, other than to point out that these may be considered a form of esoteric didactic literature as they both rely on an allegorical narrative to impart knowledge to the reader.

In fact, nearly all of the Rosicrucian texts of this period rely upon such didactic methods. As a further example, let us examine but one paragraph of a highly influential Rosicrucian source work by Theophilus Schweighardt (likely a pseudonym of Daniel Mögling), *The Mirror of Wisdom of the Rosy Cross* (Latin: *Speculum Sophicum Rhodostauroticum*). In this 1618 work, the author is attempting to describe how to find the Rosicrucians, whom he refers to as the *Collegium of the Fraternity of the Rosy Cross*, or simply, the *Collegium*,

> *And now thou askest, how shall I come thereunto? Attend unto what Iulianus de Campsis says in his epistle: "I wandered through many kingdoms, principalities, domains and provinces; I turned towards the sunrise, noon and evening and finally towards midnight etc." These words will explain the Collegium clearly enough unto thee and it helps but little if thou wander through all kingdoms and seaport towns and art not worthy to receive. Study my figure, Serpentarius and Cygnus have shewn thee the way thirteen years ago to the Holy Spirit and have not the blessed videamini called unto the brethren? What shall it avail thee if thou comest with unwashed hands and a mind desirous of money? Little can the ringing of the bell or blowing of the horn help thee, and even though thou seest the gates open before thee thou mayest not enter, for thy name stands not written there, for thus it is written: "Come ye who are worthy. Thou however must be an unworthy Christophilus though thou beest a Christophilus." Therefore the fraternity shall bethink themselves of Jehova, their leader, rather than give thee a reply. Shall we be moved? even let us be moved – that is an evil message. If that should happen thou shalt certainly either miss the Collegium or if thou art not content with this and wilt climb higher against all will, thou shalt sing the*

paenitere (penitence) in the dirt. Therefore hasten slowly. Pray, work and hope. If God pleases by many distinctions of things. At last. Thou seest that the Collegium hangs in the air, where God wills, he can direct it. It is moveable and immoveable, constant and inconstant, it relies upon its wings and wheels, and though the brethren call the "venite" with sweet trumpets, Iulianus de Campus stands with the sword, and thou must undergo his examination, wherefore beware. If thou pass not the examination and hast a bad conscience neither bridge nor rope shall avail thee. If thou comest high, high shall be thy fall, and thou must die and spoil in the pit of errors and opinions. Follow me, imitate the birds as in my figure, fly in the free air, go gently. There is no peril in delay, but in haste. Let the dove fly from thine ark and seek out the land. If she bring thee an olive branch be sure that God has helped thee, and thou shouldst in turn help the poor. But if the dove stays away without a sign then go into thy herb garden and feed thyself meanwhile upon the lovely herb "patientia" (in so far as it has been planted in thy garden), but beware, as thou lovest thy soul, of the weed "desperation", for although Iulianus says: "He who is not ready today shall be less so tomorrow" which is to be applied to presumptuous heads who would break into wisdom against the laws of God and nature - may the thrown dice fall! This I say: walk with a stick, for thou who art not ready today shall be so one day, for not all the day is evening, and what is not to be hoped for today shall yet come to pass. Do thou only what thou canst (as the aforementioned Campanus says) and thou shalt be in his good time released from the flood of ignorance.
(Schweighardt, 1618)

With some reflection, we see that in a single passage, Schweighardt has managed to convey a great wealth of information.

We learn that those with *unwashed hands and a mind desirous of money* will be denied entry to the *Collegium*. *Little can the ringing of the bell or blowing of the horn help thee,* for we must be pure of heart and not simply parodying ourselves as worthy. Our intent, represented in the text by conscience and the dove, is absolutely essential. And being a Christian is not enough if you lack humility and understanding for, *Thou however must be an unworthy Christophilus though thou beest a Christophilus.*

The text urges us to study the *Serpentarius* and *Cygnus*. Superficially, this represents the astronomical events that preceded the announcement of the Rosicrucians. But a more esoteric interpretation reveals that the text is also indicating the metaphorical alchemical vitalising of the body (*Cygnus*) and the grounding of the spirit (*Serpentarius*). Some contemplative alchemical texts might substitute these phrases for, *Solve* and *Coagula;* phrases that, whilst not entirely the same, are quite similar. In other words, we should seek out the wisdom resident in the world in which we live and aim to bring into manifestation those subtle inspirations which we gain on our mystical journey. After all, what use is inspiration if it remains locked up in our mind!

And there are no shortcuts to finding the Collegium which, Schweighardt reminds us, resides in the air, is both movable and immovable, both constant and inconstant, and has wheels and has wings. For neither *bridge nor rope* can save us from our arrogance for *if thou comest high, high shall be thy fall.*

Patiently abide by your conscience and *fly high from thine Ark*, says Schweighardt. In short, true initiation into the Rosicrucian fraternity requires sincerity, preparation, effort, patience, and perseverance.

This may seem like a lot of information that can be gained from such a small passage. But actually, there is so much more encoded here that we have not even touched upon. Many Rosicrucian texts are multi-faceted and layered with meaning like this. Whilst my commentary has reflected the text as a mystical ascent, others will see in this a practical bodily alchemy aimed at *raising the vibrations* of the body. Not to mention that this is but one paragraph of a much larger work. Truly, the full import of such a work cannot be gained by a mere superficial reading. Rosicrucian didactic texts demand from us a more contemplative approach, where meaning unfolds gradually through our own engagement and reflection[1].

Rosicrucian didactic literature during the Occult Revival

We have already discussed one of the *hallmarks* of Rosicrucianism as being, *The Rosicrucian Pulse*, describing how the Rosicrucian tradition has tended to manifest itself in a cyclical alternating pattern of activity/inactivity. When this period of activity reached its zenith in England and France at the turn of the twentieth century, we also had an increase of interest in didactic literature that could be considered quite particularly, *Rosicrucian*.

Perhaps one of the most celebrated of this era was a work titled, *Zanoni,* and penned by the Englishman Sir Edward Bulwer-Lytton. Prior to writing novels, Bulwer-Lytton had already amassed considerable professional expertise as a parliamentarian, playwright, and journalist. He was also a Cambridge alumnus.

By the time Zanoni was published in 1842, Bulwer-Lytton had already established himself as a bestselling author and a prominent literary figure. However, Zanoni did mark a significant departure from the historical and social themes of his earlier works, as he ventured into territories more occult and mystical.

---

[1] To learn more about *Contemplative Reading and Reflection*, I would highly recommend *A Rose Croix Oratory* by C. R. Dunning Jr published by *Stone Guild Publishing*, where the author provides a practical method of *reading* Rosicrucian texts.

The novel depicts the journey of a near immortal adept, named Zanoni. Aside from his incredible occult knowledge, Zanoni also belonged to an ancient and secretive Rosicrucian brotherhood. However, his centuries of life as a master of the occult had not furnished Zanoni with everything one might wish for, for his great wisdom conflicts with the more human aspect of his existence: Love. To embrace this love, which he aims to fulfill with a young and talented opera singer, Zanoni learns that he must ultimately sacrifice his immortality.

Glyndon is another character who appears in the Zanoni novel. Unlike the enigmatic and wise, Zanoni, Glyndon is a more flawed character. Ambitious for occult knowledge, he sets out on his initiatory path. He is drawn to the wisdom he sees in Zanoni and wishes to possess a power that might elevate him beyond ordinary men. But his desire is more grounded in ambition. He is impulsive, impatient, and easily swayed by others' opinions and more material pursuits. He wants all the rewards of occult knowledge but avoids the work necessary to attain them. Glyndon's inability to confront his own weaknesses and lack of inner preparedness leads him to psychological torment. When finally faced with the true challenge of initiation, Glyndon is faced with a terrifying entity: *The Dweller*

A rare image that appeared in the frontispiece of an 1888 edition of Zanoni depicting the meeting between Zanoni and Adon-Ai.

"From the column there emerged a shape of unimaginable glory. Its face was that of a man in its first youth; but solemn, as with the consciousness of eternity and the tranquillity of wisdom; light, like star-beams, flowed through its transparent veins; light made its limbs themselves, and undulated, in restless sparkles, through the waves of its dazzling hair (Bulwer-Lytton, 1862, pp. 78-79)."

on the Threshold. Fortunately, not all is lost for Glyndon and by the end of the novel, he eventually comes to recognise his failings and embarks on a more *genuine* path of self-discovery.

So what was it about this Victorian-era novel that held such fascination in the minds of Rosicrucian philosophers of this time? Perhaps they saw in this novel a reflection of their own initiatory journey. Perhaps it was the allure and mystique of all the occult knowledge mentioned in the text? Perhaps it was the references to earlier esoteric didactic texts, such as *Comte de Gabalis*. Perhaps it was because the novel reveals to the reader that Zanoni was a Rosicrucian (only one of two remaining of this *august fraternity*). More than likely, it was all of these things and more. And fortunately, for those readers that were not able to recognise the characters as representing parts of our own human nature, Bulwer-Lytton would in later editions of the novel provide his own commentary as to the meaning behind some of these mysterious allegorical characters.

Bulwer-Lytton's understanding of the mystical journey of an initiate is unmistakable. The journey of initiation, as he presents it, is an experiential process which allows the seeker to apprehend a true reality that normally resides beyond the limits of ordinary human understanding. He also recognised that those who embark on this path must overcome their fears and embrace the unknown with courage and determination as true pioneers with an unshakeable faith peering into the unknown,

> *To quaff the inner life, is to see the outer life: to live in defiance of time, is to live in the whole. He who discovers the elixir discovers what lies in space; for the spirit that vivifies the frame strengthens the senses. There is attraction in the elementary principle of light. In the lamps of Rosicrucius the fire is the pure elementary principle. Kindle the lamps while thou openst the vessel that contains the elixir, and the light attracts towards thee those beings whose life is that light. Beware of Fear. Fear is the deadliest enemy to Knowledge.* (Bulwer-Lytton, 1862, p. 59)

It is also clear that Bulwer-Lytton was well aware of the method his novels took. When discussing another of his popular esoteric didactic novels, *A Strange Story*, he would state that it was,

> ...a Romance which conducts it bewildered hero towards the same goal to which philosophy conducts its luminous student (Bulwer-Lytton as quoted by Affectator, 2025)

'Frater' Bulwer-Lytton

At a quarterly meeting of the Societas Rosicruciana in Anglia[2] held on the evening of Thursday, 14 July 1870, it was proposed that,

> *The Right Hon. Lord Lytton be elected an Hon. Member, and be requested to accept the office of Grand Patron of the Order.* (Rosicrucian Society of England, 1870, p. 114)

This motion was put forward by the Supreme Magus, Robert Wentworth Little, and the Secretary-General, William Robert Woodman. Frater Bulwer-Lytton was then inscribed in the society's *Golden Book*[3] at position 101[4], not far below John Yarker.

In an amusing turn of events, John Yarker, who had been admitted to the society shortly before Bulwer-Lytton's honorary patronage, invited him to an obligatory meeting. Bulwer-Lytton's response to this summons made it clear that, not only was he completely unaware of his honorary title, but he was also rather displeased by it. He promptly requested that his name be removed from the society's records (Greensill, 2003, p. 364).

2 Being known at this time as, *The Rosicrucian Society of England*.
3 The *Golden Book* is a membership register maintained by the S.R.I.A. in London. It contains records of every member, including their advancements in each grade. Esteemed esotericists such as William Wynn Westcott, Arthur Edward Waite, Marcus Worsley Blackden, John Yarker, Robert Felkin, and contemporary esoteric authors can be found within its pages. In 2012, the Golden Book archive was transferred to an electronic database, but it continues to fulfill the same function (Lees, 2013).
4 These numbers were added in by William Wynn Westcott a short time after becoming Supreme Magus. Further details can be found in *The Temple and the Vault* published by *Lewis Masonic*.

The Ancient and Mystical Order Rosae Crucis (A.M.O.R.C.) likewise had noted Bulwer-Lytton's contributions to the Rosicrucian tradition. In the inaugural issue of the organisation's public periodical, published less than a year after the A.M.O.R.C. was founded, there is a book recommendation stating,

> "*Zanoni.*"
>
> *By Bulwer-Lytton.*
>
> *The world's greatest of all Rosaecrucian stories. The symbolism of the Order is interestingly told in a story of love and mystery, by a Master Rosaecrucian.*
>
> *(Recommended by the Imperator.)*
>
> (The Ancient and Mystical Order Rosae Crucis, 1916)[5]

Subsequent issues of A.M.O.R.C. periodicals, even up to today, provide great praise to Bulwer-Lytton's esoteric works. Whilst clearly, Bulwer-Lytton may never have been a member of A.M.O.R.C. having passed away several decades before the organisation was founded, he nevertheless exerted considerable influence upon Rosicrucian thought leaders. Naturally, this had nothing to do with *membership*, but was due to the praise Bulwer-Lytton had given to the mysterious Rosicrucian brotherhood as well as the successful and creative way in which Bulwer-Lytton transmitted esoteric knowledge. And no doubt there were initiates in the A.M.O.R.C. tradition that could recognise Bulwer-Lytton's *Dweller of the Threshold* with a corresponding force encountered in A.M.O.R.C.'s Temple Degree Initiation tradition; *The Terror of the Threshold*.

Additionally, as both A.M.O.R.C. teachings and Bulwer-Lytton's narratives reveal the mysteries that are to be found in nature,

---

5 In a following issue of the same periodical there was published a letter to the editor querying if Bulwer-Lytton was really a member of A.M.O.R.C. as the reader was of the impression he was a member of the S.R.I.A. as well as querying the confusion between *Societas Rosicruciana in Anglia* and *Societas Rosicruciana in America* (a point that still confuses people a century later). The response given was, "*You are right Lytton did belong to a number of societies. But – what is the point of this question?*"

it would only be natural that Rosicrucian students would recognise that whilst A.M.O.R.C. teachings sounded modern, they were simply the old re-packaged as something new.

In this work by Albrecht Dürer entitled, *Knight, Death and the Devil* (1513), a lone knight rides steadfast through a shadowed gorge, flanked by Death bearing an hourglass and a horned devil lurking close behind. Yet he does not falter. This image evokes the *Terror of the Threshold*, the initiatory moment when one must confront inner fear, doubt, and mortality. The knight's calm resolve, towering mount, and faithful dog symbolise the virtues of discipline, courage, and focus.

Despite the threats, the brave knight looks ahead and continues on his way.

Elemental Inhabitants

> *At Fez he made the acquaintance of the Elementary Inhabitants (as he commonly called them), who revealed to him much of what they knew, just as we Germans could do among ourselves if we had sufficient unity and a passionate and earnest desire to search.* (Godwin, McIntosh, & McIntosh, 2016, p. 19)
> **Fama Fraternitatis**

The presence of elemental beings in esoteric thought has been a recurring theme in mystical traditions, particularly within Rosicrucianism. These beings, usually described as subtle ethereal or astral entities, are often described as intermediaries between the material and spiritual worlds.

Such unusual creatures were said to inhabit nature, their specific *habitat* being determined by their curious personalities. And it was this personality which influenced the changes which primitive man might observe around him in nature. As one author would state,

> *To the mind of primitive man, living in constant intercourse with a still hostile nature, every object of his environment seemed animate. The rock, the tree, the pond, all were inhabited by spirits from whom good or evil might come, who forced one to be on his guard constantly and who had to be placated at times. The creative genius of the Greeks lent color to these vague spirits. The heaven became Zeus, the sun Apollo, the moon Artemis, not mere forces of nature, but beings with a biography, with passions and whims very similar to those of mortal man, and thus very close to him.* (Sigerist, 1941, p. 217)

The notion of elementals played a significant role in the teachings of Paracelsus and other esoteric philosophers, influencing not only occult traditions but also the literature that drew upon them, including the works of the aforementioned Bulwer-Lytton,

As I have so often said before, magic (or science that violates Nature) exists not; —it is but the science by which Nature can be controlled. Now, in space there are millions of beings, not literally spiritual, for they have all, like the animalculae unseen by the naked eye, certain forms of matter, though matter so delicate, air-drawn, and subtle, that it is, as it were, but a film, a gossamer that clothes the spirit. Hence the Rosicrucian's lovely phantoms of sylph and gnome. Yet, in truth, these races and tribes differ more widely, each from each, than the Calmuck from the Greek —differ in attributes and powers. In the drop of water you see how the animalculae vary, how vast and terrible are some of those monster mites as compared with others. Equally so with the Inhabitants of the atmosphere: some of surpassing wisdom, some of horrible malignity; some hostile as fiends to men, others gentle as messengers between earth and heaven. He who would establish intercourse with these varying beings, resembles the traveller who would penetrate into unknown lands. (Bulwer-Lytton, 1862, pp. 45-46)

Paracelsus, the sixteenth century physician and alchemist, was one of the earliest figures to provide a systematic classification of elementals. In his writings, he divided these beings into four primary categories corresponding to the classical elements:

- **Gnomes**[6] (*Earth*),
- **Undines** (*Water*),
- **Sylphs** (*Air*), and
- **Salamanders** (*Fire*).

Paracelsus describes these beings as being distinct yet residing parallel with our human existence. These creatures would be said to mostly remain within their own elemental realms but would occasionally be perceived by humans in special circumstances. As Paracelsus would state,

---

6   Sometimes referred to as, *Pygmies*.

Off with the Fairies

There are more things, however, than those which are comprehended and recognized in the light of nature, things which are above and superior to it. But these cannot be understood against the light of nature, that is in the light of nature, but in the light of man which is above the light of nature. (Paracelsus as quoted in Sigerist (1941, p. 223)

To Paracelsus, these spirits were integral to the natural order, acting as caretakers of the elements and possessing wisdom beyond human perception. Their role, he suggested, was not merely metaphorical but practical, influencing health, alchemy, and the balance of natural forces (Sigerist, 1941, pp. 220-221).

The Comte de Gabalis, a seventeenth century esoteric text attributed to the Abbé Henri Montfaucon de Villars, built upon these ideas, presenting the elementals as beings with whom an initiate could make contact. According *to* Abbé de Villars communication with these entities could result in the revelation of secret knowledge; which the sages of old had relied upon to illuminate their disciples.

This notion of communion with elementals fascinated later Rosicrucian commentators, who viewed it as part of the greater alchemical and spiritual work of purification that was suggested in *some* medieval alchemical writings.

The incredibly well-read Bulwer-Lytton was obviously familiar with these earlier esoteric traditions when he incorporated elementals into Zanoni, particularly in his depiction of the mysterious and supernatural forces which surrounded the stories protagonist. The novel alludes to a hidden world inhabited by spirits that influence human destiny.

Perhaps even the concept of the Dweller on the Threshold could be interpreted as a distorted or fearsome version of these elementals, beings whose presence could either aid or obstruct the initiate, depending upon their worthiness.

Rosicrucian thought, particularly as preserved in the teachings of Rosicrucian organisations, continued to explore the reality of these beings. Contemporary Rosicrucian organisations often interpreted the elementals as manifestations of universal vibratory forces. This then led to a more physical approach to understanding these forces, aligning spiritual entities with those quantum forces which compose and maintain our atomic and sub-atomic world.

Will L. Garver's *Brother of the Third Degree*, a lesser-known but still influential esoteric novel, also touches upon the role of unseen forces, including elementals, as encountered upon an initiate's mystical journey. Though not as explicit as Comte de Gabalis, the novel presents the protagonist's initiatory path as one where interactions with etheric entities shape his development. Similar to the previously mentioned texts, these beings acted as both guides and obstacles, further reinforcing the idea that an initiates illumination can only be attained with the proper preparation, perseverance, and patience.

Franz Hartmann, in his work *An Adventure Among the Rosicrucians*, provides a shorter, yet highly enjoyable portrayal of elementals, depicting them as conscious entities that pervade nature. He describes them as the forces behind natural phenomena, shaping the material world through unseen influences. According to Hartmann, those trained in the mystical arts could communicate with these beings and obtain secret knowledge. As such, Hartmann's depiction aligns with earlier Rosicrucian interpretations that saw elementals not merely as folklore but as integral to the esoteric understanding of nature's hidden dimensions,

> "Oh!" answered the monk, "this shrine contains some powders for fumigations, by the aid of which a man may see the Elemental Spirits of Nature."
>
> "Indeed!" I exclaimed. "Oh, how I should like to see these lovely spirits! I have read a great deal about them in the books of Paracelsus; but I never had an opportunity of seeing them."

"They are not all of them lovely," said the monk. "The Elementals of earth have human forms. They are small, but they have the power to elongate their bodies. These gnomes and pigmies are usually ill-humoured and cross; and it is just as well to leave them alone, although sometimes they become very good friends of man, and may even show him hidden treasures and mines. The Elementals of air, the sylvans, are of a more agreeable nature; still we cannot rely upon their friendship. The salamanders, living in the element of fire, are ugly customers, and it is better to have nothing to do with them. But the nymphs and undines are lovely creatures, and they often associate with man." (Hartmann F. , 1910, pp. 161-162)

It might be possible also to make comparisons between elementals within the Western esoteric tradition and the djinn of pre-Islamic Arabian religion[7]. The djinn are described in the Quran as beings created from *smokeless fire* (Quran, *Sūrat l-Rahmān, Verse 15*). They are similarly regarded as invisible entities that co-exist with humanity, possessing the ability to influence human affairs. Just as Paracelsian elementals are associated with the four elements, Islamic traditions describe djinn inhabiting deserts, oceans, and winds, reflecting their connection to natural forces. Moreover, both traditions depict these beings as morally diverse, some benevolent, others malevolent, and many simply indifferent to human concerns. Éliphas Lévi and Manly P. Hall have both suggested that djinn correspond to the salamanders who govern the fiery realm (Waite A. E., 1910, p. 227) (Hall, 1928, pp. 327-328).

In discussing elementals within the Rosicrucian tradition though, we should be mindful of the influence from the Paracelsian tradition upon the author/s of the Fama Fraternitatis; for it was likely this influence that contributed more to the Rosicrucian thought of this period than other traditions, such as the pre-Arabic tradition.

---

7   There is also some speculation that Djinn may be of pre-Zoroastrian Persian origin, where they later arrived in Avestic literature as *Jaini,*

In considering the broad fascination elementals have had within the Rosicrucian tradition, we might be tempted to explain away these forces as merely symbolic in nature, representing more emotional or psychological tendencies. Certainly, such an interpretation would not be entirely out of place, especially within the framework of the humoral theory that shaped medieval medical thought. However, this view is far too narrow. Elementals would be better understood as a subtle external presence as well as an ongoing philosophical inquiry into the forces that govern nature and existence, whether this be through the lens of medieval alchemy, Victorian esotericism, Islamic mysticism, or modern metaphysics.

Even in the early twentieth century, the study of elementals might even be considered an attempt to bridge that gap which began to swell rapidly between the advancing scientific thought and the trailing spiritual traditions that once walked hand in hand with it. Consider the following quote from an early A.M.O.R.C. periodical,

> *It was the alchemists who first discovered and announced in their writings that the manifestations of all of nature's laws were possible through the vibrations which emanated from the spirit energy contained in the elementals of all nature. These elementals were carefully analyzed and classified by these old scientists called alchemists to such an extent that many of their writings today prove that they had a more correct understanding of the composition of matter than had the so-called scientists of the Middle Ages[...] And what about the researches of the Rosicrucians, as explained recently in Marie Corelli's books and referred to in the older writings of Lord Bulwer Lytton? Did not the Rosicrucian teachings of several centuries ago speak of the indivisible elements of universal energy which composed all atoms and which determined the nature of the composition of matter by their vibratory rate and their electrical polarity as negative or positive? Is not the modern electron another name for that same indivisible element to which the Rosicrucians referred?*
> (Thurston, 1925, p. 150)

The Rosicrucian writings of this era were the final attempts by some of the last great occult minds to reconcile two branches of study that were never meant to be severed. The effects of this division continue to influence our modern world, leaving a lingering sense of something lost; a wound that has yet to be healed.

In this alchemical mandala-like image from Basil Valentine, we can see that the Alchemist (represented by the wise old man in the centre) resides in the centre of the elements represented by the Earth (lower left), Water (lower right), Air (upper right), Fire (upper left). Before chemistry, meteorology, and biology emerged as modern sciences, the elemental spirits, gnomes, undines, sylphs, and salamanders, helped early thinkers describe and symbolically interpret the forces of nature.

The initiatic power of esoteric narrative

Esoteric didactive narratives serve an essential part of the Rosicrucian tradition. By reading these works, we participate in the *mystery*. And whilst this participation is quite unlike those curious rituals conducted in the ancient mystery rites or by modern-day Masonic and Rosicrucian organisations, these *literary mysteries* take place in silence, in solitude, and in the inner chamber of the heart and mind. Yet they still serve a very similar purpose: to educate or guide aspirants towards a revelation of a universal truth or internal insight. This universal truth, however, eludes simple articulation. It cannot be bestowed or imposed, no matter how skilled the writer or how carefully crafted the text.

Instead, the narrative serves as a mirror. It creates conditions under which intuitive insights might arise. These insights come not from the words themselves, but from what they awaken in the reader. And the truth to which these writings allude is not relative. It is perennial!

But here lies a paradox. How can it be possible that a single text can have so many inspired readers and yet their personal interpretations differ so widely? In one single esoteric narrative, one reader might reach conclusions that are morally inspired. Another might read in the characters and their relationships a description of an abstract cosmogony. And another reader might find a metaphysical narrative from which to understand reality and the meaning of existence.

It might be tempting for us to assume that there is a *correct* reading of the narrative that leads us to a similar *correct* conclusion. And naturally, what must follow is that those readers who did not reach this *correct* interpretation must have failed in their assessment. But this is not the case. In fact, the ability of the text to produce such a diversity of conclusions is (to borrow a modern idiom) *not a bug, but a feature.*

A correct reading of an esoteric narrative is not to reach a particular conclusion. Rather, it is a *quickening*; it stirs us to engage with something deeper within ourselves. It activates our emotion and imagination, and urges us to contemplate, reflect, and meditate upon those problems of human existence and thereby leads us on a holy pilgrimage into our very Self.

And in the end, many esoteric narratives do not conclude with a tidy resolution, just as the journey of an initiate does not conclude with a specific attainment. For even after finding the Philosopher's Stone, the Alchemist must continue in his work to refine and transmute the environment and people around him in order to fulfil the Great Work.

Magdalene with the Smoking Flame (c. 1640) by Georges de La Tour.

WAR OF THE ROSES

*T*hroughout this text, we have explored the Rosicrucian tradition as it has manifested throughout the ages. We have considered its many expressions and read from the writings of Rosicrucian thought leaders which has allowed us to appreciate the Rosicrucian tradition from many different perspectives. And it would appear, that despite the diverse views, many of these leaders are united in certain fundamental values: seeking out the hidden mysteries of nature, the pursuit of peace, the cultivation of harmony, and a life dedicated to service. In short, to *Know Thyself*.

Therefore, that must mean that these Rosicrucian leaders have always treated each other with respect, tolerance, and goodwill; for the *Summum Bonum*, the *Greater Good*, of humanity.

If only such were the case.

In writing a compendium of Rosicrucianism, I have sought to express to the reader that which makes the Rosicrucian tradition so incredibly valuable. And to this end, I have sought to elicit an optimistic and hopeful vision of Rosicrucian values. But the history of Rosicrucianism has not always been beautiful. And it would be an injustice to a compendium to exclude information. Especially information that has, whether we like it or not, been a large part of Rosicrucian history. So unfortunately, even as the author of this text, I must set aside that which is nice to discuss that which is factual.

It will be impossible to cover every thorn that has appeared on our tradition. So which thorns should be addressed. Some thorns are obvious for the wounds caused by them are still fresh. Although some years have passed, a sudden pain can grip the body with any sudden twists or turns toward that painful memory. Other wounds are long healed over leaving nothing but a scar. And although nobody knows where this scar came from it hinders our movement regardless.

We will have to be delicate here. The task ahead is not without risk. This *IS* going to hurt.

But you are not here alone. We are in this together. The circle of our brotherhood is neither bound by space nor time and the courage we can invoke together will be more than enough to support us as we endeavour to heal together.

The Invisible Fraternity and its Visible Critics:
Rosicrucian Conflict in the Early Modern Period

When the Rosicrucian source works first emerged in the early seventeenth century, they stirred a storm of controversy across Europe. The mysterious Rosicrucian fraternity announced in these texts proclaimed themselves to the cause of spiritual and religious reform, as well as scientific and artistic advancement. While some hailed these writings as a beacon of hope in a time of intellectual and religious tumult, others saw in them a threat, either to their authority or to the direction of public discourse, which they preferred would drift in an alternative direction.

Almost immediately after the publication of the Fama Fraternitatis, a barrage of tracts, pamphlets, and counter-narratives flooded the printing presses. The authors of these reactions were as varied as their motives.

Some were simply sceptics dubious of how anything of value could possibly come about from anonymous publications with such optimistic ideals.

Some were opportunists, looking to take advantage of the recent resurgence of public interest in ancient wisdom by promoting and selling their own pseudo-alchemical cure-alls.

Some resented the anonymity and ambiguity of the Rosicrucian project stating that those that were behind it were obviously charlatans or dreamers. Their critiques of the fraternity were usually less directed at the arguments made in the source works (which were generally quite reasonable, if a little philosophical) but at the character of the messengers. No doubt they would have attacked the messenger too could they identify them (and some, like Robert Fludd, were certainly accused of being a messenger).

But by far the most common outrage encountered came from those who had an investment in maintaining the status quo and who saw in the Rosicrucian project the potential for their undoing. And these were mostly religious authorities.

One notable critic of the Rosicrucian movement who levied all of the above critiques was the Lutheran alchemist, Andreas Libavius (1555-1616).

According to Libavius, the Rosicrucians were simply repeating the same *foolishness* found in the *Magic, Cabala, & similar ineptitudes of Paracelsus* (Libavio, 1615, p. 20). He mocked the efficacy of their *infallible secrets of the Divine Will* as they were after all locked away *within a cloud* (Libavio, 1615, p. 11). He also frequently condemned the Rosicrucians as being blasphemers, linking them with heretical groups like the Anabaptists and Donatists (Libavio, 1615, p. 9). In fact, the overuse of biblical criticism from this alchemical-scientist leads me to believe that the primary cause of Libavius's outrage came from his own religious dogmatism.

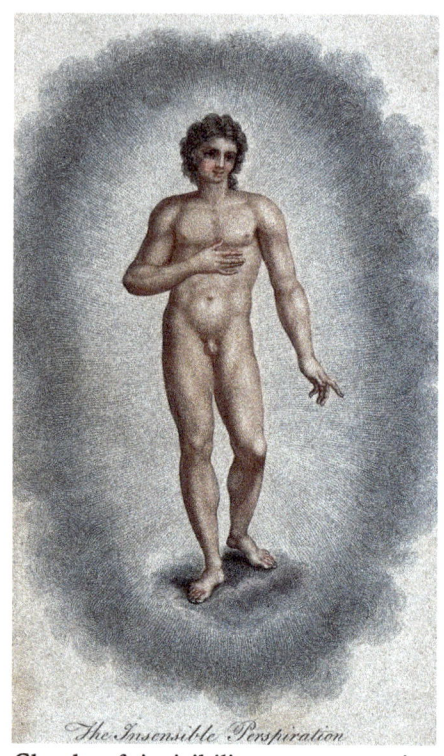

Clouds of invisibility are a recurring motif in Rosicrucian literature, symbolising the hidden nature of the adepts and the veiling of sacred knowledge away from the uninitiated.

Another German Lutheran critic was Christian Kortholt (1633-1694) who shared his concerns that the Rosicrucian movement was attempting to undermine Lutheran orthodoxy with unsound and undesirable mystical propositions.

And whilst these Lutheran religious leaders criticised the Rosicrucian movement's promotion of private revelation (which opposed the Lutheran doctrine of *Sola Scriptura*) and esoteric knowledge (which opposed *Sola Fide*), there were no shortage of Catholic critics either. Afterall, the Confessio Fraternitatis did single-out the Pope as the Antichrist!

War of the Roses

The German Jesuit Jacob Gretser (1562-1625) authored a pointed treatise defending the Catholic Church against what he saw as the slanderous assertions found in the Rosicrucian source works. He openly ridicules the grandiose representation of the so-called *Rosencreuzbruder* (Gretser, 1618, p. 83) (English: *Brothers of the Rosy Cross*) and their lofty claims to divine illumination and secret wisdom. Far from viewing them as a divinely inspired fraternity, Gretser portrays the Rosicrucians as nothing more than superstitious Paracelsians; itinerant charlatans who roamed the land disguised as mystics, deceiving honest people and profiting from their credulity (Gretser, 1618).

Friedrich Förner (1568–1630), Suffragan Bishop of Bamberg, also took a strong stand in defence of Catholic interests against the blasphemous Rosicrucians, whom he regarded with suspicion. He linked them to a dangerous occult conspiracy aimed at undermining Catholic states from within. His views are chiefly expressed in his 1621 work, *The Triumphal Palm of the Miracles of the Catholic Church* (Latin: *Palma Triumphalis Miraculorum Ecclesiae Catholicae*).

Förner condemned many Rosicrucian ideals, particularly their calls to purify science and medicine, as blasphemous, accusing them of arrogating powers that belonged solely to Jesus Christ. However, beyond theological concerns, Förner also believed the Rosicrucians were entangled in more worldly affairs, alleging that they had infiltrated the highest levels of government, including the imperial court and the princely houses of the Holy Roman Empire. He even went so far as to claim that the Rosicrucians were a major instigating force behind the Thirty Years' War (Smith, 2014).

Dame Frances Yates, in her influential book *The Rosicrucian Enlightenment*, argued that the occult philosophy expressed in the Rosicrucian source works was intertwined with a politico-religious vision linked to the marriage of Princess Elizabeth of England and Frederick V of the Palatinate. She theorised that this union symbolised a hoped-for alliance between Protestant England and the German Protestant states, and that the Rosicrucian movement, whether real or imagined, reflected a broader intellectual and spiritual current supporting a Protestant utopian ideal rooted in Hermetic and esoteric traditions. However, in more recent years, Yates' commentary has been critiqued as being too speculative and having exaggerated the role of John Dee and the political involvement of the Rosicrucian movement (Smith, 2014). Nevertheless, we can see that even during the source work era, there did exist concerns about the political involvement of the Rosicrucians.

Fortunately, the same anonymity which protected the author/s of the Rosicrucian source works also protected their message. As we've already discussed, the combination of suggestive language and anonymity fosters an esoteric mode of understanding. But it also had another effect: it prevented readers from fixating on the author's identity, political affiliations, or religious loyalties. Instead, they were compelled to engage directly with the ideas themselves.

As a result, the Rosicrucian message transcended any fixed religious or political agenda. The Lutheran yearning for deeper reform, the English Protestant's hope for spiritual renewal, the humanist philosopher's quest for wisdom, and the liberal scientist's belief in the progress of knowledge, all found something personal and affirming within the same texts. This ability to speak across ideological divides gave the Rosicrucian tradition a kind of resilience. It could weather both orthodoxy's suspicion and religion's tendency to fragment.

The Rosicrucians vs the Illuminati

Whilst there remains speculation as to whether any Rosicrucian groups actually existed during the source work era, eventually groups would arise dedicated to the study of Rosicrucian philosophy and calling themselves *Rosicrucian*.

The Order of the Gold and Rosy Cross (German: *Gold- und Rosenkreuzer*), or G.u.R.C. emerged as one of the most influential esoteric societies of the eighteenth century; although their potential origins may stretch much further back with some speculation that this may continue even as far back as the source work era. They were a Masonic-Rosicrucian society that combined esoteric Christian practices with theurgical magic and practical alchemy. Admission was restricted to Master Masons of at least thirty years of age (Westlund, 2007).

Like the formation of many Rosicrucian societies the formation of G.u.R.C. is a tangled web of fact, myth, and legend. Additionally, many of the foundational G.u.R.C. texts were backdated[1] or attributed to pseudonyms[2] making dating them challenging.

The earliest mention of G.u.R.C. appears at the beginning of the eighteenth century through the publication of *The True and Complete Preparation of the Philosopher's Stone of the Brotherhood from the Order of the Golden and Rosy Cross* (German: *Die wahrhafte und volkommene Bereitung des philosophischen Steins der Brüderschafft aus dem Orden des Gulden und Rosen Kreutzes*) by Sincerus Renatus (a pseudonym for Samuel Richter). Although this text is dated at 1710, it is not known if such a group ever existed at this time (Westlund, 2007).

G.u.R.C. were not short of critics which came not only from religious authorities, but from within the Masonic brotherhood itself. G.u.R.C. was explicitly marked by its anti-Enlightenment stance. Members aimed to regenerate humanity through alchemy, magic, and prophecy, rooted in a belief that disease and death stemmed from *Original Sin* (Westlund, 2007). The organisation upheld biblical authority alongside ancient traditions and believed in a vitalistic correspondence between gold, the Sun, and God (Tilton, 2003, p. 252). This worldview stood in direct opposition to the new German Enlightenment (German: *Aufklärung*) movement (McIntosh, 2011, p. 4).

1   Such as *Testamentum*
2   Such as, *Heavenly and supernatural mystery of the spirit and soul of the world* (German: *Himmlisches und übernatürliches Geheimnis des Geistes und der Seele der Welt*)

Another initiatic movement that gained popularity at this time and recruited from the ranks of Freemasonry, was the *Illuminati*. In contrast to G.u.R.C., the Illuminati represented the strictly reason-oriented and radical wing of the Enlightenment movement. The Illuminati championed reason, criticised superstition, prejudice, and blind faith in authority or tradition. Their goal was to spread *enlightened science* and *philosophy* (McIntosh, 2011, p. 72).

Both G.u.R.C. and the Illuminati became dominant forces within German Freemasonry in the 1780's.

Concurrent to the rise of G.u.R.C. and the Illuminati was another para-Masonic society established by Hans Heinrich von Ecker und Eckhoffen, an ex-member of G.u.R.C. This group was called, *The Asiatic Brethren of St. John the Evangelist in Europe* (German: *Die Brüder St. Johannes des Evangelisten aus Asien in Europa*).

An opposition faced by G.u.R.C. was the publication of a text called *Authentic message from the Knight and Brother Initiates from Asia* (German: *Authentische Nachricht von den Ritter- und Bruder-Eingeweihten aus Asien*) in 1787 by Friedrich Münter, a scientist, Freemason, and member of the Illuminati[3]. In this text, Münter would condemn both G.u.R.C. and The Asiatic Brethren for mixing theology with alchemy, warning that this combination threatened both reason and social order stating,

> *If the Rosicrucians continue for another half century in the way that they have begun, then philosophy and enlightened science will be ousted; we shall have no more history or philosophical theology; monkish legends, priestly hocus-pocus and superstition will possess the thrones; the princes, already deceived by swindlers, will all become royal priests and will learn from the despotism of the order yet more fearful despotism.* (McIntosh, 2011, p. 72)

---

3 Anybody wishing to learn more about the conflict between the Illuminati and the Order of the Gold and Rosy Cross would benefit by seeking out Christopher McIntosh's work, *The Rose Cross in the Age of Reason*.

In 1781, an exposé of G.u.R.C. materials appeared in the form of a book called, *The Rosicrucian in his Nakedness* (German: *Der Rosenkreuzer in seiner Blöße*). The exposé was authored by Magister Pianco, widely believed to be a pseudonym for Ecker und Eckhoffen; although, he himself denied having written it. Magister Pianco would outline his *doubts* concerning the Masonic-Rosicrucian society. He would condemn G.u.R.C. as being Godless, their magic as being wicked, their interpretation of scripture as being false and blasphemous, and even claimed that the members fees were being embezzled by the chiefs of the society. This publication caused great embarrassment to the group leading to a deterioration in their standing within masonic society. Nevertheless, like most good exposés, Pianco's does allow us a glimpse into the rituals and practices of the society, even if we must be mindful that the narrator is somewhat unreliable.

Another threat to the popularity of G.u.R.C. was a 1785 edict, or *Freemason Patent* (German: *Freimaurerpatent*) issued by Holy Roman Emperor Joseph II which restricted the operations of esoteric and Masonic groups. Although this was primarily addressed to the Illuminati, G.u.R.C. was caught up in the crossfire (McIntosh, 2011, p. 136).

By the early 1790's, all of these factors would lead to internal schisms and the decline of the once popular Masonic-Rosicrucian society. By the end of the eighteenth century, Rosicrucianism had begun to be associated with charlatanry and deceit. Despite this however, some remnants of the G.u.R.C. tradition remained active, with at least one known group continuing under the leadership of Prince Karl of Salm-Reifferscheidt (McIntosh, 2011, p. 67) in his castle located in Rájec, Czech Republic (then part of the Austrian Empire). The influence of G.u.R.C. would also continue on in contemporary Rosicrucian societies, notably with the inclusion of G.u.R.C. ideas as well as the adoption of their degree naming system, which has become commonplace in many contemporary Rosicrucian organisations.

As the years progressed, the Rosicrucian ideal became an arena in which new generations projected their own spiritual aspirations and anxieties. In the Early Modern period, the battleground was primarily theological and political. But by the nineteenth century, as the Occult Revival gained momentum in Britain and France, new lines of conflict would emerge. Disagreements about lineage, legitimacy, and interpretation would erupt between initiatic organisations, spiritual reformers, and self-styled adepts; and the Rose-Cross would become a contested symbol in an increasingly crowded esoteric landscape.

The Urim and Thummim was a device created by G.u.R.C. Magi. It was essentially a scrying mirror surrounded by Alchemically produced stones. Pictured here in *MS.4808* (1737) from the *Wellcome* collection in London.

Cloaks, Daggers, and Crosses: *Rosicrucian Conflict in the Occult Revival*

The Societas Rosicruciana in Anglia (S.R.I.A.), founded in 1867 by Robert Wentworth Little, was among the first attempts to institutionalise Rosicrucian ideas in the modern period.

In forming the S.R.I.A., Little took authority from several sources. First, he had been initiated into a Rosicrucian society in Scotland called *Edinburgh, The Grand Council of the Rosicrucians of Scotland*. This society had descended from an earlier (now extinct) group of English Rosicrucians. However, Little had only acquired the first grade in their nine-grade initiatory system[4]. Additionally, he had not been given any authority or charter from this group to establish a Rosicrucian society in England[5]. However, William James Hughan, a fellow Freemason and acquaintance of Little's, had attained the second grade of The Grand Council of the Rosicrucians of Scotland and had been given a charter to establish an English branch of this Rosicrucian society.

Together, Little and Hughan held an inaugural meeting of *The Rosicrucian Society of England*[6], under the authority of The Grand Council of the Rosicrucians of Scotland.

Despite no authority being granted from Scotland, Little would proclaim himself as Magus (the highest rank in the nine-grade system) in the Rosicrucian Society of England's membership register and act independently from the Scottish society.

Over the course of several years, several differences would arise that differentiated Little's society from the Scottish society. Perhaps the most curious difference that is relevant to our discussion pertains to the role of Freemasonry.

---

4 The names of the grades had been adapted from the German, *Orden des Gold- und Rosenkreuzer* (G.u.R.C.).
5 A more complete history concerning the foundation of the S.R.I.A. can be found in *The Temple and the Vault* published by *Lewis Masonic*.
6 Later to be renamed, *Societas Rosicruciana in Anglia*.

The Grand Council of the Rosicrucians of Scotland was not a Masonic society, nor did it request its members to be Freemasons. However, by 1879, the Rosicrucian Society of England would restrict membership to Master Masons.

Anthony Oneal Haye, the leader[7] of The Grand Council of the Rosicrucians of Scotland, would state,

> *The Rosicrucian Society [of Scotland] has nothing whatever to do with the Rose Croix, or Freemasonry in any of its degrees. The Supreme Council, with the exception of myself, is composed entirely of non-Masons [......] As there appears to be a considerable amount of misunderstanding existing relative to this society, perhaps I may be allowed to make the following explanations: The Society is purely philosophic and scientific, there are no fees exigible, the numbers never having at any time necessitated more than an interchange of letters among the members. There is no restriction as to numbers. There might be two; there might be two thousand. At least a year must elapse before advancing a step, but very few ever attain the fourth grade, and 11 years elapsed before I reached my present position. The Rosicrucian doctrines being only of interest to the members, I do not think necessary to notice here.*
>
> *The Rosicrucian Society must not be confounded with its German bastard of the 17th century, which had its exponent in the ludicrous "Fama," and gave birth to the present Royal Arch Degree.*
>
> *The searches for the Philosopher's Stone and the Elixir of Life were perfectly legitimate, and the celebrated Sir Humphrey Davy told the elder D'Israeli "that he did not consider this" (the making of gold) "undiscovered art as impossible; but, should it ever be discovered, would*

---

7 The title assumed by the leader of this Scottish society was, *Magus Maximus.*

certainly be useless." Of course, if gold could be made, and the diamond has been made, the metal might sink in value below iron and lead. A very esteemed friend of mine, an eminent chemist, is decidedly of opinion that man's life could be prolonged to the age of the patriarchs, barring accident and disease, by supplying the waste which produces old age, but he confesses that to discover this waste would occupy so much time that old age would come before the remedy was ready. The Rosicrucian Society has other matters to attend to than to take up such eccentricities of its ancient members, it has no wish to be known beyond its small circle of initiates, and as the sole end it aims at is for their good, and, by extension, the good of all they come in contact with, its ambition of outer appearance is very modest.....My principal object, however, in writing this note is to disabuse the minds of the brethren that there is any connexion between the Rosicrucian Society and Freemasonry; and if any body of men calling themselves Rosicrucians maintain the existence of such a connexion, they must be descendants of the bastard aforesaid. (Oneal Haye, 1868)

Today, the existence of Masonic-Rosicrucian societies may seem entirely unremarkable; just another branch on the ever-expanding tree of Western esoteric organisations. Yet, as Oneal Haye had argued, the Masonic and Rosicrucian traditions are, in their origins and essence, distinct. Oneal Haye's viewpoint is eerily similar to those of the Toulouse Rosicrucian movement established by Viscount Louis-Charles-Édouard de Lapasse (1792-1867) who would state,

> *Freemasonry has given one of its degrees the denomination of Rose-Croix, the vulgar confuse the masons arrived at this tenebrous dignity with the Brothers of the Rose-Croix, whose institution dates back to the fifteenth century. The vulgar are mistaken. True Rosicrucians are outside Masonic associations of High*

> Science. An alchemist, Andréas Valentin, succeeded in deciphering these talismanic inscriptions and re-established the Society of which Rosencreutz had laid the foundations. The Edelphes (as the Rose-Croix were then called) pledged to practice medicine gratuitously, to meet once a year in a general convent, to hasten the reign of the pure Spirit, to hold at last under the faith of the oath their doctrines hidden from the vulgar. They had found a new idiom to express the nature of beings. Crollius, in his Treatise on Signature Rerum, gives the alphabet. They had the secrets of longevity. They had learned all the teachings contained in the library of Ptolemy-Philadelphus. Heirs of the Eumolpides[8], depositaries of the mysteries of Isis, they had discovered the true philosopher's stone, divine nectar, terror of death, elixir of old people, joy of maturity, flame of youth! (Boissin, 1890)

Fortunately, the S.R.I.A., nor any of the daughter/grand-daughter *Societas Rosicruciana* traditions, attempt to present themselves as Masonic appendant bodies, but rather as Rosicrucian societies composed of Master Masons.

On 15 April 1880, Dr William Wynn Westcott would be initiated into Metropolitan College of the S.R.I.A. Although we know that Westcott had been seeking out Rosicrucian societies as early as February 1875[9]. Westcott seemed destined for greatness in the society and within three years he was appointed Secretary-General.

It was around this time that the name of the society would formally change from *The Rosicrucian Society of England* to *Societas Rosicruciana in Anglia (S.R.I.A.)*.

---

8 The Eumolpidae were the priests who maintained the Eleusinian Mysteries during the Hellenic era.
9 In February 1875, Westcott corresponded with Francis George Irwin, expressing his interest in joining Irwin's *Occult Order*, which Westcott believed to be affiliated with Rosicrucianism. Irwin replied, informing Westcott that his society was not currently accepting new members and instead directed him towards the S.R.I.A. (Wilson, Early History of the S.R.I.A._Chapter 3, 1937, p. 23)

War of the Roses

On 21 January 1886 William Robert Woodman and Westcott would authorise the foundation of a new College in Melbourne, Australia called, *The Demiurgus College*. This would mean that the foundation of The Demiurgus College preceded both the founding of the *United Grand Lodge of Victoria* as well as the Federation of Australia! Just why a college should be chartered in a colony on the other side of the world raises some interesting questions, which I hope someday will be explored.

Just prior to Woodman's passing in 1891, Woodman had entrusted Westcott with a letter nominating him as the next Supreme Magus (Greensill, 2003, p. 141). Accepting this esteemed position, Westcott assumed the role and held it steadfastly until 1925. Over the course of thirty-four years, Westcott played a pivotal role in the progressive development of the society, re-writing the rituals, adding all the grade lectures, printing the first S.R.I.A. rituals in 1906-08 (manuscript rituals having been used previously), and implementing numerous transformative changes that have contributed significantly to the distinctive character that we recognise today. Indeed, a substantial portion of what many Fratres would perceive as traditional practice within the S.R.I.A. today is, in actuality, derived from Westcott's interventions.

So what prompted such a transformation?

Westcott's own esoteric interests went far beyond the Masonic and Christian framework of the S.R.I.A. Although the society had always entertained a contemplative and scholarly approach to Western esotericism, it remained tightly bound to Masonic orthodoxy. Its membership was restricted to Master Masons, and its teachings were largely symbolic, not operative or practical. Westcott likely found this limiting. His own interest in the more practical dimensions of esotericism found no outlet in the S.R.I.A. Thus, in 1888, together with Woodman and Samuel Liddell MacGregor Mathers, Westcott would found a new esoteric order that abandoned the restrictions of Freemasonry and presented a fully operative magical system. This was The Hermetic Order of the Golden Dawn[10] (H.O.G.D.).

10 Although, the inaugural summons used the name, *ORDER OF THE G.D. IN THE OUTER*

The H.O.G.D. may have been, in many ways, Westcott's escape hatch: a place where he could explore and promote the magical doctrines that the S.R.I.A. was not built to accommodate. The H.O.G.D. expanded rapidly, attracting an eclectic array of artists, intellectuals, and seekers. But by the 1890's, it had begun to suffer from internal tensions and power struggles. The beginning of the end was planted quite early. Much of this was centred upon the relationship between two of its founders: Westcott and Mathers.

It is not unusual for some initiatic organisations to employ pseudohistorical legends to present how their organisation was founded. At first glance, some of these foundations may appear somewhat uncontroversial, albeit flamboyant in detail. It is only when you begin examining the story closely that you may begin to see that not all is as it appears. However, it would be a mistake to view these legends as simply childish stories used by simple founders to bolster their tradition with a fabricated authority. Instead, it would be better to view these narratives as a repeating theme in Rosicrucian organisations as well as a tool for initiates to come to an inner understanding of a particular tradition. Rosicrucian foundational legends provide a tradition with a sense of unity, lineage, and authenticity. This subject has already been explored in detail in my previous book, *The Temple and the Vault*, in a chapter called, *Foundational Legends*.

The foundational legend associated with the H.O.G.D. is not only an example of the power of a founding legend but also serves to remind us of the potential risks that may arise when the authority of a founding legend is undermined; especially when so much faith is placed upon its historicity.

In the case of the H.O.G.D., the legend surrounding the organisation's foundation held significant importance for many members and when doubts were raised about its accuracy, the members' faith in belonging to an authoritative lineage began to waver.

In 1886, Westcott claimed to have received a set of manuscripts through Rev. Adolphus Frederick Alexander Woodford. These manuscripts consisted of fifty-six encoded pages; their writing concealed using a substitution cipher. It was not until 1887 that Westcott successfully decoded the cipher, revealing the content within. Collectively, these manuscripts are referred to as the *Cipher Manuscripts*.

Once decrypted, the manuscripts proved to be primarily in English and contained rudimentary instructions for a series of graded magical rituals, adopting grade names originally derived from the German Masonic-Rosicrucian society, *Orden des Gold- und Rosenkreuzer*. These rituals would later undergo further elaboration, with the collaborative efforts of Westcott, Mathers, and Woodman. Together, they expanded upon the teachings in the cipher manuscripts, refining, and adding considerable depth to the original concepts contained therein.

On a separate slip of paper[11] contained within the manuscript cache was a note written in a different handwriting, although still encoded using the same cipher as the main manuscripts. This slip of paper makes mention of a *Fräulein Sprengel* of the *Die Goldene Dammerung* (English: *The Golden Dawn*) whose motto can be observed to be *Sapiens Dominabitur Astris*. Westcott wrote to the person named on the slip of paper using S.D.A. as the person's name (not Sprengel) and received a reply from an individual thanking him for finding the long-lost cache of private papers. Westcott identifies this respondent as, Fräulein Sprengel. Further correspondence between England and Germany would ensue when eventually S.D.A. would name Westcott, Mathers, and Woodman as *Adeptus Exempti* and charge them with the authority of establishing an English branch of S.D.A.'s Die Goldene Dammerung. Contact was maintained with S.D.A., who operated as an intermediary between the society's leaders in England and transcendent cosmic authorities known as the *Secret Chiefs*.

11 A translation of this paper provided by Golden Dawn historian, Ellic Howe, reads: *Sapiens dom ast is a chief among the members of the goldene dammerung [i.e., Golden Dawn] she is a famous soror her name is fräulein sprengel letters reach her at herr j enger hotel marquardt stuttgart she is 7=4 [figures in Hebrew characters] or a chief adept.* (Howe, 1984)

The rupture came to a head in 1900, when Mathers accused Westcott of dishonesty in relation to the origin story of the Order itself. According to Mathers, Westcott had never been in contact with these Secret Chiefs. Worse, Mathers alleged that Westcott had forged the entire correspondence with Fräulein Sprengel, the mysterious German adept who had supposedly authorised the foundation of the H.O.G.D. in England. Mathers even claimed that Westcott had privately confessed to the deception and had bound him to secrecy!

These allegations struck at the very heart of the H.O.G.D.'s legitimacy. If the secret instructions and spiritual mandate from the German Rosicrucians were a fiction, then the Order's hierarchy, its curriculum, and even its rituals were built on illusion.

This tension unfolded during a period when the H.O.G.D. was already experiencing internal instability. Many Second Order adepts in London were growing disillusioned with Mathers' increasingly autocratic behaviour and his public association with Aleister Crowley, whose reputation was controversial even then. In a dramatic bid to regain control, Mathers sent Crowley, clad in Highland regalia and armed with letters of authority, to London in 1900 to seize command of the Second Order's temple, the *Vault of the Adepti*, on his behalf (Gilbert, 1997, p. 54).

One of the senior members present at the time was Marcus Worsley Blackden who took it upon himself to protect a considerable portion of the equipment. Subsequently, some of this equipment would reappear within a H.O.G.D. splinter group, the *Independent Rectified Rite* (I.R.R.), and possibly even later, during a noteworthy event in 1924 when Blackden would reunite with Arthur Edward Waite, following a decade-long feud. During this reunion, Blackden and Waite would unite in a cathartic act of burning H.O.G.D. manuscripts, that Blackden had maintained in his possession (Davis, 2017).

The London adepts, already wary of Crowley's presence and Mathers' authoritarian ambitions, refused him entry and dismissed the commission outright. A committee of adepts was convened to examine Mathers' accusations regarding the correspondence between Westcott and S.D.A. Neither Westcott nor Mathers attended the investigation.

At the same time, Westcott found himself under pressure in his public life. He held a respected position as a Coroner and Justice of the Peace, roles that could hardly withstand the scrutiny of scandal involving secret societies and magical rituals. Some of his private esoteric papers had gone missing and surfaced publicly. Westcott became concerned that someone within the Order may have been trying to force his resignation. Intriguingly, in 1911, Aleister Crowley (using the pseudonym Leo Vincey) would make reference to this incident, suggesting that Mathers was envious of Westcott's authority, had orchestrated his removal from the society, and strongly insinuated that Mathers had leaked H.O.G.D. manuscripts with Westcott's name on them (Howe, 1984, p. 167).

On 16 March 1900, Westcott would resign from all his positions within the H.O.G.D. and its Second Order. While he never directly addressed the forgery allegations in public, his silence was perhaps as strategic as it was dignified. With his withdrawal, the fragile unity of the H.O.G.D. began to unravel. Though Mathers was initially left in sole command, his increasingly erratic leadership and controversial alliances eventually led to his own expulsion by the London adepts. The result was organisational fragmentation with the original H.O.G.D. now being splintered into several offshoots, some of which have continued in some form until today.

For Westcott, the experience appears to have been sobering. Westcott would retreat into the more stable and structured world of the S.R.I.A., where he would spend the next two decades reshaping the society with the same esoteric sensibility, but under the safer cover of Masonic decorum. Ironically, the innovations he had hoped to achieve in the H.O.G.D. may have become partially realised in a more tempered form through his reforms in the S.R.I.A.

Rosicrucian Rivalries in Belle Époque France

The *fin de siècle* in France was a turbulent and imaginative period for the Rosicrucian tradition. Just as in England, Rosicrucianism was by no means a stable tradition. It was alive and adapting to the cultural influence of the period. Two of the most compelling personalities to emerge from this occult revival period were Joséphin Péladan and Stanislas de Guaita, whose brief collaboration would culminate in one of the most memorable rifts in modern Rosicrucian history. The scars left from these events would go on to shape the way Rosicrucianism has continued to us today.

Their first contact was not through a lodge or temple, but through literature. Like his Rosicrucian contemporaries, Péladan had made his own attempt at writing esoteric didactic fiction, like those discussed in an earlier chapter. Péladan planned a monumental project of twenty-one novels which he called, *The Latin Decadence* (French: *La Décadence Latine*). Péladan envisioned the project to be a spiritual reform movement in literary form. He wanted to convey intricate mystical ideas, symbolic systems, and his own aesthetic principles. However, writing twenty-one novels of dense, esoteric, didactic fiction is a monumental task for any writer. Perhaps then it is not surprising that by the end of his life, only thirteen of these would be completed. Nevertheless, their impact was profound, and the momentum stirred by these works would lead to future projects, including Péladan's partnership with de Guaita.

In 1884, after reading the first book of Péladan's literary behemoth, *The Supreme Vice* (French: *Le Vice Suprême*), de Guaita would make contact with Péladan. In a letter dated 3 November 1884, de Guaita would express his admiration for the novel and the,

> ...hermetic gust which blows through your work.
> (Churton, 2016)

Two weeks later, he wrote again with even greater reverence,

> *It is your Vice Suprême that revealed to me (to me, sceptic, although respectful of all holy things), that the Kabbala and High Magic could be something other than a trick.* (McIntosh, 2011, p. 166)

In that same letter, de Guaita declared his intention to undertake a serious study of Hermeticism and sought Péladan's guidance,

> *If you will be so kind as to permit me, I shall come to ask for some advice to guide the researches which I hope to make.* (McIntosh, 2011, p. 166)

Péladan welcomed the request, and the two soon met in person. In his follow-up, de Guaita expressed joy at the opportunity, writing,

> *You do me a great kindness in offering to let me have a chat with you about hermetism, something which I have wanted to do for a long time... it will therefore be a great joy for me to be able to talk with a true initiate– who is greatly my senior in cabalistic studies.* (McIntosh, 2011, p. 166)

After their meeting, de Guaita acknowledged a teacher-pupil dynamic was forming. It was a formative moment for both men and for the future of French Rosicrucianism.

From this literary beginning grew the *Ordre Kabbalistique de la Rose-Croix* (O.K.R.+C.), which they co-founded in the late 1880's. To this society, de Guaita brought rigour and structure; whilst Péladan brought mystical vision and flair. The O.K.R.+C. drew on Kabbalah, Hermeticism, and Catholic symbolism. It was conceived as both a spiritual path and an intellectual academy, even offering degrees in esoteric studies. So popular was the society, that soon many Parisian occultists would join their ranks.

Despite their shared esoteric venture, Joséphin Péladan and Stanislas de Guaita were two strikingly different personalities. De Guaita was a nobleman and a poet. As an occultist, he was rather systematic. He very much embodied the intellectual and ceremonial wing of the French esoteric revival. Péladan, on the other hand, was a flamboyant aesthete, mystic, and self-styled *Sâr* who viewed art as a sacred vehicle through which the soul could express itself.

Soon, their differences would become irreconcilable. Péladan grew increasingly critical of de Guaita's emphasis on ritual magic and his admiration for Éliphas Lévi, whom Péladan viewed as doctrinally flawed as pertained to the Rosicrucian tradition. Additionally, Péladan's own Toulousain Rosicrucian pedigree, which he had inherited through his brother, Adrien Péladan, contrasted sharply with the doctrines of Lévi as championed by de Guaita (Galtier, 2017, p. 199). These recurring criticisms must have been extremely challenging for de Guaita to endure, particularly given the esteem in which he held Lévi.

The rupture would finally arrive in 1890, when Péladan broke away to form the, *Order of the Catholic and Aesthetic Rose-Cross of the Temple and the Grail* (French: *Ordre de la Rose-Croix Catholique et Esthétique du Temple et du Graal*) (Galtier, 2017, p. 201). In this new body, spiritual elevation came through beauty, art, and Christian virtue; not magical operations. Péladan would not allow any members of the O.K.R.+C. to join his new order which would become well known for its *Salons of the Rose+Cross* (French: *Salons de la Rose+Croix*), public exhibitions that showcased the works of symbolist painters and composers aligned with his vision.

At the same time, the Supreme Council of the O.K.R.+C. would issue a formal decree regarding this schismatic group founded by Joséphin Péladan. The decree asserted that Péladan's group was fundamentally opposed to the historical and authentic Rosicrucian teachings and aims as upheld by the O.K.R.+C. Primarily, the Supreme Council took issue with Péladan's behaviour which they described as childish and with his schismatic order being Catholic. Ultimately, they conclude Péladan was being *a good hoaxer* or *fraud* (French: *Un bon fumiste*) (Ordre kabbalistique de la Rose-Croix. Suprême conseil, 1891).

Péladan was a mystic in the truest sense of the word and saw art as a means to achieve spiritual elevation and believed that true art could serve as a bridge between the earthly and the divine,

> *Artist, you are a priest: Art is the great mystery, and when your effort results in a masterpiece, a ray of the divine descends as on an altar. O real presence of the resplendent divinity under these supreme names: Vinci, Raphael, Michelangelo, Beethoven and Wagner*[12].
> (Péladan, 1892)

But these were not the only voices shaping the esoteric current of the Belle Époque.

Alexandre Saint-Yves d'Alveydre, a nobleman and visionary thinker, added an entirely different strain to the Rosicrucian conversation. He formulated the doctrine of Synarchy, a divine, hierarchical form of governance that offered an alternative to the anarchic ideologies that were then becoming popular. Saint-Yves did not claim to be the inventor of Synarchy, but that this model of government was actually in action in a subterranean world known as Agartha, a city that was led by hidden masters who had occasionally made themselves known to the overworld inhabitants leading to remarkable periods of human progress. Saint-Yves Synarchic writings, which discussed Eastern and Western initiatory traditions, were incredibly popular amongst the French Rosicrucians. Though he wasn't directly involved in the O.K.R.+C. or Péladan's order, his writings influenced many amongst their ranks, as well as Martinists and later Rosicrucian and Gnostic bodies. Although, his model clashed with the more personal, artistic mysticism of Péladan and departed from the more formal ritual structures favoured by de Guaita.

---

12 French: *Artiste, tu es prêtre: l'Art est le grand mystère, et lorsque ton effort aboutit au chef-d'oeuvre, un rayon du divin descend comme sur un autel. O présence réelle de la divinité resplendissante sous ces noms suprêmes: Vinci, Raphael, Michel-Ange, Beethoven et Wagner.*

Joséphin Péladan (1858–1918), flamboyant mystic, novelist, and founder of the Order of the Catholic and Aesthetic Rose-Cross of the Temple and the Grail, saw art as a sacred path to spiritual elevation. His visionary Salons de la Rose+Croix made occult symbolism a public affair, even as his doctrinal purism fractured alliances within the French esoteric revival.

Nevertheless, Synarchy represented another avenue for those disillusioned with the theatrical politics taking place in the lodges and temples around them but who still yearned for an esoteric tradition from which to base their own personal philosophy.

Another highly influential personality of the time was Nizier Anthelme Philippe, most commonly referred to as Master Philippe of Lyon (French: *Maître Philippe de Lyon*). Papus had encountered

Master Philippe of Lyon (Nizier Anthelme Philippe) (1849-1905) was regarded by many as a living embodiment of the Rosicrucian spirit, despite no formal affiliation. Known for his radical simplicity, miraculous healings, and humble service, Philippe eschewed ceremonial excess and organisational ambition. To Papus and others disillusioned by esoteric rivalries, he was simply *The Master*.

Philippe in the 1890's. Though loosely affiliated with Papus and the Martinist Order, Philippe's influence came more through his lived example and personal influence rather than through any organisational filiation. Philippe was not one for ceremony and hierarchy, preferring a more mystical path of compassion and healing. His emphasis on simple spiritual truths and healing challenged the necessity of elaborate rites and secret initiations. Nevertheless, far from being shunned by the Parisian Rosicrucian leaders, he was actually quite highly regarded and considered Saint-like by many.

Philippe's spirituality was radically simple: love, faith, and service to others. Papus referred to Philippe as *The Master* and reportedly followed his advice in both personal and spiritual matters. Papus's regard for Philippe was not unique. The humble mystic quietly attracted the attention of many prominent esoteric thinkers, some of whom must have been rather uncomfortable with the power struggles and performative displays that plagued the Parisian orders. In true Rosicrucian fashion, Philippe dedicated himself to a life of service, including miraculous healing acts which he performed without payment. Philippe's influence would even reach the Russian court, with the Tsarina Alexandra of Russia even requesting his assistance, although his influence here was but brief (Churton, 2016, pp. 488-489).

Philippe was not a Rosicrucian in any official or organisational sense. But the fruit of his work expresses that of a Rosicrucian mystic.

By the early twentieth century, various spiritual heirs to this Belle Époque moment were already emerging, among them the Gnostic Churches. The *Gnostic Church of France* (French: *Église gnostique de France*) and later *The Universal Gnostic Church* (French: *Église Gnostique Universelle*) began to shape a more ecclesiastical expression of the Rosicrucian tradition. These bodies took inspiration from much of this French period: Papus's Martinism, Péladan's sacramental aesthetics, the Christian mysticism of Philippe, as well as the more traditional Gnostic traditions of southern France, such as Catharism.

Thus, by the turn of the twentieth century, one could speak not only of multiple *Rosicrucian-isms* but also of multiple Gnostic revivals, all born from the light and shadow of the occult revival taking place in Britain and France.

Across the Atlantic: *Rosicrucian Conflict in the Twentieth Century*

It is perhaps this chapter more than any other where readers may be tempted to look for signs of this author's own Rosicrucian persuasion. Some will scan these pages for a glimpse of bias, hoping that my own commentary might betray my allegiance. Should my thoughts and conclusions align with the reader's filiations, they may be forgiven or even welcomed. But if they do not, severe judgment may swiftly follow. But alas, this author does not treat the Rosicrucian tradition as one would a sports team, deserving of cheers even in the midst of disgrace. Here, the thorns are many, and they grow on many stems. The wounds left from this period are the freshest and, in some ways, the most bitter.

But have hope, for the night is darkest before the dawn and though the memory of these wounds are so recent, they are safely ensconced in the embrace of history's purse, from whence valuable lessons may still be drawn.

As the first World War engulfed Europe and laid waste to the old Rosicrucian world order, many spiritual movements found themselves displaced or disrupted. While the salons and societies of Paris and London fell quiet under the weight of global conflict, the Rosicrucian current sought refuge across the Atlantic.

In the minds of many esoteric thinkers, the United States came to be seen as *The New Atlantis*, the prophesied utopia that had been dreamt by Sir Francis Bacon centuries earlier. A land where ancient wisdom traditions might find safe and free expression. Amidst a culture increasingly fascinated with mysticism, personal development, and metaphysical healing, the Rosicrucian tradition began to take root in new and distinctly American forms. Yet even in this supposed sanctuary, the Rosicrucian ideal was far from immune to strife. The twentieth century would see the tradition embroiled in legal battles, ideological rifts, and personal rivalries. While some observers have described this era as marked by elitism, a closer look reveals a climate dominated more by denunciation than exclusivity. The prevailing tone was not simply *We are the true Rosicrucians*, but rather, *They are not*.

Black Magic and White Books

If the Rosicrucian tradition in America had a civil war, its fiercest front was drawn between two Rosicrucian leaders: Harvey Spencer Lewis, Imperator of A.M.O.R.C., and Reuben Swinburne Clymer, Supreme Grand Master of the Fraternitas Rosae Crucis (F.R.C.). The protracted dispute between the two men was not a mere skirmish of doctrine or a polite disagreement. It was a battle waged in pamphlets, courtrooms, and public announcements. At stake was nothing less than the right to define American Rosicrucianism.

Clymer was a second-generation U.S. Rosicrucian inheriting the legacy of Paschal Beverly Randolph and the organisation he developed. Clymer would launch a relentless campaign against Lewis, whose flamboyant marketing of the Rosicrucian tradition flew in the face of Clymer's more puritanical brand of Rosicrucianism. To Clymer, A.M.O.R.C. was simply a modern corporatisation of an ancient tradition. Perhaps, Clymer may have also harboured jealousy of this contemporary, and by all accounts, more popular form of Rosicrucianism. Nevertheless, if this were the case, Clymer would not admit it. Instead, Clymer accused Lewis of being a Rosicrucian fraud whose Toulousain initiation had been fabricated. He accused Lewis of forgery, noting that writings of various authors had been published in A.M.O.R.C. monographs. But neither of these accusations could compare to the more dastardly and more decidedly wicked accusation that Clymer levied against Lewis: that Lewis had been secretly initiated into Rosicrucianism, not by the Rosicrucians of Toulouse, but by Alisteir Crowley, and was in fact practicing black magic (Clymer, 1935, p. 72).

To bolster his argument, Clymer would bring forth evidence that the *pilfering Imperator* had incorporated various of Crowley's doctrines and symbols into the A.M.O.R.C. teachings and most importantly had been provided a *Charter* from the Ordo Templi Orientis:

> *Let us now consider the proof which Mr. Lewis has furnished—proof which he cannot question. We trust the reader—especially A. M. O. R. C. members—will carefully study this proof and follow through, closely observing and noting the links of the chain of evidence that proves, beyond a doubt, that Mr. Lewis is a follower and disciple of Aleister Crowley, the notorious "Beast of the Apocalypse"— the Anti-Christ.*
>
> *[...]*
>
> *Some time during the summer—in July, we believe, of 1921 — there was issued to H. Spencer Lewis, so he claims, a charter or document by the O. T. O.—Ordo Templi Orientis-Fraternitatis Lucis Hermeticae (see facsimile Reproduction No. 20)— to which we invite the closest examination and investigation. It bears the title Ordo Templi Orientis, with the sub-title Fraternitatis Lucis Hermeticae. In the body of the document it certifies that H. Spencer Lewis is a 33°, 90°, 95° of the Ancient and Primitive Rites of Memphis and Mizraim* and the 7° of O. T. O.—THE IDENTICAL ORDER FOUNDED BY ALEISTER CROWLEY in 1911.* (Clymer, 1935, pp. 72-73)

Lewis, for his part, did not remain silent, but swiftly denied each of Clymer's claims and presented his counterarguments in A.M.O.R.C.'s own literature, claiming that Clymer had distorted historical sources in an attempt to undermine A.M.O.R.C.'s legitimacy. Lewis even challenged Clymer to submit his accusations to an impartial tribunal or engage in public debate; offers which Clymer repeatedly denied.

Much of the vitriol between the men stemmed from a deeper ideological rivalry. Both men claimed to possess the *true* lineage of Rosicrucianism in the New World. Perhaps if A.M.O.R.C. had used its printed counterarguments to actually counter the specific evidence provided by Clymer, the issue could have been nipped in the bud, for each of Clymer's arguments are actually very easily disproven. Instead, most of the counter-arguments A.M.O.R.C. offered to support their legitimacy involved the presentation of various unusual papers and manuscripts (A.M.O.R.C. The National Membership Defense Committee, 1935) the esoteric nature of which simply provided more leverage for Clymer to issue additional criticisms.

In short however, the primary evidence that Clymer proposed, *proves, beyond a doubt, that Mr. Lewis is a follower and disciple of Aleister Crowley, the notorious "Beast of the Apocalypse"— the Anti-Christ,* was not actually a *Charter* for the O.T.O. at all, but a *concordat*. Nor had it been issued by Crowley, but by Theodor Reuss, who was at the time of its issuance, the leader of the O.T.O. (an organisation not started by Crowley).

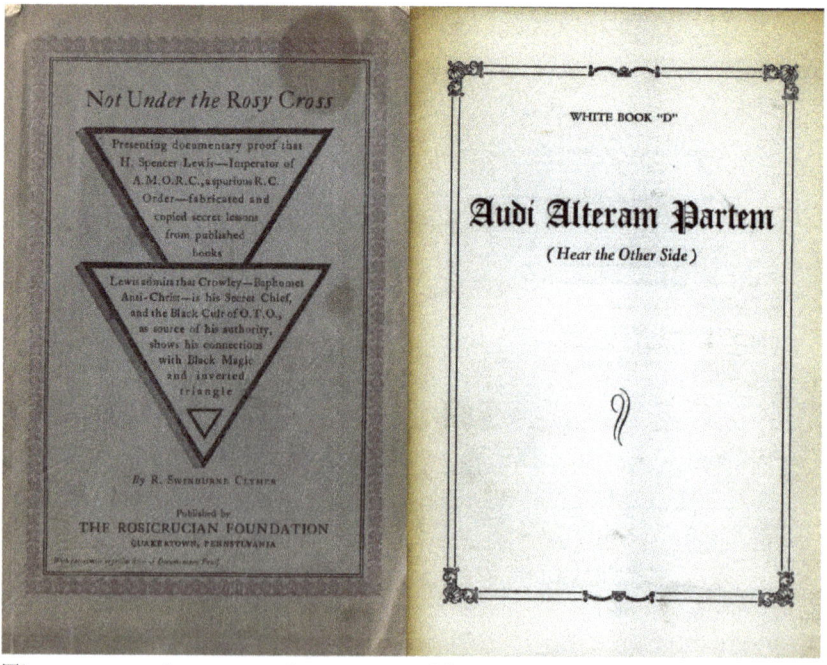

These were the two primary pamphlets used by these Rosicrucian heavyweights to proclaim/denounce. Not Under the Rosy Cross was published by Clymer's The Rosicrucian Foundation (left) and White Book "D" published by Lewis's A.M.O.R.C. (right).

This concordat was the result of a brief period of collaboration between Lewis and Reuss which commenced in 1920. With this concordat, Reuss conferred upon Lewis honorary degrees in O.T.O. (VII°) and The Ancient and Primitive Rite of Memphis-Misraim (33° 90° 95°). The collaboration between Lewis and Reuss would end in 1922.

As for the various signs and symbols which Clymer had claimed linked Lewis with Crowley, these had all pre-dated both Lewis and Crowley and their inclusion in A.M.O.R.C. materials had been unrelated to Crowley.

In truth, Lewis had gone to considerable lengths to keep A.M.O.R.C. free from controversy making any kind of collaboration with Crowley, who seemed to attract scandal like iron to a magnet, highly improbable. Lewis even delayed his collaboration with Theodor Reuss until he received explicit confirmation that Reuss had severed ties with Crowley (Rebisse, 2005, p. 422).

Nevertheless, in 1935, Crowley would make an opportunistic attempt to exploit the tensions between Lewis and Clymer for his own gain. At the time, Crowley was in dire financial trouble and had attempted to pressure Raymund Andrea, A.M.O.R.C.'s Grand Master in England. Crowley claimed that A.M.O.R.C.'s authority derived from the O.T.O. by virtue of the document Lewis had received from Reuss in 1920, and as Crowley was now head of the O.T.O., he held the power to rescind this authority. Andrea promptly contacted Lewis, who reassured him that A.M.O.R.C.'s lineage and authority had no connection whatsoever to Crowley or the O.T.O.

Perhaps growing more desperate, Crowley would record in his personal diaries between September-October 1937 his discussions and plans to take over A.M.O.R.C. including that he had been conducting sex-magic *to control A.M.O.R.C.*

Much of this episode reappeared in a 2001 series of correspondence between author Robert Vanloo and an A.M.O.R.C.

Archivist in France. While the A.M.O.R.C. Archivist had unequivocally refuted any suggestion of a lineage descending from either the O.T.O. or Crowley, the ripples from this episode still continue to surface in certain Rosicrucian circles and online forums, where speculation still clouds the historical record.

In the end, neither side succeeded in eradicating the other. Both A.M.O.R.C. and F.R.C. survived long beyond Lewis and Clymer, their conflict now preserved in archival vitriol. But the scars remain. What this feud did perhaps reveal was the fragility of esoteric authority, especially when it had been transplanted onto American soil, where initiatory legitimacy could be fought for, not in the efficacy of their initiatory work, but in courts and mass-market print media. Unfortunately, this counter-productive approach to proving legitimacy did not end here, but continued on and resulted in both organisations forming alliances with initiatory peer groups to help bolster their own claims; with A.M.O.R.C. co-establishing *Fédération Universelle des Ordres et Sociétés Initiatiques*[13] (F.U.D.O.S.I.) and F.R.C. co-establishing *Fédération Universelle des Ordres, Fraternités et Sociétés Initiatiques*[14] (F.U.D.O.F.S.I.).

These ambitious Pan-European Rosicrucian federations, characterised by charismatic and egoistic leaders, would eventually succumb to internal conflicts. The breakdown of F.U.D.O.S.I. resulting from allegations of racism and an inability to compromise, despite their acknowledgment of the importance of individual group autonomy. And with disappearance of F.U.D.O.S.I., so would F.U.D.O.F.S.I.'s *raison d'être*.

Perhaps it was the Great Depression or perhaps it was the sense of another international conflict on the horizon, but 1935 would be a big year for esotericists battling it out. Not only do we have the war ongoing between Lewis, Crowley, and Clymer, but Lewis would be about to be engaged in a conflict on another front with another big name: *Paul Foster Case*.

13 English: *Universal Federation of Initiatic Orders and Societies*
14 English: *Universal Federation of Orders, Fraternities, and Initiatic Societies*

War of the Roses

Paul Foster Case, founder of Builders of the Adytum (B.O.T.A.) and author of *The True and Invisible Rosicrucian Order*, held a rather different approach to the nature of Rosicrucianism compared to Lewis. From Case's perspective, the Rosicrucian Order was *invisible* partially because it lacked a formal external organisation (Case, 1989, p. 5).

This position directly contradicted the more public and institutional model presented by Lewis and A.M.O.R.C., with its structured degree system, international conventions, and physical temples. It is quite possible that these represented to Case precisely the kind of *visible* organisation that the Rosicrucian tradition was never meant to become. In fact, Case asserted that any modern societies claiming a direct institutional descent from the original Rosicrucian source works should be *judged as invalid* (Case, 1989, p. 5), no doubt referring to A.M.O.R.C.

In 1935, Case would write to Lewis expressing his viewpoints as well as throwing in a few more accusations that A.M.O.R.C. represented a *clumsy adaptation of Golden Dawn material*. The latter argument would appear quite astounding to those who have familiarity with both organisations as they are vastly different systems. And whilst Case was intimately familiar with the Golden Dawn system, we might forgive him for not knowing much about the work of A.M.O.R.C., likely never having been a member.

Lewis's response to Case was quite positive and hopeful in tone. Lewis appeared to have had quite a positive regard for Case and on multiple occasions, expresses his respect for Case's work and contributions, including his commentaries on the work of Franz Hartmann.

In his reply, Lewis would state,

> *You have evidently selected a path of your own which you have more or less consistently followed and I am on an entirely different path, from your point of view. Our paths may cross some day but I hope it will be in a humorous situation so that both of us—since we are both lovers of humor—can enjoy it to the fullest extent.*

A photograph taken from within the F.U.D.O.S.I. Temple in Brussels, Belgium.

From the left: Sar Akhnaton (unknown), Sar Placidus (Jan Coops), Sar Elgim (Jean Mallinger), Sar Validivar (Ralph Maxwell Lewis), Sar Puritia (Jeanne Guesdon).

This was actually not the first communication between Lewis and Case[15]. In May 1917, Case would write to Lewis accusing him of plagiarism in a public A.M.O.R.C. periodical. Lewis would respond to Case explaining that the supposed plagiary had not been authored by him, but by another member of A.M.O.R.C. But in any case, the member who wrote the article was a close friend and colleague of the original author, with an additional justification that the original author in question had actually only been responsible for compiling still earlier information.

Lewis would end his letter by stating,

> *I know of course that this explanation will not satisfy you but I have the satisfaction of knowing that you can no longer make such statements in ignorance of the facts and there I have done my duty, in illuminating your mind in this regard. I thank you for your compliments and assure you that so long as there is breath in my*

---
15 Whether Lewis recalled this earlier communication is not known.

body, I will continue to concentrate my efforts on that very good part of the public which Lincoln said could be fooled all of the time, I hope thereby to some day enable them to rise upon that condition where they can no longer be fooled. Those, like yourself, who cannot be fooled do not need our teachings or our help.

With all good wishes for Peace Profound,

I am Yours very truly,

H. S Lewis
Imperator

Despite the voluminous critiques levied at Lewis during his lifetime, A.M.O.R.C. would continue on relatively unscathed. In fact, it would increase in membership still. After Lewis passed away in 1939, the A.M.O.R.C. torch would be handed over to the Supreme-Secretary and Lewis's son, Ralph Maxwell Lewis.

Under Ralph's tenure, the organisation's educational correspondence system (the monograph catalogue) would also be completed and updated. Whilst the monographs of this period would lose that personal style of A.M.O.R.C.'s founder, they would increase in number and take on a more academic tone. A.M.O.R.C. would gain in popularity and spread further across the globe. Perhaps fortunately for Lewis Senior and Junior, they would not be around to see the impending tidal wave about to hit their organisation, the ripples of which would affect the whole Rosicrucian tradition.

A.M.O.R.C. vs Gary L. Stewart

Under Ralph's tenure, A.M.O.R.C. membership reached its peak. Rosicrucianism was no longer a niche domain studied by only the most philosophical of thinkers. A.M.O.R.C. had been quite successful in couching ancient doctrines in such a contemporary fashion that it was now being studied by individuals from all walks of life. In addition, Ralph's own psychological approach to mysticism struck a chord with more modern sensibilities and helped bring A.M.O.R.C. out of its esoteric shadows and into more mainstream spiritual discourse.

Public lectures, well-designed correspondence courses, and global outreach made the organisation highly visible. Whether Rosicrucianism was ever meant to become so popular, is a fair question, but no matter the answer, Rosicrucianism would become more popular in the world than at any other period of history.

Under Ralph's tenure, A.M.O.R.C. would reach all corners of the Western world. Yet as Rosicrucianism became more accessible, some would argue that it was becoming increasingly misunderstood.

Ralph M. Lewis would spend nearly five decades serving as Imperator of A.M.O.R.C., his death in January 1987 marking the end of an era for the organisation.

A.M.O.R.C.'s Board of Directors would elect Ralph's successor, Gary Lee Stewart to the role of Imperator at a meeting held on January 23 1987. This would be followed by a ritualistic installation ceremony held during the occasion of the organisation's traditional New Year celebrations which took place on March 20 1987. Stewart had been a long-serving member of the organisation and had previously held various administrative and ceremonial positions over the years.

The following two years would be exceptionally busy for the new Imperator as he prepared plans to establish a *Rosicrucian University*, and travelled to conferences and events in France, Switzerland, Germany, Belgium, the Netherlands, Japan, Brazil, and Australia.

At the New Year celebrations in the following year, Stewart would provide some information regarding his work on the structural reorganisation of the organisation's headquarters (*Rosicrucian Park* in San Jose, California) as well as his plans for instituting financial seminars based upon *Rosicrucian perspectives* (Stewart, 1988). Over the next two years, when not travelling, Stewart would remain close to the headquarters attending various local events and installing new officers.

However, by early 1990, concerns were being raised about his leadership. Stewart's plans would be cut short following an extraordinary meeting of the Board of Directors held between April 11 1990 and April 12 1990, the details of which were provided to the general membership as follows,

> *A vote of confidence had been demanded by the Grand Masters concerning Frater Gary Stewart. Following the discovery of grave facts of which we had learned, no member of the Board could give him a vote of confidence, and Frater Gary Stewart was therefore immediately dismissed of his function as Imperator for placing in peril the philosophy and the good of the Ancient and Mystical Order of the Rosae Crucis. In the minutes which followed, on the nomination of the Grand Masters, I assumed the Presidency of AMORC on April 12 of the Rosicrucian year 3343. I was unanimously elected to the position of Imperator. By common accord, we decided to propose to Frater Gary Stewart that he tender his resignation but he refused.* (Bernard, 1990)

The *grave facts* that led to the vote of no confidence in Stewart's leadership were partially revealed in court documents which details that *The Rosicrucian Order, AMORC, Inc.*, along with its Secretary-Treasurer *Burnham Schaa*, filed a civil lawsuit against Stewart in the *Santa Clara County Superior Court* in California (Case No. *700028*). Also named in the suit were two banks: *Silicon Valley Bank* (based in California) and *Banc Agricol I Comercial* (based in Andorra).

The plaintiffs alleged that Stewart, while acting as President and Imperator, had misappropriated over three million dollars of the organisation's funds. Stewart was accused of transferring these funds between March and April 1990 from A.M.O.R.C.'s account at Silicon Valley Bank to an external trust account, and ultimately to Banc Agricol I Comercial in Andorra, without the necessary board authorisation or the required co-signatures as stipulated in the organisation's financial policies. The funds, the plaintiffs asserted, were unaccounted for and possibly being used for personal benefit.

Compounding this issue was Stewart's alleged refusal to fully disclose details of the transactions or provide access to the relevant account numbers, fuelling suspicions and urgency among the board members.

The timing of the transfers and the secrecy surrounding them triggered alarm amongst the Board of Directors. These tensions culminated in the extraordinary board meeting alluded to above. Over the course of two days, the Board of Directors questioned Stewart regarding their concerns, primarily related to the transfers of large sums of money.

Stewart provided his response, to which the Board of Directors expressed dissatisfaction. Consequently, Stewart was requested to leave the room so that a vote of no confidence could be conducted. The result: no director present voted in support of Stewart. The Board members did agree however to offer Stewart the opportunity to resign from his position.

After re-joining the meeting, Stewart requested a short recess to contemplate his decision. After the recess, Stewart came back with his response.

Rather than resign, Stewart attempted to dismiss all the board members from their positions before announcing the meeting adjourned and departing the room. However, the meeting still constituting a quorum reconvened under the direction of the Vice-President. All board members present agreed to dismiss Stewart as Imperator, President, Board member, as well as a member of good standing in the organisation.

Stewart, however, disputed the legitimacy of these actions, asserting that his authority as Imperator in particular, had been conferred directly by Ralph M. Lewis and was not subject to board removal. He continued to act in an official capacity, reportedly attempting to assert control over the organisation's assets. The following day, A.M.O.R.C. filed for a temporary restraining order and a preliminary injunction to prevent Stewart from representing himself as the Imperator or accessing organisational resources.

War of the Roses

Stewart countered with a cross-complaint, asserting that he had not been acting improperly with the organisation's finances and had in fact been attempting to stabilise the organisation's finances through legitimate means; specifically, by negotiating a secured line of credit and establishing a European trust to support A.M.O.R.C.'s international operations. He also claimed that internal rivals had conspired to remove him and that he had been the victim of a politically motivated coup rather than guilty of any wrongdoing.

Over the next three years, the legal case dragged on. By August 10 1993, the case concluded. Both sides agreed to drop their respective suits. A.M.O.R.C. provided no official explanation for the withdrawal. Stewart, by contrast, would go on to speak publicly about the affair in various interviews and forums, portraying himself as the victim of a political coup.

The above represent the matter as presented through available court documents.

Naturally, you will observe that there remains a great deal of questions, the answers to which may never reach the light of day. Nevertheless, whilst there are a great deal of unknowns regarding the motives and exact circumstances, what we can be more sure of is the fallout that would follow.

In the aftermath, Stewart's supporters claimed that his ousting had been part of a wider agenda to shift the organisation's centre of gravity from the United States to Europe, pointing to concurrent structural reforms that redistributed power across newly established autonomous Grand Lodges. They framed the conflict as a betrayal of A.M.O.R.C.'s American roots. A.M.O.R.C. loyalists, on the other hand, maintained that Stewart had been rightfully removed for misconduct, and that the reforms were necessary to prevent similar crises in the future.

Over the course of several years, claims and counterclaims would also be made out-of-court among the membership in the form of interviews, pamphlets, and periodicals.

Stewart never relinquished his claim to the Imperatorship. In the wake of the conflict, multiple individuals would take the opportunity to establish and promote their own Rosicrucian organisations. The most significant would be developed by Stewart himself who would found the, *Confraternity of the Rose Cross* (C.R.+C.).

A.M.O.R.C. groups across the world would be bombarded with pamphlets and materials advancing the cause of a myriad of newly emerged splinter groups hoping to represent the phoenix that would arise from the ashes of the chaos.

In addition, opponents of A.M.O.R.C. would seize upon the raging controversy in order to further advance their own claims against the organisation framing A.M.O.R.C. as an illegitimate Rosicrucian group more concerned with legal proceedings then advancing the Rosicrucian tradition.

All of the above would lead to a mass exodus of A.M.O.R.C. members. Some members claimed allegiance to the office of Imperator, leading to a great deal of very senior members resigning from A.M.O.R.C. and assisting with the C.R.+C. cause. Some resigned having been influenced by the conversations that had begun in the aftermath. But many likely left simply as a result of frustration and confusion.

And whilst the organisation has never released membership data for this period, the impact was readily apparent and felt globally.

This episode not only did lasting damage to A.M.O.R.C.'s public image, but also to the Rosicrucian tradition more broadly, sowing seeds of suspicion, rivalry, and confusion that still linger today.

Following this period, Rosicrucian dialogue would increasingly feature themes concerning validity, legitimacy, and lineage. The gaps between Rosicrucian groups would widen. And any hope for inter-organisational collaboration would all but cease.

Echoes in the Chamber: *Rosicrucianism in the Internet Age*

In the wake of the institutional conflicts that closed the late twentieth century, Rosicrucianism entered a new and more diffused phase, one increasingly shaped by digital discourse.

The rise of online forums, social media groups, and discussion boards have given Rosicrucian initiates and aspirants unprecedented access to a wide variety of teachings and traditions. Vast catalogues of teachings once deemed precious and collected privately by initiates over many years of fraternal affiliation can now be found online with minimal effort.

The esoteric internet has become a patchwork of echo chambers, each one reinforcing its own legitimacy and tradition. Rather than fostering a genuine inquiry or fraternal dialogue, many online communities have cultivated a culture of partisanship. Participants become entrenched in the belief that various Rosicrucian groups might represent *true* Rosicrucian organisations. Debates about lineages, charters, and authenticity dominate discussions. Yet these arguments often rest on a fundamental misunderstanding of the original Rosicrucian ideal, which tended towards being anonymous, decentralised, and non-institutional; not a registered trademark.

And yet, many modern seekers seem obsessed with the question: *Which group is real?* Naturally, this is not their fault but is the consequence of the way organisations have framed the Rosicrucian tradition in recent years.

It is perhaps this desire for certainty in an ever-elusive tradition that has led to widespread suspicion between different Rosicrucian organisations. Some groups openly discourage dual-affiliation. Others quietly engage in subtle gatekeeping. The result is a culture in which inter-group fraternity is near impossible as groups police individual spiritual exploration to ensure the doctrinal purity of its members.

Usually, this culture is something only ever observed at a grassroots level. But occasionally, this culture solidifies into rules or reprimands from organisational leaders. An example of this occurred in late-2024, when the S.R.I.A. released an internal communication clarifying its position on other Rosicrucian organisations. The document, titled, *Guidance on Compatible Organisations*, was circulated on December 3 2024 and rapidly circulated publicly online. The document made explicit that A.M.O.R.C. was considered *incompatible with SRIA membership*.

The letter reads in part:

> *For the avoidance of doubt, UGLE have confirmed that this is still current policy and that any member of a Lodge in amity with UGLE found to be holding membership of AMORC is liable for disciplinary procedures leading to expulsion from the Craft and therefore from the SRIA.*

This blanket incompatibility ruling is drawn from a dated entry in the *United Grand Lodge of England* (U.G.L.E.) Provincial Grand Secretary's handbook, which states that some organisations are incompatible with the Craft, including,

> *Any organisation where men and women sit together in Lodges purporting to be Masonic*

This rule seems to conflate A.M.O.R.C. with pseudo-Masonic or co-Masonic organisations, despite the fact that A.M.O.R.C. has never claimed to be Masonic in any sense, nor conducted any rites remotely similar to Craft Freemasonry. And rather than question the soundness of the rule, the S.R.I.A. chose to seek out and uphold the policy without qualification.

Following this ruling, the S.R.I.A. has taken the posture of enforcement, actively restricting its members' private affiliations and, in some cases, reprimanding and even removing individuals from the society. This for many signalled a confusion between institutional loyalty and personal initiation. It reflects a defensiveness more typical of ecclesiastical gatekeeping than of the open-minded curiosity that originally defined the Rosicrucian impulse. It is clear, the online world has changed how esotericism is explored, and it has also exposed the fragility of Rosicrucian organisational identities.

But the digital age has also ushered in rare opportunities for the Rosicrucian tradition.

Where once the serious seeker would need to embark on a miniature pilgrimage to reach remote libraries gatekept by occasionally reluctant librarians, today's initiate can now access a great deal of information with minimal effort. Many of the world's most prestigious libraries, who have been responsible for caring for rare texts related to the Rosicrucian tradition, have been busy digitising manuscripts, correspondence, and pamphlets. The fruits of these efforts have allowed unprecedented access to information. This presents a new horizon for the Rosicrucian tradition; a tradition that has always maintained a peculiar relationship balancing the scales of secrecy and publication.

There is no doubt that digital archives have empowered the initiate with an academic interest.

Additionally, *Artificial Intelligence* (A.I.), whilst still in its infancy, has been playing an increasingly supportive role in navigating the influx of new information. Digital translation, once quite clumsy, has matured rapidly with A.I. as its partner. Latin, German, and French Rosicrucian texts which would have been inaccessible to many are now revealing their insights across the boundaries of language and time. And whilst A.I. translation has yet to prove a worthy substitute to a human translator (who still has the upper hand when traversing linguistic and cultural nuances) its promise is becoming more obvious.

Perhaps someone can soon use A.I. to help answer outstanding questions regarding the Rosicrucian tradition. Could A.I. one day be used to cross-analyse Rosicrucian source works with potential authors, utilising its advanced pattern recognition ability to finally determine who was responsible for writing the foundational Rosicrucian source works?

Naturally, the digital age is not without its thorns especially when dealing with esoteric knowledge. The value of this knowledge is literally *eso*-teric, that is, comes from within: it cannot be given. The information may be transmitted, but understanding arises only through a personal process. In a way, esoteric knowledge resembles the right side of an equation: the outcome. On the left, we have the *initiate* and the *information*, inputs that must be brought together to yield esoteric insight. Without the active presence of the initiate, the equation will remain unsolved. Access to information will not yield gnosis. A certain reverence is required when approaching esoteric knowledge and there is no substitute for personal effort.

Effort + *Information* = **Esoteric insight**

But the accessibility of information and sharing of information via social media has not been without fruit. The digital age has also sowed the seeds of hope to raise the Rosicrucian tradition to a new height. The digital age has restructured how information is shared, and it has also begun to re-shape the next generation of initiates. The aspirants who now approach initiatory organisations do so with unprecedented knowledge. They are more well-versed in our histories, their arrival at our portals more likely the result of sincerity than mere curiosity. And whilst this may not be reflected in membership growth (a poor indicator of efficacy) it may just produce a great generation of academically coherent and humble initiates, without dogmatic baggage. This might just lead to a Golden Age of esotericism if only these new initiates resist the temptation to commercialise or fossilise the Rosicrucian tradition. Truly, the Rosicrucian tradition has never been more vulnerable and yet so full of promise.

Crown of Thorns

In truth, the history of the Rosicrucian tradition has not been free from the very human failings it so often sought to transcend. Rosicrucian organisations have broken apart and splintered due to internal conflicts. Inter-organisational disputes abound with rival groups accusing others of incorrect interpretations of Rosicrucianism. Questions of legitimacy have flourished with some groups promoting themselves as the only true heir to the Rosicrucian tradition.

What a mess!

How did we get here? How can we possibly share the same name, the same foundational history, and distrust each other so much?

And yet, through all this drama and discord, the spirit of Rosicrucianism persists. The ideals of peace, harmony, and service have not vanished just because they are not perfectly upheld. They have, and will continue, to remain as a source of aspiration for sincere Rosicrucian initiates. Our tradition has not always succeeded in achieving a harmonious community, but it has always strived towards this goal despite our past failings.

Another point that warrants consideration is to consider that conflicts within the Rosicrucian tradition may serve as examples of dialectics or masked polemics, such as those utilised in the classical period as an educational device. Afterall, dialogues are a common theme in Platonic and Hermetic texts where fictional disputes are often reenacted to present to the reader opposing worldviews.

Whilst we have no direct evidence of Rosicrucian thinkers deliberately staging their conflicts, such would not be out of place. In any case, whether staged or real, the examined Rosicrucian polemics have served to elucidate the underlying values that the Rosicrucian tradition ever sought to express.

What is the Rose without the Cross? To be Rosicrucian is not merely to proclaim ourselves as superior. It means occasionally setting aside our pride and seeking reconciliation. It means journeying together to rediscover that shared root from which our branches have descended. To labour patiently in service of the Rose-Cross.

Let us conclude therefore, not with an idealised vision for our future...but a hopeful one. That we, and each subsequent generation of Rosicrucian initiates may learn from the struggles and mistakes of those who came before us and in so doing help bring our tradition a little closer to the spirit which we have always sought to exemplify.

SUB UMBRA ALARUM TUARUM, JEHOVA[16]

---

16 *Under the Shadow of thy Wings, Jehova.* This was the closing line of the Fama Fraternitatis.

Rosicrucianism in the digital age. Artificially developed using Microsoft Copilot A.I.

AN OPEN LETTER TO ROSICRUCIAN OFFICERS

Dear Brothers and Sisters,

I write to you now as a fellow traveller on the Rosicrucian path; not as a scholar or a critic. If you are reading this, it is likely because you hold a position of some responsibility within your Rosicrucian body, whether as an organisational leader, a ritual officer, a guide, or a mentor. Or maybe you are simply a dedicated student entrusted with some portion of the Work.

This letter is an appeal, from one initiate to another.

We all know that the Rosicrucian tradition is broad, scattered, and at times painfully divided. Many of us belong to groups with long histories, old charters, complex initiatory structures, and deeply cherished teachings. We invest much into these bodies: our time, our energy, our trust, our devotion. It is no wonder that we feel protective of them. But in guarding what we love, we must be careful not to let our reverence for one path turn into disdain for others.

There is no single authentic Rosicrucian organisation. There never was.

From the moment man first became self-aware, the primordial tradition whispered out. From the moment the Rosicrucian source works were released into the world, anonymous and unclaimed, the Rosicrucian tradition was revealed as a living current, one that each generation must interpret anew.

Some groups interpret it through ritual, others through mysticism, others through scientific philosophy, spiritual alchemy, or symbolic study. Some require Christian faith; others are more universal in approach. None of these are inherently right or wrong. They are different vessels attempting to carry the same light.

To the officers and leaders of these vessels, I urge: lead with generosity of spirit. Let tolerance be your highest badge of honour. It is easy to critique the outer forms of another group. It is harder, but far nobler, to recognise the sincerity behind a different structure, a different symbol, or a different emphasis. We do not have to agree on everything to recognise one another as fellow seekers.

We must be especially cautious not to mistake administrative boundaries for spiritual ones. No organisation owns the Rose-Cross. We are its custodians, not its proprietors.

To those who feel caught in the middle, between traditions, between loyalties, between accusations and ideals, let me say this plainly: *you have the right to find your Rosicrucian home.* Whether it is an old and established order, a newer fellowship, or a solitary practice inspired by the Rosicrucian source works, follow your heart. If a group brings you closer to Truth, Beauty, and Virtue, then it is worthy of your time. If it nourishes the Spark within, then it is doing the Great Work.

And to those who have been told that their path is invalid, that their lineage is flawed, that they are not *real* Rosicrucians, I offer you comfort. You are not alone. Many of us have heard these things. But remember: the Invisible College is not limited by paper, practice, or prestige. *It knows its own.*

Let us then focus on what truly matters.

Let us seek wonder again. Let us be enchanted by the Mystery, not distracted by politics. Let us encourage study, contemplation, humility, and fraternity. Let us teach our members that disagreement need not mean division, that questions are not threats, and that silence is sometimes more powerful than rebuttal.

Open Letter

There is work to do, and we will need each other to accomplish it. Not as rivals, but as companions.

May we each tend the garden we have been given. May we each build the temple we are called to serve. And may our labours, though scattered across many lodges, temples, and sanctums, reveal in time the one *Invisible Rose*.

With fraternal affection and in the Spirit of the Work,

I remain your fellow seeker,

RECTIFICATOR

CONCLUSION

THE ROSICRUCIAN SECRET REVEALED

Today, we stand on the threshold of a new phase of Rosicrucian renewal and as such, it is an opportune time for us to reflect upon the impact our own thoughts, words, and actions can wield upon the trajectory of our cherished tradition.

These signs of renewal are not always visible in public displays or sweeping membership booms. Instead, they are most clearly seen in the quiet seriousness of the new initiate: the brother or sister who approaches this path not for spectacle or status, but for truth, for service, and to *Know Thyself*.

Now is the time when we may thoughtfully and purposefully shape the future of Rosicrucianism by engaging with its past, its present, and our shared hopes for the future. In this era of Rosicrucian renewal, let us not merely be passive recipients of the tradition but active participants in its unfolding narrative. By engaging in a conscious dialogue with the Rosicrucian legacy, we become co-authors of its ongoing story. Through our own intentional efforts, we can ensure that the future of the Rosicrucian tradition remains vibrant, relevant, and true to its essence. Like the Rosicrucian pioneers of yesteryear, may our thoughts, words, and actions create a legacy that resonates through the corridors of time, guiding future seekers on their own journey within the Rosicrucian tradition. Afterall, no tradition, no matter how noble its origin can remain alive without the breath of sincere practitioners.

In this book, we began with the *Whisper of the Rose*. This call came, not from a temple or mountaintop, but from within. We explored the foundational Rosicrucian source works whose peculiar blend of satire, sincerity, and allegory gave the tradition much of its outward character. We examined the figure of *Christian Rosenkreuz* as a historical possibility. We also explored this character as an initiatory symbol whose own journey from *Aspirant*-to-*Initiate*-to-*Adept* encapsulates our own personal journey to *Know Thyself*. We considered the *Hallmarks* by which we might recognise the *Fruit* of the true Rosicrucians. In the *War of the Roses* we trudged through the dark and uncomfortable conflicts of Rosicrucian history, tracing how the Rosicrucian tradition has weathered misunderstanding and criticism, both from within and from without, for centuries. But, despite this friction, the Rosicrucian flame has lived on.

But now, let us look forward into the unwritten possibilities our future holds.

Unlike previous waves of Rosicrucian renewal that were defined by explosive public announcements or the establishment of initiatory federations, I expect this present-day renewal to be somewhat quieter. This new renewal is currently being witnessed in the maturing of the initiate. It will not be about whether organisations use the right language or hold the *correct* lineage. It will be about initiates living a meaningful life of service.

If anything defines the Rosicrucian today, it is someone who sees their work on themselves as but the beginning of their work in the world.

Perhaps this might appear somewhat grey for some initiates who are experienced with the colourful pageantry resident in many of our modern initiatory groups. But I can assure you, this will be as good and even more fulfilling. In our modern-era dominated by efficiency and empirical validation, the esoteric approach may seem out of step. The archaic tone utilised by our Rosicrucian ancestors doesn't always mesh with our sterile, hyper-digital culture. Be assured, Rosicrucianism does not need to conform in order to thrive. But it must, and always will, find ways to speak meaningfully to contemporary seekers. This means upholding its mystery, but without becoming obscure. It means encouraging exploration, but without stifling the imagination. Just as the rose blooms upon the cross, so too should the Rosicrucian tradition bloom upon the landscape upon which it grows.

The Rosicrucian will always recognise the sacred interrelationship that exists between *Man*, *Nature*, and *God*. Their life will always be their work. And their *Temple* will not be built with stone, but with their intention and action. They may study the arcane, but only to better understand themselves and their world. They will continue to use ritual to bring into conscious awareness their true nature. And they will always heed the *Whisper of the Rose* that comes from within; that still small quiet voice of conscience.

Some Rosicrucian groups will experience an influx of interest. But this will not be sustainable for all. Some Rosicrucian groups have been guilty of working as if they alone hold the light. Such an insular attitude does not reflect all the glory of the Rose-Cross today. The new generation of Rosicrucian initiates can recognise cynicism and dismissal coming from organisational leaders as if it were on broadcast. The inner Rosicrucian fraternity, the *Invisible College*, transcends organisational boundaries. It is not built by charters or lineages.

Personally, I do not believe the future lies in the tired old attempts at federations or alliances. But I do see a future of respectful collaboration and shared spirit. It is important that each path maintains its independence; but not its suspicion. Let us be confident enough in our Égrégore to respectfully and kindly acknowledge our Rosicrucian neighbours, for our paths of service transcend organisational boundaries.

Rosicrucian Community

Being a Rosicrucian is not something that we are granted by birth or title, nor even by initiation into a Rosicrucian group. It is something we aspire to be and may grow to become by living a life in accordance with Rosicrucian ideals. Although much of the labour of a Rosicrucian life is inward, the Rosicrucian path is not a solitary one. Our personal growth is amplified when we offer ourselves to the greater whole. This may be in a formal lodge environment or may simply be via the quiet interaction with kindred spirits who share our ideals.

To live a Rosicrucian life is to be of service, to contribute to the upliftment of humanity. In this willingness to serve, aspiration transforms into belonging, and belonging into a sense of *esprit de corps*. This we might call a *Rosicrucian community*. A Rosicrucian community is not therefore defined by structures or boundaries. One may join a Rosicrucian group and discover that the bonds of shared work and ritual are highly rewarding. Yet this same spirit can exist outside of any formal group where this principle remains the same. Our *fraternity* comes alive through our active participation. Whether this be working in a formal group or by studying and applying Rosicrucian principles in our daily life. In so doing, we come to discover that our refuge is not to be found in a withdrawal from this world, but in our commitment to it. A Rosicrucian community then is not something one passively inherits or joins. It is something that one continually creates and re-creates. In other words, it is *living*.

As such communities endure, they take on a life of their own. The thoughts, aspirations, and devotion of its members generate a subtle but potent psychic presence, almost like a personality. And just like a human personality, such a tradition may be generous or severe, welcoming or aloof, flexible or rigid. Each of these traits may prove to be strengths or weaknesses depending upon our own understanding and maturity. To participate in such a community is therefore to enter into a relationship, not only with the people around us, but also with the *soul* of the tradition itself. Each

Rosicrucian community could be considered to be a custodian of a living inheritance, a kind of invisible current that influences and shapes the tradition and those who come into contact with it. Yet an important caveat must be kept in mind: if a group that calls itself Rosicrucian does not serve the upliftment of humanity, then it is not an authentic Rosicrucian body, whatever its name may claim. By engaging with an authentic Rosicrucian community, we actively contribute to this psychic life, strengthening its virtues, tempering its faults, and working to ensure that it remains a beacon of light for humble seekers.

Thus, we may see that the Rosicrucian community is threefold in nature. It is a fellowship of kindred seekers. It is also a living psychic organism, shaped by the devotion and aspiration of its members. And it is a channel of service, striving to radiate peace and benevolence into the world. To live a Rosicrucian life is to recognise this triunity: to walk in fellowship with companions, to nurture the invisible soul of the tradition, and to help channel the light of divine beneficence to a world in need.

A Rosicrucian Home

Throughout this book, we have explored many individual Rosicrucian groups. Many readers may already belong to one of these groups. And there will be readers who belong to no group at all. Perhaps you may be wondering which group you should join? Or if your current group is the best one for you.

In this age of Rosicrucian renewal, there will be some who will take the approach that we need to develop a new group. A new foundation, with a new name, new leadership, new rituals, and new practices. Is this the correct approach? Should we now, being equipped with the beauty of hindsight and the knowledge bequeathed to us from our ancestors, attempt to *correct* the errors of existing Rosicrucian groups and develop a new Rosicrucian organisation?

Speak to any person that has had extensive experience working within an initiatory organisation and you will likely hear some similar reflections. In fact, these reflections are so common, they reveal a truly universal initiatic experience. And yet, many experienced initiates do not speak of these experiences out loud. Usually, this is for an altruistic reason. Groups are made of people, and people are flawed. And yet, even us scarred romantics can still recognise the value, however naïve, that may be found in the optimism and enthusiasm of a sincere seeker.

So what does this universal initiatic experience look like that many experienced initiates have encountered? Well, it almost looks like the journey taken by C.R.C. in the Fama Fraternitatis.

To better understand this universal initiatic experience, let me offer a fictional, but familiar story.

The below description is not based on a real life individual. But because of its commonality to real life initiatic journeys, some may be tempted to assume that I am referring to a real person. Let me be clear, this is hypothetical. This character is imagined purely for illustrating the archetypal journey many initiates will undertake.

Rian always felt a little different to the rest of the world. As a child, he was slightly more introverted compared to his peers. He was sensitive, and perhaps because of this, he often felt misunderstood. He felt compassion for those that were suffering and took solace in nature and around animals.

Adolescence proved to be a period marked by significant developments and personal setbacks. His distinct characteristics became increasingly apparent, and the divide between him and his peers in mainstream circles grew more pronounced. Identifying as an outlier often led to participation in specialised support groups and social networks. Within these communities, attributes that once caused feelings of isolation now fostered a sense of individuality and value.

But Rian always felt like there was something more to life that was always just out of reach. His curiosity led him down many paths. And whilst he learned a lot, it always seemed like he was still searching.

Eventually, a chance encounter led Rian to discover a Rosicrucian group. Obligations were taken and promises were returned. His sincerity and optimism led to a rapid advancement in his grasp of esoteric knowledge. And whilst he met some incredibly wise people (the number of which could be counted on one hand), many of the members seemed a bit odd. Nevertheless, he knew that this was where he belonged. How could it not be? For whilst he never seemed to be a complete adept with the skills he encountered, it was easy to see the internal changes that were affected by his work.

Soon, Rian was no longer the *new guy*. He would take on various roles in the group and generally had a good time. This brought him closer to the members and he got to know them quite well. No longer was he simply a witness to the ritual dramas, but he was participating in them as a ritualistic officer.

Unfortunately, peeking behind the curtain was not all that it appeared to be. The sublime ceremonies that he had seen… well…they became just choreographed dramas poorly acted out by people. And some of these people, well, they seemed to not understand the point. Sure, they could *talk the talk*, but it was becoming increasingly apparent that they could not *walk the walk*. Eventually, Rian worked his way through this tradition. He learned all of the secrets. He received all of the passwords. He did all the right things. And many of the people that he had started out his journey with had left. He was a big fish in a small pond, growing increasingly disgruntled by the way things were operating.

One day, after a great deal of reflection, Rian did something that he never thought he would ever find himself doing. He left.

And you know what, this decision, whilst it was challenging to make, turned out to be fairly effortless to enact. In fact, this decision came with an air of freedom. Rian began to explore with other communities and for the first time he really felt like he was putting into practice many of the skills he had acquired over the years. This would be like a second life in his initiatory journey.

Now, let's pause our fictional narrative here for a moment. And let me again reiterate, that Rian is not based on any real person. There are many *Rian's* out there. And for many of them, this is about where their initiatic journey plateaus. Some Rian's may carry a bit of disgruntlement for *other* groups or individuals, but generally, they live out a fulfilling life. They become mentors, not just for initiates, but for people in general. And the world is often benefitted by their kindness and wisdom. But often, this is where Rian's initiatic journey will end.

However, on rare occasions Rian's journey will continue. His mentorship attracts a growing circle of seekers. Soon, Rian is faced with a challenge. Does he dare establish his own initiatory group?

Many of us have seen this scenario play out multiple times. And whilst it would be great to state that this story ends with the foundation of a new circle of inspired initiates empowered by the impulse of the Rose-Cross, more often than not, this initiative starts with a big bang before the flames quickly settle into a smouldering ember of *what could have been*. And the bigger the *bang*, the sooner and more acute tends to be the *fall*.

So ends the story of Rian. It is quite a tragic and yet all too familiar story.

So is that it? Is that the end for all initiates who complete their journey? Are we all Icarus prototypes, destined to fly close enough to the sun only to be burned?

Like all good Rosicrucian philosophies however, the fulfilling resolution to this narrative is invisible, but has been in front of us the entire time.

Conclusion 291

Not all initiatic journeys need to end like Rian's. There are happy endings.

You may have recognised how closely Rian's journey aligned with that of C.R.C. in the Fama Fraternitatis. And yet, C.R.C.'s vision succeeded where Rian's did not. Why?

Like Rian, C.R.C. sought something greater than himself. He went searching and found a group that taught him all manner of secret teaching. He was altruistic enough to endeavour to help others. He even failed to succeed...at first. But something else happened. Where Rian chose to establish himself as a leader of a group, directly managing its affairs and curating it as a *rectified* system, something which he had perceived as being *broken* which he had endeavoured to *fix*, C.R.C. did something else entirely. He died. He sacrificed his earthly personality thereby removing his ego from the story completely. And here defines a true Rosicrucian adept. It is not somebody that will necessarily be found at the head of the group. But more often than not, will only leave traces of inspiration, beauty, and kind words of encouragement in their wake. They may work within groups. But their role here is more one of support and guidance; not of leadership. We should not conclude from this summary that all leaders are egotists. Such is certainly not the case, and there are countless Rosicrucian groups being led sincerely by talented and virtuous individuals. But the trajectory as outlined in this section and illustrated by Rian is a common occurrence.

In *A Rose by any other Name,* we explored how some organisations and movements may be Rosicrucian in all but name. In other words, they may be empowered by the Rose-Cross, even if they do not necessarily have Rosicrucian in their name or conform to an initiatic rite.

Many of these groups, some now household names, have contributed meaningfully to the advancement of humanity. And at their commencement, their aspiration to serve was guided by a hidden hand. Yet, like Rian, even the most inspired physical enterprises eventually must face a choice: re-invent themselves or risk becoming a parody of what they once were.

This short synopsis and contrast I have represented here can also be found in the esoteric didactic literature discussed in an earlier chapter, with similar narratives being found in these works (albeit, presented by far better storytellers than myself). For instance, in *Zanoni*, Edward Bulwer-Lytton introduces two characters, Glyndon and Zanoni, who can be compared in several respects to Rian and C.R.C. respectively.

So how may we best become a living embodiment of the Rose-Cross?

I'm going to give you some advice that will supercharge your advancement by allowing you to participate now in the characteristics usually reserved for the Adept.

You do not need to wander endlessly in search of a long-lost, perfect, and unblemished Rosicrucian fraternity. Nor do you need to create one from scratch.

The perfect group, in the worldly sense, is an illusion, and the sooner we let go of it, the sooner we are free to discover that every organisation is made of imperfect human beings, and that this imperfection is a part of the initiatory landscape[1]. The Great Work is not bound to any group, but by the way we labour within it. And any initiate who works with sincerity, humility, and steadfastness will find within it the same alchemical fire that has burned through every Rosicrucian temple since the beginning. And if we begin now to live and emulate our lives like that of an adept, then when the dark night comes, we need not be undone.

---

1 It is important to distinguish between understanding human imperfections and condoning unacceptable conduct. Behaviours such as bullying, harassment, corruption, and abuse are not acceptable in any initiatory group and should be addressed immediately and courageously.

Conclusion 293

The truth is many existing groups already provide the fertile soil for your growth; if you approach them with the right spirit. Existing groups, rituals, and symbols are already there. They have produced adepts before, and they may do so again. But you must engage with them with effort, patience, and sincerity. That is not to say that all Rosicrucian groups are equal. They are not. Some are better suited to your needs than others and it's important to reach out and determine which group (if any) feels right for you.

And here lies a key to supercharging your advancement: do not wait until you *become* an adept to begin behaving like one. Live now as though you already carry the quiet responsibility of the Rose-Cross. Speak with care, act with integrity, and serve without seeking recognition. Such habits will refine your character and build within you the resilience you need to pass through the dark night which will inevitably come. And when that night comes and threatens to consume your zeal, as it did to Rian and Glyndon, you will already have cultivated the hallmarks of an adept. Your work will not depend upon the rise and fall of any group. You will be a living embodiment of the Rosicrucian tradition. You will be a Rosicrucian.

If this book has spoken to you, then take it as a gentle nudge. Begin where you are. Join a Rosicrucian group that resonates with you, but do not expect miracles. Be sincere. Be patient. As the old adage goes, *When the student is ready, the Master will appear.* That *Master* is within you. Or perhaps another ancient adage, *Many are called, but few are chosen.* Perhaps you can decide now who it is that does the *choosing*.

Whether you choose to join a Rosicrucian group or not, it will certainly be beneficial to take up some Rosicrucian habits. Find time to regularly step out of the fray of life and reflect. Meditate. Create. Celebrate the mystery that unfolds from within. Know that the Rosicrucian life is not an escape from this world, but an exploration into it.

The Rosicrucian Secret Revealed

It is here, seemingly at the end of our journey that a great *Rosicrucian Secret*, that was lost, can now be found. But like all esoteric secrets, this is not secret because its meaning has been concealed, but that its meaning, by its very nature, is hidden. I cannot reveal this to you with my words, for I am lacking the tools which you may use to find it. But it just so happens that you have these tools. It is the heat from that divine spark resident within you. As one Rosicrucian adept once said, *Within us are powers and abilities that are like invisible sparks waiting to be fanned into brilliant flames.*

It might have seemed odd to you that this book contained two blank pages in the centre of the book. The fact of the matter is, that this book is unfinished. But this was not an overlooked editing issue or a printing error. This was quite deliberate. This might seem odd, but it is the truth. How can one possibly create a *Rosicrucian Compendium* on their own? It betrays the very definition of what it means to be *Rosicrucian*.

Now that you have finished the book, it is time to go back to the centre and seek for that which was lost. It is here that you may hope to find a real Rosicrucian Secret.

Think of these pages like a living mirror. I want you to stand in front of them. Take a few deep breaths and become comfortable. Ask yourself, what does it mean to be *Rosicrucian*. And then create. There are no rules. You may write a poem. Design a symbol. Draw a sketch. Compose a ritual. Write a prayer. Take some time to reflect, and when you are ready let your heart and mind dance. Let it be sincere.

Only when you have added a piece of your inspiration to these pages will this book be complete. From this act, you will be able to see that you are the co-creator of the Rosicrucian tradition. This is a path we share together, and you are a part of the Rosicrucian renewal.

But most of all, you will remember that the greatest *Rosicrucian Secret* cannot be told. It can only be *awakened*.

REFERENCES

A.M.O.R.C. The National Membership Defense Committee. (1935). *White Book D: Audi Alteram Partem (Hear the other side).* San Jose: Rosicrucian Press, LTD.

Algeo, J. (1996). *Blavatsky, Freemasonry, & the Western Mystery Tradition.* London: The Theosophical Society in England.

AMORC.org.au. (2023). *About the Rosicrucian Order (AMORC).* Retrieved from AMORC.org.au: https://amorc.org.au/about/

Bacon, F. (2020). *New Atlantis (1626)_Edited by Gerard B. Wegemer.* Dallas: CTMS Publishers.

Bernard, C. (1990). New Imperator Elected. *Rosicrucian Digest, 68*(3), p. 5.

Blackden, M. W. (1914). *Ritual of the Mystery of the Judgement of the Soul. From an Ancient Egyptian Papyrus. Translated and edited by M. W. Blackden, S.R.I.A., VII°., Late of the Archaeological Survey, Egypt Exploration Fund.* London: Societas Rosicruciana in Anglia.

Blavatsky, H. P. (1878). *Isis Uneveiled: Volume 1.* Theosophical University Press Online Edition. Retrieved from https://www.theosociety.org/pasadena/isis/isis_unveiled_volume_1.pdf

Blavatsky, H. P. (1918). *The Secret Doctrine Volume 3.* London: The Theosophical Publishing House.

Blavatsky, H. P. (1981, August). Pen and Ink Sketch of Ramsgate Harbour by H. P. B. *The Theosophist*, pp. 558-559. Retrieved from http://iapsop.com/archive/materials/theosophist/theosophist_v52_n4-n12_jan_1931-sep_1931.pdf

Blavatsky, H. P. (n.d.). *File:Blavatsky_handwriting.jpg*. Retrieved from https://commons.wikimedia.org: https://commons.wikimedia.org/wiki/File:Blavatsky_handwriting.jpg

Böhme, J. (1624). *The Way to Christ*. Grand Rapids: Christian Classic Ethereal Library. Retrieved from https://www.ccel.org/ccel/b/boehme/waytochrist/cache/waytochrist.pdf

Böhme, J. (2016). *The Three Principles of the Divine Essence*. Kraus Haus. Retrieved from https://jacobboehmeonline.com/assets/docs/three_principles_jbo_vers.18693636.pdf

Boissin, S. (1890). *Excentriques Disparus*. Toulouse: De la petite libraire di xix siecle.

Bulwer-Lytton as quoted by Affectator, S. E. (2025, February). Edward Bulwer-Lytton. *The Rosicrucian*(99), pp. 27-31.

Bulwer-Lytton, S. E. (1862). *Zanoni*. Philadelphia: J. B. Lippincott & Co.

Case, P. F. (1989). *The True and Invisible Rosicrucian Order*. Boston: Weiser Books.

Christian Cynosure. (1898, July). News of our Work. *Christian Cynosure*, p. 91.

Churton, T. (2016). *Occult Paris: The Lost Magic of the Belle Époque*. Rochester: Inner Traditions.

Clausen, D. J. (n.d.). *Origins of Masonic Templarism in the French Ordre du Temple*. Ordre Souverain et Militaire du Temple de Jérusalem.

Clemens, M. L. (1953). *Autobiography of Marie Louise Clemens*. Boston: Bruce Humphries, Inc.

Clymer, R. S. (1935). *Not under the Rosy Cross: An expose of Imperator of AMORC with black magic connections.* Quakertown: The Rosicrucian Foundation.

Copenhaver, B. P. (2000). *Hermetica: the Greek Corpus Hermeticum and the Latin Asclepius in a new English translation with notes and introduction.* Cambridge: Cambridge University Press.

Corpus.Quran.com. (2017). *Verse (55:15) - English Translation.* Retrieved from Corpus.Quran.com: https://corpus.quran.com/translation.jsp?chapter=55&verse=15

Cranston, S., & Williams, C. (1993). *H.P.B. The Extraordinary Life and Influence of Helena Petrovna Blavatsky.* Santa Barbara, California: Path Publishing House in cooperation with the Institute of Noetic Sciences.

Craven, J. B. (1902). *Doctor Robert Fludd (Robertus de Fluctibus), the English Rosicrucian: life and writings.* Kirkwall: William Peace & Son.

Craven, R. J. (1968). *Count Michael Maier- Doctor of Philosophy and Medicine, Alchemist, Rosicrucian, Mystic.* London: Dawsons of Pall Mall.

d'Alveydre, S.-Y. (1910). *Mission de l'Indie en Europe.* Paris: Librairie Dorbon Ainé.

Davis, S. (2017). *HERMETIC ORDER OF THE GOLDEN DAWN: BIOGRAPHIES OF MEMBERS.*

Democritus Junior. (1883). *The Anatomy of Melancholy: A New Edition.* Philadelphia: E. Claxton & Company.

Dionysius the Areopagite. (1899). *The Celestial Hierarchy.* (1899). www.tertullian.org. https://www.tertullian.org/fathers/areopagite_13_heavenly_hierarchy.htm

Eckartshausen, K. V. (2003). *The cloud upon the sanctuary* (I. de Steiger, Trans.). Ibis Press.

etymonline.com. (2024). *Manifesto*. Retrieved from etymonline.com: https://www.etymonline.com/word/manifesto#etymonline_v_6805

Faulks, P., & Cooper, R. L. (2018). *The Masonic Magician: The Life and Death of Count Cagliostro and his Egyptian Rite*. Watkins Publishing.

Fletcher, M. (2020). The History of the Societas Rosicruciana in Anglia. *SRIA*.

Frizium, J. (1629). *Summum Bonum*. Frankfurt. Retrieved from https://archive.org/details/robert-fludd-summum-bonum-1629/

Galtier, G. (2017). *Maçonnerie égyptienne, Rose-Croix et néo-chevalerie: Les fils de Cagliostro*. DU ROCHER.

Gilbert, R. A. (1987). *Magician of Many Parts*. Northhamptonshire: Crucible.

Gilbert, R. A. (1997). *The Golden Dawn Scrapbook. The Rise and Fall of a Magical Order*. York Beach: Samuel Weiser, Inc.

Gilly, C. (2000). The 'Midnight Lion', the 'Eagle' and the 'Antichrist': Political, religious and chiliastic propaganda in the pamphlets, illustrated broadsheets and ballads of the Thirty Years War. *Brill*.

Gladwin, I. H. (2019, May 19). *Revealing Westcott's Lodge of Secret Chiefs: Lichte, Liebe, Leben - A Golden Dawn Origins Revelation*. Retrieved from Pansophers.com: https://pansophers.com/licht_liebe_leben/

Godwin, J., McIntosh, C., & McIntosh, D. P. (2016). *Rosicrucian Trilogy*. Massachusetts: Weiser Books.

Gould, R. F. (1951). *The Concise History of Freemasonry. Revised Edition*. London: Gale & Polden Limited.

GreekMythology.com. (2025). *Adonis and Aphrodite*. Retrieved from greekmythology.com: https://www.greekmythology.com/Myths/The_Myths/Adonis_and_Aphrodite/adonis_and_aphrodite.html

References

Greensill, T. M. (2003). *A History of Rosicrucian Thought and of the Societas Rosicruciana in Anglia. Second (revised) edition.* Premier Metropolis.

Greer, J. M. (2006). *The Element Encyclopedia of Secret Societies.* London: HarperElement.

Gretser, J. (1618). *Syntagma de S. R. Imperii Sacrosanctis Reliquiis, et Regalibus Monumentis, præsertim de Quadruplici Lancea.* Ingolstadi: Ex officina Ederiana, apud Elisabetham Angermariam Viduam. Sumptibus Ioannis Hertzroi Bibliopolæ Monacensis. Retrieved from https://www.prdl.org/

Hall, M. P. (1928). *The Secret Teachings of All Ages.* San Francisco: H.S. Crocker Company, Incorporated.

Hartmann, F. (1910). *With the Adepts: An adventure among the Rosicricoans. Second edition, revised.* New York: The Theosophical Publishing Co.

Hartmann, F. M. (1888). *Secret Symbols of the Rosicrucians.* Boston: Boston Occult Publishing Company.

Harvey, S. (2023, August 16). *A brief history of the rose.* Retrieved from https://www.worldhistory.org: https://www.worldhistory.org/article/2264/a-brief-history-of-the-rose/

Heindel, A. F. (2012). *Birth of the Rosicrucian Fellowship. The History of its Inception.* Oceanside, California: The Rosicrucian Fellowship.

Heindel, M. (1911). *The Rosicrucian Cosmo-conception.* Chicago: M. A. Donohue & Co. Printers, Binders, Publishers.

Heindel, M. (1922). *The Rosicrucian Philosophy in Questions and Answers. Third edition.* London: L.N.Fowler.

Heindel, M. (2011). *THE TEACHINGS OF AN INITIATE. Eighth Edition.* Retrieved from Rosicrucian.com: https://www.rosicrucian.com/tin/tineng01.htm

Holme, R. H. (1988). Who was C.R.? A Essay to commence discussion. *Societas Rosicruciana in Anglia. Series No. 13.*

Howe, E. (1972). *Fringe Masonry in England, 1870-85*. London: Transactions of the Quatuor Coronati Lodge No. 2076. Retrieved from https://freemasonry.bcy.ca/aqc/fringe/fringe.html

Howe, E. (1984). *The Magicians of the Golden Dawn. A documentary history of a magical order 1887-1923*. Maine: Samuel Weiser, INC.

Huffman, W. (2001). *Western Esoteric Masters Series: Robert Fludd*. Berkeley, California: North Atlantic Books.

Jinarajadasa, C. (1939). *The Meaning and Purpose of the Ritual of the Mystic Star*. Wheaton, Illinois: The Theosophical Press.

Johnsen, D. C. (2014). *Observations in Eddic Astronomy How Passages in the Eddas Act as References to Constellations*. Retrieved from GermanicMythology.com: https://www.germanicmythology.com/ASTRONOMY3/EddaPassages.html

King, F. (1971). *The Rites of Modern Occult Magic*. New York: Macmillan Company.

Lees, A. M. (2013). Some Interesting people from the SRIA Golden Book. *SRIA High Council Library*.

Lévi, É. (1910). *Transcendental Magic: A complete translation of 'Dogme et Rituel de la Haute Magie' by Arthur Edward Waite*. Chicago: de Laurence, Scott & Co.

Lewis, H. S. (1904). Four Special Lessons in Personal Influence hypnotic Suggestion and Treatment by Suggestion. The Essential Points. *The Metropolitan Institute of Sciences Correspondence Course*. Retrieved from http://iapsop.com/archive/materials/wing_lessons/1902__mcintyre_lewis___metropolitan_institute_of_science_correspondence_course.pdf

Lewis, H. S. (1927). *Rosicrucian Manual*. Charleston: Lovett Printing Co.

Lewis, H. S. (1929). *Rosicrucian Questions and Answers with Complete History of the Rosicrucian Order*. San Jose: Rosicrucian Press.

Lewis, H. S. (1930). *Mansions of the Soul*. San Jose: Rosicrucian Press.

Lewis, H. S. (1990). *Rosicrucian Manual.* San Jose: Rosicrucian Order, AMORC.

Libavio, A. (1615). *D.O.M.A. Analysis Confessionis Fraternitatis de Rosea Cruce, pro admonitione et Instructione eorum qui, quid, iudicandum sit de ista noua factione, scire cupiunt.* Frankfurt: Francofurti ad Moenum. Retrieved from https://www.google.com.au/books/edition/D_O_M_A_Analysis_confessionis_fraternita/Rpxj80meCxUC?hl=en&gbpv=0

MacParthy, F. (2021). *The Divine magic of the Golden Rosicrucians (V. Veritatis, Trans.).* Nontron: Sesheta Publications.

Magre, M. (1932). *Magicians, Seers, and Mystics.* New York: E. P. Dutton & Co., Inc.

Maier, M. (1656). *Laws of the Fraternity of the Rosie Crosse (Themis Aurea) with introductionary preface by Manly P. Hall.* Los Angeles: Philosophical Research Society.

Markham, S. E. (2019). *Markham's Brotherhood: The Rosicrucian Manifestos in Modern English.* Ferret Books.

McIntosh, C. (1998). *The Rosicrucians_ The History, Mythology, and Rituals of an Esoteric Order.* San Francisco: Weiser Books.

McIntosh, C. (2011). *Eliphas Levi and the French Occult Revival.* Albany: Suny Press.

McIntosh, C. (2011). *The Rose Cross and the Age of Reason. Eighteenth-Century Rosicrucianism in Central Europe and its relationship to the Enlightenment.* Leiden: Suny Press.

McLean, A., & Godwin, J. (1991). *The Chemical Wedding of Christian Rosenkreutz/ translated by Jocelyn Godwin; introduction and commentary by Adam McLean.* Massachusetts: Phanes Press.

Merriam-Webster. (2024). *Allegory.* Retrieved from merriam-webster.com dictionary: https://www.merriam-webster.com/dictionary/allegory

Merriam-Webster. (2024). *manifesto*. Retrieved from merriam-webster.com dictionary: https://www.merriam-webster.com/dictionary/manifesto

Merriam-Webster. (2024). *Treatise*. Retrieved from merriam-webster.com dictionary: https://www.merriam-webster.com/dictionary/treatise

Montfaucon de Villars, A. H. (1670). *The Comte de Gabalis. 2nd Edition*. Obernkirchen: Black Letter Press.

Noel, D. P. (1995). *The Genesis of the Grade of Scottish Master of St. Andrew*.

Olcott, H. S. (1895). *Old Diary Leaves_The True History of The Theosophical Society*. New York and London: G. P. Putnam's Sons.

Oneal Haye, A. (1868, December 12). The Rosicrucian Society. *Freemasons Magazine and Masonic Mirror*, p. 471.

Ordre kabbalistique de la Rose-Croix. Suprême conseil. (1891). Le Suprême conseil de la Rose-Croix / Ordre kabbalistique de la Rose-Croix. Retrieved from https://gallica.bnf.fr/ark:/12148/bpt6k9613099m

Osborne, M. R. (2025). *Rosicrucian Death: The Manner and Meaning of Death in Modern Rosicrucianism*. Bayonne: Rose Circle Publications.

Péladan, J. (1892, March-April). Ordre de la Rose+Croix du Temple. *Catalogue du Salon de la Rose+Croix*. Retrieved from projectawe.org: https://www.projectawe.org/blog/2015/8/4/making-the-invisible-visible-pladans-vision-of-ensouled-art

Philalethes, E. (1651). *Lumen de Lumine or A new Magicall Light discovered, and Communicated to the world*. London: H. Blunden at the Castle in Corne-Hil. Retrieved from https://archive.org/details/lumendelumineorn00vaug/page/n3/mode/1up?view=theater

Philalethes, E. (1658). *The fame and confession of the Fraternity of R: C: commonly, of the Rosie Cross. With a praeface annexed thereto, and a short declaration of their physicall work*. London: J.M. for G. Calvert. Retrieved from https://archive.org/details/b30340159/page/n9/mode/2up

Pike, A. (1871). *Morals & Dogma of the Ancient and Accepted Scottish Rite of Freemasonry*. Chareleston: Ancient and Accepted Scottish Rite Southern Jurisdiction of the United States.

Profundis, B. (1918). *Confessio R. C. Fraternitatis*. California: Ancient Mystcial Order Rosae Crucis.

Rebisse FRC, C. (2016). The Chymical Wedding. *Rosicrucian Digest, 1*, pp. 2-10.

Rebisse, C. (2005). *Rosicrucian History and Mysteries*. San Jose: Supreme Grand Lodge Of The Ancient and Mystical Order Rosae Crucis.

Robinson, S. (2021). *Alois Mailander: A Rosicrucian Remembered*. Oberstdorf: Pansophic Press.

Rocks, D. T. (1996, July). Mrs. May Banks Stacey. *Theosophical History, VI*(4), pp. 144-150.

Rosicrucian Society of England. (1870, October). Secretary-General's Report. *The Rosicrucian; A Quarterly Record of the Society's Transactions, with occasional notes on Freemasonry, and other kindred subjects*(X).

Samson, C. (2004, July 14). *Secret fraternity roiled again by lawsuit over leadership*. Retrieved from The Morning Call: https://www.mcall.com/2004/07/14/secret-fraternity-roiled-again

Schmidt-Biggemann, W. (2004). *Philosophia Perennis: Historical Outlines of Western Spirituality in Ancient, Medieval, and Early Modern Thought*. Berlin: Springer.

Schultze, H. (1849). *Johannis Valentini Andreae, Theologi Q. Wurttembergensis, VITA, Ab Ipso Conscripta, Ex Autographo, In Bibl. Guelferbytano Recondito, Asumtis Codd. Stuttgartianis, Schorndorfiensi, Tubingensi, nunc primum editit, F. H. Reheinwald, Dr*. Berlin.

Schweighardt, T. (1618). *Speculum Sophicum Rhodostauroticum*. Retrieved from https://www.alchemy-texts.com: https://www.alchemy-texts.com/book/speculum-sophicum-rhodostauroticum/

Sédir, P. (2006). *The Histroy & Doctrine of the Rose-Croix (translated by Piers A. Vaughan)*.

Sigerist, H. E. (1941). *Four Treatises of Theophrastus von Hohenheim called Paracelsus*. Baltimore: The John Hopkins Press.

Sinnett, A. (1886). *Incidents in the Life of Madame Blavatsky*. New York: J. W. Bouton.

Smith, W. B. (2014). Resisting the Rosicrucians: Theories on the Occult Origins of the Thirty Years' War. *Church History and Religious Culture, 94*, 413–443.

Societas Rosicruciana in America. (2025). Retrieved from sria.org: https://sria.org/

Southern California Earthquake Data Center. (2023). *San Jacinto Earthquake*. Retrieved from Southern California Earthquake Data Center: https://scedc.caltech.edu/earthquake/sanjacinto1918.html

Sri Ramatherio. (1927). *The Light of Egypt: The Strange Story of the Rosicrucians*. Tampa: The Ancient and Mystical Order Rosae Crucis.

SRIA Province of Greater London. (2023). *Metropolitan Study Group*. Retrieved from srialondon.org: https://srialondon.org/metropolitan-study-group/

Steiner, R. (1912, February 09). *The Mission of Christian Rosenkreutz GA130*. Retrieved from The Rudolf Steiner Archive: https://rsarchive.org/Lectures/GA130/English/RSP1950/19120209p01.html

Stephenson, A. (1988). Who was C.R.? An essay to commence discussion. *Societas Rosicruciana in Anglia. Series No. 13*.

Stewart, G. L. (1988). Thought of the month: Moving ahead into the future. *Rosicrucian Digest, 66*(4), p. 4.

References

Suedharz-Kyffhaeuser.de. (2021). *Sagen & Mythen*. Retrieved from region-suedharz-kyffhaeuser.de: https://www.region-suedharz-kyffhaeuser.de/sagen-mythen

SuperSummary.com. (2025). *Didacticism*. Retrieved from SuperSummary.com: https://www.supersummary.com/didacticism/

The Ancient and Mystical Order Rosae Crucis. (1916, January). Books Recommended for Study. *The American Rosae Crucis, 1*(1).

The Chicago Sunday Tribune. (1898, April 17). Women organise a Masonic Lodge. p. 1.

The Rosicrucian Digest. (1937, July). The Ancient Tomb of Christian Rosenkreutz? *The Rosicrucian Digest, 15*(6), p. 201. Retrieved from https://archive.org/details/IAPSOP-rosicrucian_digest_v15_n6_1937_jul

Thurston, R. (1925, October). The Science of Alchemy. *The Mystic Triangle, 3*(10).

Tilton, H. (2003). *The Quest for the Phoenix. Spiritual Alchemy and Rosicrucianism in the Work of Count Michael Maier (1569 -1622)*. Berlin, Boston: De Gruyter. doi:doi.org/10.1515/9783110896572

Tilton, H. (2016). The Urim and Thummim and the Origins of the Gold-und Rosenkreuz. Retrieved from https://www.researchgate.net/publication/332697084

Trinca, T. (2024). *The Temple and the Vault: Exploring the Initiatic Stories of Freemasonry, Rosicrucianism and the Western Esoteric Tradition*. London: Lewis Masonic

Volker, J. (2021). *The Brothers Grimm: Astronomical relations to German fairy tales*. Retrieved from Judy-Volker.com: http://judy-volker.com/StarLore/Myths/BrothersGrimm.html

Waite, A. E. (1887). *The Real History of the Rosicrucians*. London: George Redway, York Street, Covent Garden.

Waite, A. E. (1894). *The Hermetic and Alchemical Writings of Aureolus Philippus Theophrastus Bombast of Hohenheim, called Paracelsus the Great. Vol. 1.* London: James Elliott and Co.

Waite, A. E. (1910). *Transcendental Magic. Its Doctrine and Ritual. A complete translation of Dogme et Rituel de la Haute Magie.* Chicago: de Laurence, Scott & Co.

Westcott, W. W. (1888, March 1). ACTA. S.R.I.A. Archives.

Westcott, W. W. (1894, March 2). Rosicrucians, their History and Aims. *Ars Quatour Coronatorum being the transactions of the Lodge Quatour Coronati No. 2076, London*, pp. 36-47.

Westcott, W. W. (1897, March). Notice reporting Dr W. Wynn Westcott's resignation from the Golden Dawn. Ref code GBR 1991 GD 2/5/3/6. Museum of Freemasonry in London.

Westcott, W. W. (1900). *History of the Societas Rosicruciana in Anglia.* London: Privately Printed.

Westcott, W. W. (1908, March). Handwritten Note on Origins of the SRIA- Communicated by the Supreme Magus Dr. W. Westcott. SRIA High Council Library.

Westcott, W. W. (1915). *The Rosicrucians Past and Present, At Home and Abroad.* London: S.R.I.A. High Council Library.

Westenberg, g. (2014). *Max Heindel and The Rosicrucian Fellowship.* Madison, Wisconsin: The Rosicrucian Fellowship MMX U. A.

Westlund, T. (2007). An Overview of the alchemical and magical system of The Gold- und Rosenkreuz Order. Retrieved from https://www.rosae-crucis.net/gurc.pdf

Wilson, H. C. (1937). *Early History of the S.R.I.A._ Chapter 3.*

Wilson, H. C. (1937). The History of the Societas Rosicruciana in Anglia - Part 1. *SRIA HIGH COUNCIL LIBRARY.*

Yates, F. A. (2003). *The Rosicrucian Enlightenment.* New York: Taylor & Francis e-Library.

APPENDIX ONE:
ROSICRUCIAN GROUPS

The decision of whether to include this list is something that I considered carefully. On one hand, a summary of many of the below mentioned Rosicrucian groups has already been presented in other books. I do not desire to repeat the same information that is already available via other authors, organisational propaganda, or Wikipedia.

However, as this book is a *Compendium* and as I have made reference to many of these groups throughout this book, it would be helpful to have a handy quick reference for the reader who may not be already familiar with the facts concerning many of these groups. Secondly, there is still a great deal of information concerning these groups that has not reached the public, either due to the novelty of the research or because of a lack of interest.

But the foundation of many of these groups still has a lot of surprises left in store and you will observe that in some of these summaries, there is a great deal of new information. This is especially the case with G.u.R.C., the Rosicrucians of Toulouse, A.M.O.R.C., and Societas Rosicruciana.

But I wish to make one thing absolutely and abundantly clear: *the inclusion of the below groups suggests nothing about their inherent value.* They have not been included due to any personal bias. And they have not been included because I think their work is in any way superior. Indeed, there are many small Rosicrucian circles existing around the world whose names have never been printed and whose positive influence in the world can be readily observed by those who have familiarity with them. And yet, their names are not included below.

The inclusion of the Rosicrucian groups below is based upon one point, and one point only. These are Rosicrucian groups who have had a significant influence upon the public understanding of the Rosicrucian tradition. It is not an exhaustive list and their inclusion has been purely at my discretion.

However, as it is my belief that such a list is primarily valuable as a reference material, it has not been included in the main body of the book.

Order of the Gold and Rosy Cross (G.u.R.C.)

The Order of the Gold and Rosy Cross (German: *Gold- und Rosenkreuzer*), or *G.u.R.C.* emerged as one of the most influential esoteric societies of the eighteenth century; although their potential origins may stretch much further back with some speculation that this may continue even as far back as the source work era. They were a Masonic-Rosicrucian society that combined esoteric Christian practices with theurgical magic and practical alchemy. Admission was restricted to Master Masons of at least thirty years of age (Westlund, 2007).

Like the formation of many Rosicrucian societies the formation of G.u.R.C. is a tangled web of fact, myth, and legend. Additionally, many of the foundational G.u.R.C. texts were backdated[1] or attributed to pseudonyms[2] making dating them challenging.

The earliest mention of G.u.R.C. appears at the beginning of the eighteenth century through the publication of *The True and Complete Preparation of the Philosopher's Stone of the Brotherhood from the Order of the Golden and Rosy Cross* (German: *Die wahrhafte und volkommene Bereitung des philosophischen Steins der Brüderschafft aus dem Orden des Gulden und Rosen Kreutzes*) by Sincerus Renatus (a pseudonym for Samuel Richter). Although this text is dated at 1710, it is not known if such a group ever existed at this time (Westlund, 2007).

Attempts to trace its history have revealed connections to alchemical societies in Italy as well as to pre-existing European mystical currents. One possible influence is the sixteenth century alchemist Heinrich Khunrath, whose writings describe artefacts fashioned from an alloy known as *electrum magicum,* a material that was used by G.u.R.C. in the construction of instruments that were used for divine communication.

---

1 Such as *Testamentum*
2 Such as, *Heavenly and supernatural mystery of the spirit and soul of the world* (German: *Himmlisches und übernatürliches Geheimnis des Geistes und der Seele der Welt*)

Another more established thread emerges from the work of Ulrich Pfeffer (?–1680), a physician and spiritual writer from Holstein, Germany who had connections to the Quakers as well as to mystics such as Jakob Böhme and Jan Baptist van Helmont. The connection between Pfeffer and G.u.R.C. is partially observed via similarities between a foundational G.u.R.C. text called *Treasure of Treasures* (Latin: *Thesaurus Thesaurum*) and Pfeffer's own works (Tilton, 2016, p. 48). Although Pfeffer himself does not appear to have been a member of any Rosicrucian society, his Kabbalistic and Paracelsian ideas appear to have been quite influential on G.u.R.C.'s doctrines.

However, Pfeffer's spiritual legacy was not restricted to influencing only G.u.R.C., but also to an Italian magical society known as the *Knights of the Golden Cross* (Italian: *Cavalieri dell'Aurea Croce*) which had been active in Venice under the guidance of an enigmatic figure named Friedrich Gualdi (Tilton, 2016, p. 55). In fact, many of the practices of the Italian Knights of the Golden Cross, such as spirit conjurations and angelic operations, would later reappear in the rituals of the German G.u.R.C.

It is likely that a later contributor, often referred to as *pseudo-Gualdi*, played a role in merging these two traditions. Pseudo-Gualdi appears to have respected both Pfeffer and the original Gualdi, and introduced these Italian elements into a new grade system and hierarchical structure, that would go on to become G.u.R.C.

The hierarchical structure of G.u.R.C. is outlined in a compendium of G.u.R.C. alchemical-magical texts, referred collectively as the *Testamentum* (Tilton, 2016, p. 36), which outlines an inner circle of seven *Magi* and seventy-seven initiates. At the heart of their organisational system was the *Ark of the Covenant* which represented a figurative and literal repository for the society's most sacred text: the *Treasure of Treasures*. It is possible that the Ark of the Covenant was real ritual object, but it has not ever been found. However, affiliated initiated societies (such as the *Asiatic Brethren*) are known to have employed a ceremonial representation of the Ark of the Covenant in their ritualistic work.

The leader of G.u.R.C. assumed the title of *Imperator* and was responsible for coordinating and maintaining an extensive network of meeting places. Some temples that we know of were located in Hamburg, Nuremberg, and Amsterdam. After pseudo-Gualdi, the Imperator-ship was likely assumed by a man named *Tobias Schultz*, of whom very little is known.

The society included initiation rituals some of which resembled Masonic ceremonies. These ceremonies employed a variety of ritual implements including bells (likely to resemble those found in the Tomb of C.R.C. in the Fama Fraternitatis) made of electrum magicum and various alchemical stones. The development and use of these devices partially made up their initiatory curriculum. The final grade of the society culminated in the construction of an impressive instrument, incorporating all previously studied techniques. This was referred to as the *Urim and Thummim* (MacParthy, 2021), named after the oracular objects set into the breastplate of the High Priest of Israel, as described in the Book of Exodus. This device was ultimately a very elaborate black mirror which could be used for, amongst other things, scrying.

The teachings of G.u.R.C. included a rather dense amalgam of alchemy, Christian Kabbalah, Hermetic mysticism, and angelic magic. Their system was built upon the assumption that divine knowledge could be recovered through disciplined inner work that incorporated the study of the relationships and correspondences that exist between Man, Nature, and God.

Their alchemical practice was by no means purely speculative but involved serious laboratory experimentation. Some of the ingredients used included substances that could be considered dangerous, such as antimony and mercury, as well as those that would be considered more grotesque, such as animal blood and urine. A recurring motif involved ingesting gold dissolved in one's own urine to achieve visionary states, in an attempt to communicate with planetary intelligences.

G.u.R.C. would rise to prominence following the collapse of Baron von Hund's *Rite of Strict Observance* in 1782 (Tilton, 2003, p. 252). Certain segments of German nobility became rather enchanted by the Rosicrucian ideals presented by G.u.R.C; including Crown Prince Friedrich Wilhelm of Prussia, who was initiated into the rank of Magus (the highest grade) in 1783 (Tilton, 2016, p. 44).

In addition to the Testamentum and Treasure of Treasures, several other manuscripts related to G.u.R.C. have survived. However, most of these manuscripts received little attention from later Rosicrucian organisations, with the notable exception of the widely circulated, *The Secret Symbols of the Rosicrucians* (German: *Geheime Figuren der Rosenkreuzer*) which became quite popular in contemporary Rosicrucian groups.

The Secret Symbols of the Rosicrucians was first published in Altona in 1785 and re-printed in 1788 as a compendium of emblematic plates. It was almost certainly tied to G.u.R.C., although its author and compiler remain unknown. Many of the aphorisms and motifs in the Secret Symbols of the Rosicrucians overlap with language found in the Testamentum, suggesting their shared authorship and values. The book's layout resembles that of a devotional text with emblems and text being presented for contemplation and reflection.

Franz Hartmann was likely the first to present translations of some of the emblems of The Secret Symbols of the Rosicrucians in 1888. In 1935, A.M.O.R.C. would produce their own translation and reproduction of the text, including some manuscript sources that were unavailable to Hartmann. The Secret Symbols of the Rosicrucians remains a fantastic contemplative text from this era of Rosicrucianism.

Yet, the popularity of G.u.R.C. was not without opposition. Another para-Masonic society would be established by Hans Heinrich von Ecker und Eckhoffen, an ex-member of G.u.R.C. This group was called, *The Asiatic Brethren of St. John the Evangelist in Europe* (German: *Die Brüder St. Johannes des Evangelisten aus Asien in Europa*). This rival group was more inclusive then G.u.R.C., welcoming Jewish members, and also incorporated Jewish mysticism into its doctrines. This rivalry would reduce G.u.R.C.'s popularity.

In 1781, an exposé of G.u.R.C. materials appeared in the form of a book called, *The Rosicrucian in his Nakedness* (German: *Der Rosenkreuzer in seiner Blöße*). The exposé was authored by Magister Pianco, widely believed to be a pseudonym for Ecker und Eckhoffen; although, he himself denied having written it. In this work, Magister Pianco outlined his *doubts* concerning the Masonic-Rosicrucian society. He condemned G.u.R.C. as being Godless, their magic as being wicked, their interpretation of scripture as being false and blasphemous, and even claimed that the members fees were being embezzled by the chiefs of the society. This publication caused great embarrassment to the group leading to a deterioration in their standing within masonic society. Nevertheless, like most good exposés, Pianco's does allow us a glimpse into the rituals and practices of the society, even if we must be mindful that the narrator is somewhat unreliable.

Another opposition faced by G.u.R.C. was the publication of a text called *Authentic message from the Knight and Brother Initiates from Asia* (German: *Authentische Nachricht von den Ritter- und Bruder-Eingeweihten aus Asien*) in 1787 by Friedrich Münter, a scientist, Freemason, and member of the Illuminati[3]. In this text, Münter would condemn both G.u.R.C. and The Asiatic Brethren for mixing theology with alchemy, warning that this combination threatened both reason and social order stating,

> *If the Rosicrucians continue for another half century in the way that they have begun, then philosophy and enlightened science will be ousted; we shall have no more history or philosophical theology; monkish legends, priestly hocus-pocus and superstition will*

---

[3] Anybody wishing to learn more about the conflict between the Illuminati and the Order of the Gold and Rosy Cross would benefit by seeking out Christopher McIntosh's work, *The Rose Cross in the Age of Reason*.

possess the thrones; the princes, already deceived by swindlers, will all become royal priests and will learn from the despotism of the order yet more fearful despotism. (McIntosh, 2011, p. 72)

Another threat to the popularity of G.u.R.C. was a 1785 edict, or *Freemason Patent* (German: *Freimaurerpatent*) issued by the Holy Roman Emperor Joseph II which restricted the operations of esoteric and Masonic groups. Although this was primarily addressed to the Illuminati, G.u.R.C. was caught up in the cross-fire (McIntosh, 2011, p. 136).

By the early 1790's, all of these factors would lead to internal schisms and the decline of the once popular Masonic-Rosicrucian society. By the end of the eighteenth century, Rosicrucianism had begun to be associated with charlatanry and deceit. Despite this however, some remnants of the G.u.R.C. tradition remained active, with at least one known group continuing under the leadership of Prince Karl of Salm-Reifferscheidt (McIntosh, 2011, p. 67) in his castle located in Rájec, Czech Republic (then part of the Austrian Empire). The influence of G.u.R.C. would also continue on in contemporary Rosicrucian societies, notably with the inclusion of G.u.R.C. ideas (mostly from *The Secret Symbols of the Rosicrucians*) as well as the adoption of their degree naming system, which has become commonplace in most contemporary Rosicrucian organisations.

Appendix One

The Rosicrucians of Toulouse

The French city of Toulouse has an enduring association with mystical activity.

Toulouse was the capital of the old French province of Languedoc, where Lord Raymond VI, Count of Toulouse, maintained an atmosphere of tolerance and intellectual freedom.

This atmosphere attracted Troubadours, Gnostic sects, and esoteric thinkers who flourished in the late-twelfth and early-thirteenth centuries.

The region became a haven for diverse spiritual movements some of which challenged the authority and dogma of the Catholic Church. The Cathars especially with their dualistic worldview and emphasis on inner purity, posed a theological threat to the Catholic Church, which responded with the brutal Albigensian Crusade wherein over 200,000 Cathars were brutally killed.

Nevertheless, the romance of the region popularised ideas such as divine love, inner rebellion, and mystical idealism. This legacy would echo centuries later in the symbolic language of Rosicrucianism, which championed very similar ideals and also under the shadow of orthodoxy (albeit, without the threat of genocide).

The Rosicrucians of Toulouse were Catholic but they were anything but conventional. In fact, it is likely that their religious beliefs protected them from censure and also allowed them to participate in some of the more militaristic chivalric societies, the spirit of which can still be seen preserved in some Rosicrucian societies today; most notably A.M.O.R.C. and O.K.R.+C.

Another common association we see amongst the Rosicrucians of Toulouse is a shared aversion to Freemasonry. In fact, they were not shy in pointing out the differences between the *Rose-Croix* of Freemasonry (which they deemed as sacrilegious) and the true *Rose+Croix*.

When it comes to self-identification, the Rosicrucians of Toulouse seldom overtly proclaimed themselves as Rosicrucians, and if they did, it was typically done in an ambiguous or cryptic manner, such as including cryptic symbols like a '+' in their signature.

The Rosicrucians of Toulouse were actively involved in various professional and academic societies, some of which still continue in Toulouse today. These include:

- **The Archaeological Society for the South of France** (French: *La Société archéologique du Midi de la France*);

- **The Floral Games Academy** (French: *Académie des Jeux Floraux*);

- **Toulouse Academy of Sciences** (French: *Académie des sciences de Toulouse*);

- **Academy of Inscriptions and Belle-Lettres** (French: *Académie des Inscriptions et Belles-Lettres*).

And several initiatic organisations, such as:

- **Sovereign Pyramid of the Friends of the Desert** (French: *Souveraine Pyramide des Amis du Désert*);

- A Catholic chivalric society possibly derived from *The Knights of Faith*.

Their affiliation with these academies suggests that their pursuits were not only mystical but also intellectual, artistic, and civic.

The earliest traceable figure in this network is Viscount Louis-Charles-Édouard de Lapasse (1792–1867), a nobleman and parliamentarian whose legacy would influence the cultural and spiritual milieu of Toulouse. From Lapasse, a lineage of thinkers, artists, and mystics gradually emerged who can be loosely defined as the *Rosicrucians of Toulouse*.

Appendix One

Lapasse was born in Toulouse on 21 January 1792. Born into Spanish nobility that settled in Languedoc in the thirteenth century[4], Lapasse's early life included military service and diplomatic roles. However, the Revolution of 1830 disrupted his career, affording him the freedom to pursue his esoteric interests.

During his travels, Lapasse resided in Palermo, Sicily. Here he became an archaeologist and discovered alchemy, Hermetic sciences, and Rosicrucianism. We learn from Lapasse's disciple that Lapasse was initiated here by an elderly man, Prince Balbiani who himself had been a student of Cagliostro (Boissin, 1890).

Prince Balbiani possessed a vast library of occult manuscripts, instructed Lapasse in Kabbalah and alchemy. He emphasised the distinction between the true Rosicrucians and their Masonic namesakes, asserting that genuine Rosicrucians operated outside Masonic associations.

In a conversation related to Lapasse, Balbiani would state,

> *Freemasonry has given one of its degrees the denomination of Rose-Croix, the vulgar confuse the masons arrived at this tenebrous dignity with the Brothers of the Rose-Croix, whose institution dates back to the fifteenth century. The vulgar are mistaken. True Rosicrucians are outside Masonic associations of High Science. An alchemist, Andréas Valentin, succeeded in deciphering these talismanic inscriptions and re-established the Society of which Rosencreutz had laid the foundations. The Edelphes (as the Rose-Croix were then called) pledged to practice medicine gratuitously, to meet once a year in a general convent, to hasten the reign of the pure Spirit, to hold at last under the faith of the oath their doctrines hidden from the vulgar. They had found a new idiom to express the nature of beings. Crollius, in his Treatise on Signature Rerum, gives the alphabet. They had the secrets of longevity. They*

---

4 Although another biographer, Fernand de Rességuier put this date at 1090.

> *had learned all the teachings contained in the library of Ptolemy-Philadelphus. Heirs of the Eumolpides[5], depositaries of the mysteries of Isis, they had discovered the true philosopher's stone, divine nectar, terror of death, elixir of old people, joy of maturity, flame of youth!* (Boissin, 1890)

Prince Balbiani supposedly kept a small crystal vial filled with a transparent liquid. The biographer does not state what the liquid is, other than that he had inherited it from a hermit and that it had been blessed by Pope Benedict XIV.

Of the Rosicrucians, Prince Balbiani further relates,

> *Their only common bond today is the study of doctrines which prolong life while preserving health; their aim is the search for the formula which will realise these doctrines and facilitate their practical application. Persevere, my young friend, in the study of science par excellence, and you will be able to render services to humanity much more effective than those which it derives from official medicine.* (Boissin, 1890)

It is not known who Prince Balbiani was. Tobias Churton speculates that his name may refer to the title of *prince* in an Egyptian Masonic Rite (Churton, 2016, p. 257). This is a fair speculation. However, this was during the Kingdom of Two Sicily's, so narrowing down Princes can prove challenging as their were no doubt many at the time who felt they deserved this title. There was a Bishop in Trent by the name of Prince Pietro Vigilio Thun who had links with Cagliostro and who was interested in the occult (Faulks & Cooper, 2018, p. 81). However, he died when Lapasse was only a young boy. Lapasse then departs for France with a letter of recommendation addressed to Marquis d'Ourches[6]. The Marquis maintained a tremendous library of occult

---

5   The Eumolpidae were the priests who maintained the Eleusinian Mysteries during the Hellenic era.

6   Upon his death, Marquis d'Ourches offered two prizes of a grand-total of 5000 francs in his last will and testament to any person that could provide

literature and it was here that Lapasse became further acquainted with magic, magnetism, and natural medicine, particularly the works of Paracelsus, Robert Fludd, and David de Planis-Campy. At the age of sixty, Lapasse registered as a student at the Faculty of Medicine in Paris and commenced a medical degree that he would not complete.

Afterwards, Lapasse returns to Toulouse and establishes medical clinic. In true Rosicrucian fashion, he did not charge patients. This is despite the fact that most of his patients received an alchemical elixir made with gold. Lapasse asserted that this recipe was from Cagliostro himself. Lapasse was not short of admirers and from them we learn that he was intelligent, well-read, multi-lingual (including fluency in several dead languages), and was an admirer of the arts; especially poetry, of which he was said to have composed many himself. By all accounts Lapasse was a talented physician, even if his treatments were unorthodox. He was easily recognisable in Toulouse by his eccentric hats and habit of breathing with pursed lips and puffed cheeks; an unusual breathing technique attributed to his belief in breath hygiene and capturing vital force from the air.

From Lapasse, we find an array of individuals whom he introduced into the Rosicrucian tradition.

One such person was an archaeologist, Alexandre Du Mège (1780-1862). Du Mège was an initiate in an Egyptian styled initiatic group called, The Sovereign Pyramid of the Friends of the Desert[7]. The Sovereign Pyramid itself was founded by Baron Philippe Picot de Lapeyrouse, another of Toulouse's cultural luminaries. Lapeyrouse, like many of his intellectual contemporaries, was a member of

evidence of how to discern real death from apparent death. This was to prevent accidental live burials. His request defines the conditions of the submissions. The major prize was to utilise a simple method that could be employed by the layman. The second minor prize was to utilise more advanced methods that could only be employed by skilled individuals. Given the Marquis' peers, library, and generosity, it may be that he was also initiated into the Toulouse R+C.

7 Further information regarding The Sovereign Pyramid including reproductions from original manuscripts can be found in The Temple and the Vault, published by Lewis Masonic.

multiple academic societies and also an active Freemason. During Du Mège's time, Lapeyrouse held the role of Archivist and contributed to furnishing the initiatory spaces of the society. Du Mège himself took the title *Sovereign Prince*.

The ideal layout of a pyramid (or lodge-room) for The Sovereign Pyramid of the Friends of the Desert was a triangle, although rectangles could be used if space was an issue. The entrance to the pyramid is guarded by two sphinxes and the walls were painted to look like granite with the walls lined with hieroglyphics.

There are some similarities between The Sovereign Pyramid and Egyptian Freemasonry including an Osirian version of the Hiramic myth (where Hiram is substituted by Osiris and the ruffians are replaced by Typhon).

Initiates were encouraged to read the works Antoine Court de Gébelin, notably his magnum opus (a considerable unfinished nine volume book series that remained unfinished upon his death) *Primitive World analysed and compared with the Modern World* (French: *Monde Primitif, analysé et comparé avec le monde modern*) which explored ancient mythology as allegory. In this work, Court de Gébelin analysed the origins of language and writing, suggesting that language emerged naturally with man's interaction with nature and the heavens. Court de Gébelin's pioneering investigations into the tarot as a repository of esoteric wisdom is also notable. Other recommended readings for the society included Herodotus's *History of Egypt* (likely the source of the Osiris allegory used in the society's rituals) and Iamblichus's Neoplatonic philosophy.

An example of an opening address that Du Mège offered in The Sovereign Pyramid was,

> *The Seventh Sun of the month of Thoth the year 3601, the most August and Most Sovereign Pyramid of the Friends of the desert extraordinarily assembled, the session opened by the ordinary invocation to the God of the worlds.*
> (Trinca, 2025, p. 120)

A pivotal figure in the later Rosicrucian current of Toulouse was Adrien Péladan (1844–1885), elder brother to the more well-known Joséphin Péladan. While Joséphin would become an iconic figure in Parisian occultism, Adrien's role was foundational to his brother's Rosicrucian beliefs. In Joséphin Péladan's book *How to become a mage* (French: *Comment on devient mage*), Joséphin credits Adrien with his *Rose+Croix initiation*, portraying him as one of the last true Rosicrucians of Toulouse.

After Adrien's death, a poignant obituary appeared in a Toulouse journal called *Messager de Toulouse*. In this obituary, the author states that Adrien was a Rosicrucian and he asks the readers, '*...not to confuse Catholic Rosicrucians with Freemasonry Rosicrucians...*' the latter of which he calls '*imbeciles*' and '*scoundrels*'. He states that the true Rosicrucians have nothing in common with their Masonic namesakes, and that the true Rosicrucians are more interested in the,

> *...mysterious law of numbers, the secrets of alchemy and spagyrics, the mysteries of nature, all for improving progress, for the relief of human suffering and for the greater glory of God.* (Galtier, 2017, p. 240)

The author goes on to call Adrien,

> *A learned generaliser above all, who desired a universal synthesis which, going back to the very sources of science, would make it possible to consider it as a whole, to cover all its developments, to decipher all the hieroglyphs, and to demonstrate that, upon all the manifestations of nature God has inscribed his revelatory Word.* (Galtier, 2017, p. 240)

The author also suggests that Adrien was a disciple of Viscount de Lapasse. This obituary was signed by, '*A Catholic R+C*'. Gerard Galtier in his impressive work on Egyptian Freemasonry states that Firmin Boissin (1835-1893) was the person concealed behind this pseudonym. This is most likely the case, evidenced by Boissin having been in the habit of signing his name in a similar manner on other occasions and by the fact that he was editor of the journal at the time of its publication.

The Péladan family's Catholic loyalties also extended into a Neo-Templar lineage. Joséphin records receiving a Neo-Templar affiliation from his father, who was associated with the *Neo-Templery of Genoude and Lourdoueix*. These figures, defenders of traditional Catholic values, had founded a newspaper to counter monarchist influence, a publication eventually edited by Adrien and Joséphin's father, Adrien Péladan Sr (1815-1890). This Neo-Templar group may have descended from the *Knights of the Faith*, a Catholic secret society formed by Ferdinand de Bertier in 1810. Convinced that Freemasonry had catalysed the Revolution that led to his father's death, Bertier established the Knights of the Faith as a counter-Masonic organisation, comprised of four hierarchical grades: *Charity Member, Equerry, Knight Hospitaller*, and *Knight of the Faith*. Curiously, the A.M.O.R.C. Temple initiatory tradition also includes a reference to the *Knight of the Faith*.

The continuity of Toulouse's Rosicrucian current is also seen in Firmin Boissin's own career. Known under the pseudonym *Simon Brugal*, Boissin was a respected writer, journalist, and eventual Keeper of the Floral Games Academy. Joséphin Péladan referred to him as *Commander of the Rose+Croix of the Temple and Prior of Toulouse*, indicating his central role in the final expressions of the movement. Anybody interested in exploring the personalities involved in the Toulouse Rosicrucian movement would benefit from obtaining a copy of, Boissin's 1890 work *Excentriques Disparus* which offers a short biography of many of these figures. In a similar spirit, local Toulousain Christian Attard has recently released *Etranges Toulousains* (published by *Editions Philomène Alchimie*) which provides a similar biography to some strange Toulousains, many of whom were acquainted with the R+C of Toulouse. Additionally, collaborative efforts between myself and Lyonnaise researcher, Francis Meinsohn have recently revealed the identity of *Frater Donjon* from H. Spencer Lewis's *A Pilgrim's Journey to the East* legend as *Rozes de Brousse* (1876-1960). De Brousse was a journalist, poet, lawyer, as well as Permanent Secretary of the Floral Games Academy. Truly, there is still much more waiting to be discovered by this mysterious group of Rosicrucian noblemen.

By the early nineteenth century, the Rosicrucian current that appeared in Toulouse with Viscount de Lapasse appeared to have gone dormant, details being maintained by only a few individuals. It was these individuals which H. Spencer Lewis would encounter in 1909.

Kabbalistic Order of the Rose-Cross

The Kabbalistic Order of the Rose-Cross (French: *Ordre Kabbalistique de la Rose-Croix*) or O.K.R.+C. was established in Paris in 1888 by the poet and occultist Stanislas de Guaita, together with the mystic and artist Joséphin Péladan. Conceived as both an initiatory fraternity and a teaching body, the O.K.R.+C. quickly became a nexus for esoteric revival in fin-de-siècle France. Among its prominent early members were Gérard Encausse (better known as, Papus), the spiritual writer Paul Sédir, Albert Faucheux (better known as, F.-Ch. Barlet), Calixte Mélinge (better known as, Abbé Alta), and the composer Claude Debussy.

The O.K.R.+C. distinguished itself by combining initiatory symbolism with formal instruction in esoteric sciences. It operated as a university for the study of Hermeticism, Christian Kabbalah, and occult philosophy. Members could attain academic-style degrees through a structured program involving written theses and oral examinations. These degrees reflected the O.K.R.+C.'s aspiration to bridge the gap between spiritual discipline and intellectual rigour. This dual commitment, to inner spiritual development and outer cultural influence, was perhaps what placed the O.K.R.+C at the heart of the French occult revival.

Tensions within the Order itself soon emerged. In 1891, Péladan split from de Guaita and the O.K.R.+C, publicly rejecting operative magic and what he saw as an overly rationalised occultism. In its place, he founded the, *Order of the Catholic and Aesthetic Rose-Cross of the Temple and the Grail* (French: *Ordre de la Rose-Croix Catholique et Esthétique du Temple et du Graal*). Péladan's new order was devoted less to occult instruction and more to spiritual renewal through art, beauty, and Catholic mysticism. His flamboyant persona and theatrical sensibilities attracted a following among Symbolist artists, culminating in the famous *Salons de la Rose+Croix*. Though the schism was never formally reconciled, both strands of Rosicrucianism went on to influence later esoteric currents in Europe and the U.S.A.

Appendix One

After its energetic beginnings the O.K.R.+C., faded from prominence in the early twentieth century, largely due to the deaths or withdrawal of its key figures and the fragmentation of the French occult milieu.

Stanislas de Guaita died in 1897 at the age of 36, cutting short his intellectual and spiritual leadership of the Order. Papus, who had been a central figure in both the O.K.R.+C., and the broader Martinist movement, became increasingly occupied with his own initiatory systems and eventually focused his energies on the Martinist Order (French: *Ordre Martiniste*), which grew to overshadow the O.K.R.+C., in terms of institutional longevity.

With the loss of its founders and the absence of any strong organisational successor, the O.K.R.+C., gradually ceased to function as a formal body. Unlike some contemporary esoteric groups, it did not evolve into a mass-membership organisation or leave behind a robust administrative structure that could outlast its charismatic leaders. However, its teachings and influence were absorbed into related currents, especially the Martinist Order, the Gnostic Church of France, and certain strands of fringe French Masonic rites.

In the modern era, various independent groups have arisen that claim inspiration or lineal descent from the original O.K.R.+C.

Societas Rosicruciana

The Societas Rosicruciana in Anglia (S.R.I.A.) was founded in London on June 1 1867 by two Freemasons, Robert Wentworth Little and William James Hughan.

In 1866, Little and Hughan came into contact with a non-Masonic Rosicrucian society in Scotland named, *Edinburgh, The Grand Council of the Rosicrucians of Scotland* (sometimes referred to as *The Rosicrucian Society of Scotland*- not to be confused with the later *Societas Rosicruciana in Scotia*).

The origins of this Scottish Rosicrucian society are not entirely known, but they were descended from an earlier English Rosicrucian society about which even less in known, save that they had members based in Cambridge university. There has been some speculation about whether this could be related to the *Cambridge Platonists,* who also have some tenuous links with Rosicrucian settlements on the west coast of the USA. However, any link between the Cambridge Platonists and the Rosicrucian society based in Cambridge would need to account for the approximately 100-year gap between the two movements.

This Scottish society met in Edinburgh and was led by their *Magus Maximus,* Anthony Oneal Haye. While Little and Hughan's progression within this society was documented within the S.R.I.A.'s membership register, the *Golden Book,* it is highly unlikely that these events actually took place, with later evidence suggesting that Little and Hughan had only attained the grades of Zelator and Theoricus respectively. Nor is it likely that either of these men were given an authority to establish a new Rosicrucian society. However, Hughan did receive a charter which provides permission for an English branch of the non-Masonic Scottish Rosicrucian society.

Regardless, Little and Hughan proceeded to form an English Rosicrucian society that adopted the rituals of the Scottish Rosicrucian society. The original name of the English society was *The Rosicrucian Society of England or Brethren of the Rosy Cross.* In the 1890's, the society would formally adopt a Latin variation of this name, *Societas Rosicruciana in Anglia*.

The inaugural meeting of this society took place on June 1 1867 at the George Hotel in Aldermanbury, London. There were seven Fratres in attendance which was chaired by Little. Hughan was not present but was elected Deputy Master-General.

Around the turn of the twentieth century, particularly under the influence of Dr William Wynn Westcott, a legendary foundation history for the S.R.I.A. would begin to emerge. The primary motivations behind employing this legendary foundation is not known for certain. Although, it is possible he was trying to divert attention away from Little's account of how the society was founded[8].

Westcott's legend was first presented in 1894 and expanded upon in 1900. It consists of two main parts:

1. **Mackenzie and the German Adepts**
   This part claims that a fellow Freemason Kenneth R. H. Mackenzie had made contact with descendants of an old Rosicrucian fraternity while in Germany. He was allegedly initiated into their system and received permission to form a Rosicrucian society for Freemasons in England. In this account, Westcott presents Mackenzie as the *philosophical* founder of the S.R.I.A.

2. **The Venetian Ambassador and the Freemasons' Hall Vault Rituals**
   This part suggested that prior to the S.R.I.A.'s founding, a Venetian Ambassador conferred Rosicrucian grades and knowledge upon students in England. Westcott states that the last remaining custodian of this lineage was Brother William Henry White, who served as the Grand Secretary of the United Grand Lodge of England (between 1813-

---

8 This theory is detailed more completely in *The Temple and the Vault* published by *Lewis Masonic*.

56) and that White preserved the ritual documents in the vaults of Freemasons' Hall and used these to initiate Little into a German Rosicrucian lineage. When White retired, he passed these imperfect ceremonial papers onto Little.

According to Westcott's legend, Little, now being equipped with Mackenzie's Rosicrucian authorisation and White's incomplete ritual manuscripts from the vaults of Freemasons' Hall, thereby held an authority to establish a Rosicrucian society in England. As we can see, in Westcott's version of the S.R.I.A. history, Oneal Haye and his Scottish Rosicrucian society become of secondary importance. In fact, Oneal Haye is only ever mentioned in passing as an *assistant* in Little's endeavours.

However, like all legends, we should not pass this one off as completely fictional as there certainly are some elements worthy of consideration, especially regarding the noble Austro-Hungarian Apponyi family.

Nevertheless, given that William Henry White passed away in 1866 and Kenneth R. H. Mackenzie in 1886, they were unable to contest Westcott's assertions, leaving him with the opportunity to shape the narrative as he pleased. It seems plausible that Westcott integrated factual elements with a touch of mystique to construct a new legendary history for the S.R.I.A.

Mackenzie was a member of the S.R.I.A. and a respected scholar. Yet, a letter written by Mackenzie in 1881 explicitly states that he believed the S.R.I.A. rituals were unrelated to *"real Rosicrucianism,"* and that the *"real degrees"* he possessed were different and could not be communicated freely. This contradicts Westcott's portrayal of Mackenzie as the source of the S.R.I.A.'s Rosicrucian lineage and rituals. Furthermore, a letter cited by Westcott to support the story of White and the vault rituals has been shown to refer to a different society altogether, the *Red Cross of Constantine and Rome*, and the author, Ravenshaw, had never been an S.R.I.A. member.

It is more likely that Westcott may have been attempting to rebrand or reinvent the history of the S.R.I.A. to divert attention away from Little's historical deceptions about lineage or to inject new life into the society. By using imaginative language and symbolic elements like a *vault* and *German adepts*, Westcott crafted a legendary history that resonated with the broader Rosicrucian mythos.

Ultimately however, like other Rosicrucian organisations, the physical S.R.I.A. is partially shaped by the inspiration derived from the Rosicrucian mythos, and its foundational legend. Regardless of its historicity, it served the purpose of uniting members by claiming a connection to a pre-existing tradition and bolstering the society's sense of authenticity. In the end, what could be more Rosicrucian then a group of seekers, united together in purpose, attempting to discover *The Hidden Mysteries of Nature and Science*.

Since its establishment as a single college in London on 1 June 1867, the S.R.I.A. has undergone remarkable expansion, evolving into an international society with a prominent global presence. Presently, it encompasses twenty-two provinces and boasts over eighty active colleges worldwide. The cumulative membership of the S.R.I.A. is nearing eleven thousand (Fletcher, 2020) with a current membership of nearly two thousand members. It fosters a vibrant community of dedicated fratres who actively engage in and contribute to the society's pursuits.

Additionally, the S.R.I.A. has facilitated the formation of several daughter/granddaughter societies, which operate independently (although, usually with great amity). These include *Societas Rosicruciana in Scotia* (S.R.I.S.), active in Scotland, Hong Kong, Finland, and Australia; *Societas Rosicruciana in Civitatibus Foederatis* (S.C.R.I.C.F.), active in the United States of America, Canada, the Philippines, Panama, Brazil, and Bolivia; and *Societas Rosicruciana in Lusitania* (S.R.I.L.), active in Portugal and Italy. Together, these independent organisations are often referred to as *Societas Rosicruciana* or as *SocRos*.

As you can see, there is a rather systematic naming convention that has been applied to the daughter and grand-daughter societies of the Societas Rosicruciana in Anglia. But there is one very obvious and confusing outcast to these; the *Societas Rosicruciana in America*. Locally, this organisation is often given the acronym, *S.R.I.A.* Naturally, you can imagine how confusing this can be when considering the broader Societas Rosicruciana tradition and how it can be confused for the London-based Masonic-Rosicrucian society that bears the same acronym. Nevertheless, the Societas Rosicruciana in America is strictly independent of the former Societas Rosicruciana traditions.

The Societas Rosicruciana in America was formed in 1907 by Sylvester Clark Gould and George Winslow Plummer, both of whom had connections with Freemasonry and esoteric circles in the United States. The inspiration came from the Societas Rosicruciana in Anglia (S.R.I.A.).

However, unlike its British counterpart, the American branch broke away from requiring Masonic membership, making it open to non-Masons, including women in 1916 (Societas Rosicruciana in America, 2025). The reason for this divergence would appear to be both practical and philosophical. Certainly, the American founders believed Rosicrucianism should be more inclusive and should not be confined to Freemasons.

Like many Rosicrucian societies, the Societas Rosicruciana in America has experienced periods of decline and revival. A significant revival period occurred under Plummer (nomen mysticum, Frater KHEI), who would assume leadership of the society following Gould's death in 1909. Plummer was instrumental in giving the group a more public face as well as helping to provide it with much of the distinguishing character that it has today.

Under Plummer's leadership, The Societas Rosicruciana in America developed its own distinct system of degrees and teachings, many of which incorporated Christian mysticism, alchemy, Kabbalah, and Hermeticism.

The Hermetic Order of the Golden Dawn (H.O.G.D.)

The Hermetic Order of the Golden Dawn[9] (H.O.G.D.) was an initiatic society that taught occult Hermeticism and metaphysics in Great Britain at the turn of the twentieth century. As a magical order, it taught and practiced theurgy and spiritual development. This influential group played a significant role in the shaping of modern magical and ritual practices that would go on to influence countless later magical fraternal societies.

The H.O.G.D. was established by three Freemasons: William Robert Woodman, William Wynn Westcott, and Samuel Liddell Mathers. However, it was Westcott who was the driving force in the establishment of the organisation. The H.O.G.D. was an initiatory order arranged in a hierarchical organisational structure, admitting both men and women on an equal basis.

In a similar manner as S.R.I.A. the H.O.G.D. contained nine grades over three orders. The curriculum of the First Order was one of personal development that explored an esoteric philosophy rooted in Hermetic Kabbalah as well as including the study of astrology, tarot, and geomancy. In contrast, the Second or Inner Order, known as *Rosae Rubeae et Aureae Crucis*, included more advanced practices, such as scrying, astral travel, and alchemy. Finally, the Third Order comprised the *Secret Chiefs*, highly skilled beings thought to communicate with the chiefs of the Second Order and guide the lower two orders through spiritual communication.

The H.O.G.D.'s fusion of ancient wisdom, mystical symbols, and occult practices would become a hallmark of their teachings, attracting seekers and scholars alike to join their ranks and would pave the way for the H.O.G.D. to become a renowned and enigmatic esoteric society that would leave a lasting mark on the landscape of Western occultism.

---

9   The inaugural summons used the name, *ORDER OF THE G.D. IN THE OUTER.*

The first temple of the H.O.G.D., was established in London in March 1888. Westcott claimed that this temple was affiliated with a German Order called *Golden Dawn* (German: *Goldene Dammerung*), from which they derived their authority. The founders received this authority from an enigmatic individual known as *Fräulein Sprengel*, often referred to by the magical motto, *Sapiens Dominabitur Astris* or *S.D.A*. Westcott discovered the contact information for S.D.A. in a set of coded manuscripts he had received from the late Rev. Adolphus Frederick Alexander Woodford.

The organisational structure of the H.O.G.D. was led by three chiefs: the Imperator to command, the Praemonstrator to instruct, and the Cancellarius to record (Gilbert, 1997, p. 60). The functions of these chiefs mirrored the functions of the three leaders in an S.R.I.A. College (Gilbert, 1987, p. 107). Woodman assumed the role of Imperator (similar to an S.R.I.A. College *Celebrant*); Westcott assumed the role of Cancellarius (similar to an S.R.I.A. College *Secretary*); and Mathers assumed the role of Praemonstrator (similar to an S.R.I.A. College *Conductor of Novices*)[10].

In 1888, the three chiefs established Isis-Urania Temple No.3. According to *The Golden Dawn's Official History Lecture* composed by Westcott, the first Golden Dawn Temple was named, *Light, Love, Life*[11] (German: *Licht, Liebe, Leben*) and was formed by, "*...a group of Continental Mystics who have not been in the habit of performing ceremonies in open Lodge but have conferred the grades chiefly in privacy and in the presence of two or three members...*". The second Temple was Hermanubis No. 2 which had, "*...ceased to exist owing to the decease of all its Chiefs*".

---

10 Westcott's personal notebook states, "*The S.M. (Woodman) Sec. Gen (Westcott) & S.L.M. warranted the 0° grade for outsiders for practical work* (Westcott W. W., ACTA, 1888)".

11 Indeed, a *Light, Love, Life* lodge did exist in Germany, but a question remains as to whether this provides evidence to confirm a pre-existing H.O.G.D. current or whether Westcott had come across this information and used it to bolster his own narrative (Gladwin, 2019).

Appendix One   337

In December 1891, Woodman would pass away after a brief illness, leaving Westcott and Mathers in control of the order. Woodman also left a private letter nominating Westcott as head of the S.R.I.A. In 1892, a Second Order would be added to the H.O.G.D. curriculum. This Second Order would be known as, the *Ordo Rosae Rubeae et Aureae Crucis*. The rituals for the Second Order were largely credited to Mathers.

In 1896, Westcott would dissolve his association with the H.O.G.D[12]. This was likely influenced by pressure from his employer after some of his personal papers were misplaced and became public.

There are indications that someone might have been attempting to force Westcott out of the society. In a letter dated March 1897 to Frederick Leigh Gardner (1857-1930), Westcott expressed,

> *So I had no alternative - I cannot think who it is that persecutes me - someone must talk.* (Howe, 1984, pp. 165-166)

This was followed by descriptions of Mathers' *wrath* against him.

Intriguingly, in 1911, Aleister Crowley (using the pseudonym Leo Vincey) made reference to this incident, suggesting that Mathers was envious of Westcott's authority, had orchestrated his removal from the society, and strongly insinuated that Mathers had leaked H.O.G.D. manuscripts with Westcott's name on them (Howe, 1984, p. 167).

Mathers would nominate Henry Burry Pullen and Florence Farr to leadership roles, although Mathers maintained himself at the top of the leadership hierarchy. In 1899, dissent emerged within the adept ranks. The dissent resulted from several causes. Firstly, there was a general concern regarding Mathers' leadership and his

---

12 Notice written in the hand of Dr W. Wynn Westcott to the Adepti in Britannia, stating that for personal reasons S. A. [Sapere Aude, 5=6, degree motto of Dr W. W. Westcott] has been obliged to resign from all the offices he held within the Golden Dawn and Second Orders from 16 March. With an annotated pencil note by Dr Westcott stating that this note remained pinned up in the office until June (Westcott W. W., 1897).

association with Aleister Crowley whose advancement through the society had been authorised by Mathers, although opposed by the leaders of the Temple to which Crowley belonged. Secondly, Mathers had accused Westcott of having forged the S.D.A. correspondence thus undermining the legendary narrative that supported the H.O.G.D.'s authority. This led to internal turmoil and challenges to the organisation's leadership.

As a result, a meeting of Second Order members was called to investigate Mathers' claims which resulted in the removal of Mathers from office. With doubts cast upon the authority of the Secret Chiefs and the expulsion of the last founding Chief Adept, the H.O.G.D. experienced a swift transformation.

The Second Order underwent organisational adjustments, and as a result, numerous splinter groups emerged, attracting with them many high-ranking members.

Some of the primary groups that would arise from this schism were:

- **Alpha et Omega-** Led by Mathers from Paris.
- **Stella Matutina-** Led by Dr Robert Felkin.
- **Isis-Urania Temple**[13]**-** Led by Waite, Blackden, and Ayton.
- **Independent and Rectified Rite (I.R.R.)-** Established in 1903 and led by Waite, Blackden, and Ayton.

Each of these newly formed groups carried on the legacy of the H.O.G.D. in their own distinctive ways, perpetuating its teachings and traditions under different banners and visions.

Today, there are many groups maintaining the tradition and practices of the H.O.G.D. some of whom claim a direct connection to one of the original or splinter groups, whilst some maintain a more philosophical or spiritual connection.

---

13 Evelyn Underhill (author of *Mysticism* (1911) was a member of this group (King, 1971, p. 112).

The Fraternitas Rosae Crucis (F.R.C.)

The Fraternitas Rosae Crucis (F.R.C.) is one of the oldest Rosicrucian organisations established in the United States. It was founded by Paschal Beverly Randolph in 1856. Randolph, a spiritualist and medical practitioner, emphasised the integration of esoteric philosophy with practical healing and moral development, which he incorporated into F.R.C. practices.

Following Randolph's death in 1875, leadership passed to Freeman Benjamin Dowd (1875-1907), who continued to develop the order's teachings and structure. Edward Holmes Brown succeeded Dowd (1907-1922), and under his guidance, the F.R.C. expanded its reach and influence. In 1922, Reuben Swinburne Clymer became Supreme Grand Master, a position he held until 1966. Clymer was instrumental in formalising the F.R.C.'s doctrines and establishing its headquarters at Beverly Hall in Quakertown, Pennsylvania. It was during this period that F.R.C. would participate in public battles with A.M.O.R.C.

Clymer's son, Emerson Myron Clymer, would go on to lead the organisation from 1966 to 1983, maintaining its traditions and overseeing its educational and healing initiatives. Gerald Eugene Poesnecker followed (1983-2003) and was most notable for integrating naturopathic medicine into the F.R.C.'s practices. Poesnecker's election was not universally supported however with Ronald Swinburne Clymer (Emerson Myron Clymer's son/Reuben Swinburne Clymer's grandson) claiming that he was the rightful Grand Master (Samson, 2004) eventually leading to a section of F.R.C. membership splintering to form their own group (Greer, 2006, p. 199).

The current Supreme Grand Master is William Glen Kracht, who assumed leadership in 2003 and continues to guide the organisation today.

The F.R.C. also operates a church called the *Church of Illumination*.

Unlike under Clymer's tenure, these days F.R.C. tends to prefer discretion and avoids more spirited public displays. The organisation maintains that true Rosicrucians are recognised by their character and conduct, not by symbols.

The Rosicrucian Fellowship (T.R.F.)

The Rosicrucian Fellowship (T.R.F.) was founded by Max Heindel[14] (1865-1919), a Danish-born engineer who spent much of his early life traveling the world as a marine engineer (Heindel A. F., 2012, p. 5). These global experiences broadened his outlook and eventually sparked a great interest in metaphysics. Heindel had served as vice-President of a branch of The Theosophical Society in Los Angeles in 1904-1905 (Heindel A. F., 2012, p. 6).

By 1905, Heindel had become seriously engaged in the study of esoteric and spiritual teachings which would lead him on a pilgrimage to Germany in 1907, where he encountered the Rosicrucian tradition that would shape the rest of his life's work (Heindel A. F., 2012).

It was here in Germany that Heindel claimed to have met an *Elder Brother* who would charge him to establish the T.R.F. as a vehicle to promote the mission of the *Aquarian Age* and conduct a renewed *campaign of education and enlightenment* (Heindel M. , 2011, p. 58). The Elder Brother, who appeared to Heindel in his *vital body*[15], had expressed grave concerns about the direction of humanity and the *fate of the Western World* (Heindel M. , 1911, p. 113), which was facing increased materialism. As such, they were looking to develop a new vehicle for the Rosicrucian Order and were seeking out a suitable candidate to lead this tradition. Allegedly, they had evaluated several candidates to carry the Rosicrucian torch, all of whom had been deemed unworthy.

Eventually, Heindel was put through a test, and after having passed, he was given permission to share occult knowledge with humanity. This occult knowledge could only be communicated by reaching the *Temple of the Rose Cross*, which resided *between the border of Bohemia and Germany* (Heindel M. , 2011, p. 9) where Heindel was instructed by

14 Born *Carl Louis Von Grasshoff*.
15 Within the teachings of The Rosicrucian Fellowship, the *Vital Body* is the second of the human being's seven bodies. The Physical Body is the first body. As such, the Vital Body is very closely associated with the physical body and may appear as an etheric double of it.

the same Elder Brother who had previously tested him, only this time he appeared in his regular physical form (Westenberg, 2014, p. 68).

In this legendary account, Heindel would conceal specific details, particularly regarding his personal associations.

For instance, one of the candidates who had been deemed unsuitable by the Elder Brother in 1905 was eventually revealed to have been Rudolf Steiner; the Elder Brothers thinking it unsuitable to have a Rosicrucian leader who was promoting both Western and Eastern occultism (Westenberg, 2014, p. 63). Steiner would eventually go on to establish The Anthroposophical Society in 1913[16].

In fact, prior to being contacted by the Elder Brother it was the teachings of Steiner that had appeared to most occupy Heindel's attention. Heindel was financially assisted in this trip by *Alma von Brandis*, a member of Steiner's group, who hoped Heindel would disseminate Steiner's teachings in America (Westenberg, 2014, p. 55). Like Heindel, Steiner had a background in The Theosophical Society, having been President of Berlin Lodge, General Secretary for Germany, and inducted into the Esoteric School of Theosophy by Annie Besant; all of these appointments occurring in 1902 (Westenberg, 2014, p. 259).

Another character some have speculated to be hidden by the identity of one of the Elder Brother's is Franz Hartmann. Although I'm not familiar with any evidence to prove this to be so, the locations and relationship dynamic between Heindel, Steiner, and Hartmann do lend considerable weight to this speculation.

The teachings imparted to Heindel in Germany there became the foundation of *The Rosicrucian Cosmo-Conception*; the cornerstone text of the Fellowship. Consequently, T.R.F. members do not necessarily view its teachings as the personal philosophy of Heindel but rather as an extension of the wisdom of the Elder Brothers. Furthermore, the members of the Fellowship are considered servants of the Elder Brothers.

16 For anybody wishing to investigate further the relationship between Steiner and Heindel, I would recommend the work, *Max Heindel and The Rosicrucian Fellowship* by Ger Wesenberg.

The first draft of The Rosicrucian Cosmo-Conception was made while Heindel was still in Germany. After completing the first draft, Heindel would be told by his teacher that the writing style would not satisfy the more *electric atmosphere of America*, and he would need to rewrite the entire book. Although initially reluctant, Heindel soon agreed and rewrote the book (Heindel A. F., 2012, p. 10).

Upon his return to the United States, Heindel would go on a lecture tour, presenting upon Rosicrucianism and mystical Christianity, eventually establishing a Rosicrucian centre in Columbus, Ohio, on November 14 1908 (Heindel A. F., 2012, p. 11). Less than a year later, *The Rosicrucian Fellowship* would be formally founded in a small cottage in Ocean Park, California on August 8 1909, at 3:00 p.m. (Westenberg, 2014, p. 72).

The Rosicrucian Cosmo-Conception was finally published in November 1909, with the first edition dedicated to Rudolf Steiner (Westenberg, 2014, p. 67). Steiner however was less than impressed with Heindel's book, publicly and privately accusing Heindel of copying and plagiarising his work. Heindel insisted that this was not the case and that he had improved and added upon Steiner's lessons with teachings he had received independently of Steiner. The dedication would be removed in subsequent editions (Westenberg, 2014, p. 68).

One reader who was profoundly inspired by The Rosicrucian Cosmo-Conception was Augusta Foss who would go on to marry Heindel and become his closest ally and supporter.

On May 3 1911, Heindel purchased forty acres of land in Oceanside, California and relocated the organisation's headquarters. This location became *Mount Ecclesia* and is where the T.R.F. headquarters remains to this day.

Max Heindel would work diligently in writing and expanding the organisation until his passing on January 6 1919, whereupon Augusta Foss Heindel became his successor.

Appendix One

Shortly after its founding, many of Heindel's works were translated into Dutch, French, German, Italian, Portuguese, and Spanish, gaining an international readership. By the 1920's, T.R.F. Centres had begun to appear across the globe.

In the Netherlands, however, an internal schism led to the formation of a rival group. On September 25 1935, one faction would break away from the existing Dutch headquarters of the Fellowship and established an independent organisation called Het Rozekruisers Genootschap (English: *The Rosicrucian Society*). In 1946, this group would change their name to Lectorium Rosicrucianum (Westenberg, 2014, pp. 349-350).

The main teachings promulgated by T.R.F. are referred to as the *Western Wisdom Teachings* or *Esoteric Christianity*. The philosophy aims to explain the mystery of Life and Being from a scientific standpoint in harmony with religion and to throw occult light upon the Christian religion. It is considered a religious philosophy for the coming *Aquarian Age*.

Key concepts include the study of the visible and invisible worlds, the constitution of man, evolution, rebirth, the Law of Cause and Effect, Christ and His mission, and initiation.

Membership in T.R.F. has several different stages: *students*, *probationers*, and *disciples*. Probationers make a voluntary vow to themselves regarding diet (they must be vegetarian), abstinence (from alcohol, recreational drugs, and tobacco), and living according to Christian principles.

After Mrs. Heindel's passing in May 1949, the T.R.F. would be governed by an elected Board of Directors.

The Rosicrucian Fellowship continues to operate today with centres and study groups in numerous countries around the world, including the United States, Germany, the Netherlands, and Brazil. Its international headquarters remains located in Oceanside, California, where the Mount Ecclesia campus serves as a spiritual and administrative centre.

The Fellowship offers a variety of services, including correspondence courses, spiritual healing services, and distribution of study materials focused on astrology, esoteric Christianity, and metaphysical philosophy. Public lectures, spiritual retreats, and Sunday services are regularly held at various centres. Their teachings continue to be grounded in Heindel's synthesis of Rosicrucian, Theosophical, and Christian esotericism.

Appendix One

The Ancient and Mystical Order Rosae Crucis (A.M.O.R.C.)

The Ancient Mystical Order Rosae Crucis (A.M.O.R.C.) would have to be the most recognisable Rosicrucian group in the world today. The A.M.O.R.C. claims to have over 200,000 members found in over 450 cities worldwide and has its teachings translated into nineteen different languages (AMORC.org.au, 2023). Whilst I dare say the membership number is not reflective of the organisation today, A.M.O.R.C. nevertheless commands a dominant position in the Rosicrucian market. However, being the largest Rosicrucian organisation does not come without controversy and A.M.O.R.C. has had no shortage of critics.

Researching the early period of A.M.O.R.C. can pose considerable challenges, and it may be necessary to accept that certain details may forever remain unknown. Throughout the development of A.M.O.R.C., both critics and well-meaning members and officers have propagated falsehoods and half-truths.

For those who are wishing to read a thorough overview of Lewis's upbringing, professional career, and to become familiar with the official history of A.M.O.R.C., you may wish to read the excellent book, *Rosicrucian History and Mysteries* by Christian Rebisse[17].

The Rosicrucian Order A.M.O.R.C. was started in New York in 1915 by thirty-one-year-old, Harvey Spencer Lewis. Lewis was only young but had ample experience working with esoteric matters. In fact, his own spiritual awakening could be considered to have been sparked when he was only thirteen years old where he states,

> *I slowly became cognizant of extreme degrees of those things which seemed to make little to no impression upon others. The clean things, the noble things and*

---

17 Christian Rebisse is not a pseudonym for Christian Bernard (A.M.O.R.C. Imperator emeritus) as is occasionally cited by modern Rosicrucian commentators.

sacred things of life affected me so deeply at times that I dropped into a period of meditation resulting in hours of tears and a day or so of such sweet sadness that I could not fathom its significance; secondly, I found myself prophetic to the extent that, without intending to do so and even without knowing at the time that such was the case, I would make statements which became or rather later proved to be correct predictions. (Profundis, 1918)

As a teenager Lewis was active in a New York Methodist Church operating from the Metropolitan Temple of New York. He was a keen musician and participated in the community choir and would also spend more time than many teenagers discussing mystical matters with the Pastor of the church, Dr S Parkes Cadman (Rebisse, 2005, p. 362). His talents as a musician and artist would come to serve him well with his future business endeavours.

During the initial stages of his professional journey, Lewis occupied numerous editorial positions and held official roles in various organisations committed to exploring paranormal phenomena. As early as 1904 Lewis was providing correspondence lessons on hypnotic suggestion in periodicals published by *The Metropolitan Institute of Sciences* which operated from an office on 126 West Thirty-Fourth street, New York (Lewis, 1904).

The most notable role Lewis held during this period was as President for the *New York Institute for Psychical Research*. It was during his tenure there that he was introduced to the term *'Rosicrucian'* supposedly by an elderly visitor named Mary Henrietta Banks[18] (Rebisse, 2005, p. 372). This introduction occurred while engaged in a discussion on the concept of reincarnation. In 1918 and in reference to this discussion, Lewis would state,

---

18 Mary Henrietta Banks is most often known as *May Banks-Stacey*, taking on the name of her husband.

Appendix One

> *But there was one point revealed in the discussion I had regarding the theory and its relation to my problem, which makes me feel very grateful to the dear old lady who tried her very best to have me accept her explanation. In questioning her as to what mystical or scientific sect or fraternity she thought the previous incarnation might have belonged, she mentioned the name of the Rosicrucians of Egypt. I remember distinctly that in the many days which followed its first mention she never spoke of the Rosicrucians as having been anywhere else than in Egypt, despite the fact that all references I could find regarding such a sect spoke of its existence in Germany only.* (Profundis, 1918)

Very little is known about the relationship between Lewis and Banks, however, Lewis would maintain her important role in the founding of A.M.O.R.C. and bestow upon her the title of *Grand Matre*; although Banks's signature would not appear at the bottom of A.M.O.R.C.'s founding charter. Banks was well travelled and was involved in several fraternal organisations, including being a member of the Esoteric School of Theosophy (E.S.T.) which constituted the inner circle of The Theosophical Society. The E.S.T. worked closely with their founder, Helena Petrovna Blavatsky. For a prominent woman of her time, there are still a lot of unanswered questions regarding Banks. In a letter she wrote in August 1898 to US President William McKinley, concerning her son, she makes mention of being a *"Mason"* (Rocks, 1996). Such a statement seems unusual considering Freemasonry is a male-only fraternal order and co-Masonry had not yet been established in the U.S.A. It is possible that she was referring to the Manhattan Mystic Circle (The Chicago Sunday Tribune, 1898), which was formed in February 1898, and which did work a form of Masonic Rite of Adoption[19]. Banks led this order for a time and in New York on 16 April 1898, she swore in twenty women as *Masonesses*.

19 Rite of Adoption is a Masonic Rite which first appeared in France in the eighteenth century, and which admits female members.

The Manhattan Mystic Circle utilised Masonic style grips, passwords, and distress signals. Their insignia was a circle, a Maltese cross, and a rose. The pre-requisite for membership was that members must be the wife, widow, daughter, sister, or granddaughter of a Freemason (Christian Cynosure, 1898). The leader of the Manhattan Mystic Circle held the title, *Illustrious Mistress* (Rebisse, 2005, p. 376). It is likely the rituals used by this society would be of a similar appearance to what would later emerge in the Order of the Eastern Star.

During A.M.O.R.C.'s early years, Lewis would occasionally make mention that he held an honorary membership in *The Philomatic Society of Verdun*[20] (French: *La Société philomathique de Verdun*). Unfortunately, limited information is available regarding Lewis's affiliation with this society. The archives and meeting Registers of the society, spanning the years 1898-1916, were destroyed in a bombardment event during the *Battle of Verdun* in March 1916. Despite this loss, there is evidence suggesting that Lewis had access to the society's periodicals. In a series of private member monographs from 1918, Lewis introduced a new language called '*The Rosaecrucian Language*' for use by A.M.O.R.C. members. Its purpose was to facilitate international communication and allow for the transmission of private teachings among members. Lewis claimed that this language was the result of the work undertaken by the '*Delegation for the adoption of an international auxiliary language*,' which had previously worked on Esperanto. However, it appears that the Rosaecrucian Language was actually based on a lesser-known auxiliary language called *Ido*, which Lewis had renamed for A.M.O.R.C.'s use. Interestingly, reports from this delegation were also included in the periodicals of *The Philomatic Society of Paris*. Furthermore, a number of proficient linguists[21] who conducted research alongside the Philomatic Society possessed expertise in Indo-European languages and the Avesta. Their contributions may have influenced Lewis's early A.M.O.R.C. doctrines, including

---

20 For example, see *The American Rosae Crucis Vol. 1, No. 2, February 1916*.
21 For example, Jean-Baptiste Thomas, François Bonnardot, and Lawrence Heyworth Mills.

Appendix One

the acquisition of the *Lost Word* of the A.M.O.R.C. tradition. It is conceivable that Lewis became acquainted with The Philomatic Society, which had collaborations with academic institutions in the U.S.A., through the influence of his father's work.

In 1909, Lewis would visit Toulouse, France where he would claim to have been initiated into a Rosicrucian Order and state that it was the Rosicrucians of Toulouse who granted him the authority to establish a Rosicrucian Order in the U.S.A.

In February 1915, in preparation for establishing a new Rosicrucian organisation Lewis and his colleague Thor Kiimalehto printed a document titled *Pronunziamento Number One* which announced that A.M.O.R.C. would commence activity in the U.S.A.

On Thursday, 1 April 1915, the charter of A.M.O.R.C. was signed and it is from this date that A.M.O.R.C. was officially established.

Between 1915 to 1917, A.M.O.R.C. expanded modestly in size. By 1917 there were ten Grand Lodges throughout North America.

Between 31 July to 4 August 1917, A.M.O.R.C. held its first national convention in Pittsburgh, Philadelphia. It was the success of this convention that greatly expanded A.M.O.R.C.'s membership, and it is perhaps due to the success of this convention that A.M.O.R.C. is still in operation today. It was also during this convention that the first Constitution of A.M.O.R.C. was adopted and ratified. This Constitution would outline the function of a National Lodge which would allow for National Lodge Membership.

Whilst the doctrines of A.M.O.R.C. during this period were somewhat similar to today, the way the work was conducted was quite different. There were twelve degrees and A.M.O.R.C. teachings were given in person as discourses by a lodge Master during meetings. Members were permitted to copy information into their own personal notebook. Initiations were also provided to members in lodges across North America.

In 1918, the first correspondence course would be established under the authority of the National Lodge and was available to those members who were unable to regularly attend a physical lodge. One of the first correspondence courses that was for circulation to members was a series of seven booklets called CROMAAT. Although only small, these booklets provide a great deal of information pertaining to the infant organisation. Throughout the CROMAAT series, there are some teachings that can still be seen today whilst some others would be modified or removed entirely from A.M.O.R.C.'s system of instruction.

In 1919, A.M.O.R.C. moved its headquarters from New York to San Francisco. It was during this time that members who commenced A.M.O.R.C. in the first year of operation were now beginning to reach the end of the ninth degree. Of this period, Lewis would later state in personal correspondence to members of the tenth degree,

> *I was certainly puzzled as to what to do with these members. The work of the tenth and higher degrees had not been released to me, because in jurisdictions of other countries they have class meetings only once a month instead of once a week and it had been figured that none of the members in New York or any other lodge in this jurisdiction would reach the ninth degree until the years of 1923 or 1924. It was not until 1922 that I had all of the tenth degree work completely in my own possession and was able to polish off many of the rough points in my own progress and understanding, for I had worked personally under special instruction and special lessons by mail in brief form. But always my ambition was to reach that day when members studying under me or studying in our North American jurisdiction would advance above the tenth and reach that high goal at the borderline of new life. I was as anxious about it as a mother is to have her son grow up to manhood, reach his twenty-first birthday and be able to face the world as a man....But think of it! Those members who went*

Appendix One

> *into the ninth degree in New York in 1919 had to wait until 1926 before the first of them could enter into the tenth degree work and some of them did not reach into the tenth degree until 1927 and 1928.*

Keep in mind that the teachings Lewis is referring to here are given as lectures in a lodge.

In this intimate writing, we can observe that Lewis is maintaining that he is still in contact with a Rosicrucian Order active in some other location and that A.M.O.R.C. receives its teachings (at least in part) from this other group.

By 1927, the correspondence course had expanded and was now in the form of three grades, each grade running for approximately nine months in duration. Each of these grades would be preceded by an initiation ritual that the member could perform in their own personal sanctum. National Lodge members during this time were also able to attend physical lodges should they so desire (Lewis, 1927, p. 3). It was also in 1927 that A.M.O.R.C. would relocate their headquarters to San Jose in what would become Rosicrucian Park. Rosicrucian Park remains today the headquarters for the English language Grand Lodge for the Americas as well as a very popular attraction for tourists and school groups.

In 1931, A.M.O.R.C. would establish a National Grand Lodge. With this development, regional Grand Lodges would no longer be chartered. Instead, nine Inspectors General would be appointed to work as intermediaries between A.M.O.R.C. groups and the National Grand Lodge. A new initiative developed as a part of this reorganisation would expand the correspondence course from three grades to a complete system of instruction covering all twelve degrees. The original three grades would continue to function in a modified form as a preliminary *Neophyte* degree. This new system would completely replace the graduated lodge lectures. From this point onwards, members were under no obligation to ever visit a group, although it was always encouraged, especially for initiations and special events.

Most degrees in the correspondence course continued to contain an initiation ritual that could be performed in the members personal home sanctum. Much of the content of these monographs were dictated by Lewis and put to print by his assistant, which provided a personal style which many members appreciated of Lewis's writings. Lewis was still in the process of writing monographs for higher grade members upon his passing in 1939.

Lewis would be succeeded by his son and A.M.O.R.C.'s Supreme Secretary, Ralph Maxwell Lewis. Ralph would complete the monograph catalogue as well as add an additional section for members beyond the twelfth degree. Under Ralph's tenure, the monograph system would also be updated. Whilst the monographs of this period would lose that personal style of A.M.O.R.C.'s founder, they would increase in number and take on a more academic tone.

Gary Lee Stewart would succeed Ralph as Imperator upon the latter's death in 1987. Imperator Stewart would be removed from office in 1990. As can well be imagined, little change could take place to the monograph system during this short time.

Stewart would be succeeded by Imperator Christian Bernard. Under his tenure, the monograph system would again receive an update. The monographs of this period were under the supervision of a monograph committee. The overall structure was more consistent than in previous periods, although members of previous eras would question whether they had lost their personal touch.

Bernard would be succeeded by Imperator Claudio Mazzucco in 2018. At the time of writing, the monographs have maintained a similar structure. However, I expect to see some reforms to the system soon and wish Imperator Mazzucco the greatest success in what must be a challenging and demanding endeavour.

Like many Rosicrucian organisations, A.M.O.R.C. has a hierarchical grade structure. Members progress through twelve degrees plus a preliminary Neophyte section. Advancement through the grades is usually only dependent upon maintaining active membership. As an initiatory organisation, members are provided with initiations prior to most degrees. However, there are some curious exceptions to this rule.

Shortly after joining, members will be introduced to the *Neophyte* section where they will be known as a *Neophyte*. After approximately one and a half years, they will progress to the *Temple Degree* section where they will be known as an *Initiate*. After several years, they will then be introduced to the *Illuminati* section where they will be known as an *Illuminatus*. The complete run of monographs takes a little over thirty years to complete.

Each degree in the Temple section is preceded by an initiation ceremony that can be performed at home. The exception to this rule is the First Temple Degree initiation ceremony which can only be performed in a lodge.

Whilst there are home initiations for the Illuminati section, the Illuminatus is explicitly advised that the true initiation for each of these degrees can only be received psychically.

It is conceivable that during the initiation of the First Temple Degree, the candidate may receive a lineal succession that establishes a connection between the initiate and the Rosicrucian tradition inherited by Lewis from Toulouse, France. This can be evidenced by some curious points within the ceremony itself as well as its similarity to the initiation Lewis receives as described in the Toulouse legend.

This legend is outlined in several locations, including,

- **A Pilgrim's Journey to the East by H. Spencer Lewis**
  This account was published in The American Rosae Crucis in May 1916.

- **Confessio R.C. Fraternitatis by Bro. Profundis**[22]

---

22 Many high-ranking members of A.M.O.R.C. employ *Nomina Mystica* or *Mystical Names*. In this time-period, Lewis employed the mystical name, *Profundis*. This name would be replaced by *Alden* after 1918.

This series of manifestoes was initially shared exclusively with limited members and later made more widely available by Ralph M. Lewis.

- **Rosicrucian Questions and Answers with Complete History of the Rosicrucian Order by H. Spencer Lewis**
  First published in 1929, this work includes relevant information pertaining to the Toulouse Legend.

- **Restorer of Rosicrucianism by Christian Rebisse**
  This article was featured in the Rosicrucian Digest, 2019, Issue 1.

Lewis always claimed to have been initiated in 1909 by a group of Rosicrucians in Toulouse, France who entrusted him with the authority to establish a Rosicrucian Order in North America. The authenticity of these events has been a subject of debate amongst researchers.

Amongst many Rosicrucian students and A.M.O.R.C. officers whom I have met, the Toulouse initiation is often considered a symbolic narrative, that whilst elaborating a lineage transfer, this transfer was something undertaken psychically. However, both the literal and the purely symbolic approaches to Lewis's journey to Toulouse fail to fully express the importance of this profound story.

More recent research has confirmed that Lewis did in fact travel to France and engage with individuals that can be confirmed as being associated with the Rosicrucians of Toulouse.

First, let us consider Lewis as an individual. This was a man who was quite young and many of his early writings express his youthful sentiments. Although it is clear that he had many talents, we should not confer upon him in his early twenties an adept understanding of Rosicrucian philosophy that he had achieved by his fifties. At no point in any of Lewis's writings have I ever read his explicit wish to establish a Rosicrucian Order. His purpose was simply to find out who the Rosicrucians are. This desire was so great that it occupied his mind every day since he was first introduced to their supposed existence. Establishing A.M.O.R.C. appears to have come about as a secondary consequence of his personal search. Lewis was only 25 years old when he journeyed to Toulouse and although he had already some professional esoteric experience, his understanding of initiatory institutions was likely still in its infancy. However, what he did possess were impressive verbal and written communication skills, great artistic talents, and what would appear to be an impressively attuned psychic mind. We know this from the work that he had accomplished pre-A.M.O.R.C. as well as by commentaries provided by those that knew him. For example, one account of Lewis's psychic abilities as provided by a Soror in 1917 describes how Lewis had influenced her music student to deliver a stirring song during a convention,

> *He was a magician – had learned many ways by which one's mind can be influenced by another. He held her objective mind in abeyance as Svengali did Trilby's, and her soul came through in its soul-stirring rendering of a Love Song which she sang to him.* (Clemens, 1953, p. 107)

If we commence an analysis of the story from this starting point, we may begin to appreciate the legend and perhaps gain a glimpse of what is tangible and what is symbolic.

Aaron Lewis (H. Spencer Lewis's father) was a genealogist who specialised in a form of document analysis that was used to verify forged documents. Aaron was commissioned to perform genealogical research that required him to travel to France. In need of an assistant during this journey, he called upon his young son, Harvey. Together, they departed New York on the *Hamburg Amerika* line on the 24 July 1909. The ship would arrive in Cherbourg in the north of France on 1 August 1909. They then continued to Paris aboard a train. Online passenger records provide substantial evidence that Lewis indeed embarked on the journey described, leaving minimal room to dispute its occurrence.

Whilst on the boat to France, the legend states that Lewis meets *Mr. P* who was the confidential agent of his *Madame* who lived, *on the Banks of the Hudson where she maintained her American villa and directed her American charitable work.* No doubt this is an allusion to Mary Henrietta Banks, indicating, at least in Lewis's mind, a connection between the man and Banks.

There has been some speculation in Rosicrucian circles that Mr. P may have been Albert Karl Theodor Reuss (also known by his nomen mysticum, Sar Peregrinus). At the time, Reuss was head of the Ordo Templi Orientis (O.T.O.).

However, the argument for Reuss being on the ship all hinges on one detail: that there is a crew list from a Hamburg-Amerika line during a similar time-period that mentions *A. Reuss* as a first officer. This is a wild and tenuous link to base such a connection. Reuss was also not Persian or Egyptian (as Mr. P is described in the Toulouse legend). He had no known association with Mary Henrietta Banks.

However, we do know that Lewis did work for a brief period with Reuss commencing in 1920. This short engagement would result in a signed concordat between their two organisations. With this concordat, Reuss conferred upon Lewis honorary degrees in O.T.O. (VII°) and The Ancient and Primitive Rite of Memphis-Misraim (33° 90° 95°). Although a meeting between the pair certainly warrants our curiosity, not least of which is due to Reuss's enormous peer group which contained numerous esotericists from England, France, and Germany, we must not attempt to force a connection where there is none. With no evidence to place Reuss on the ship and with Occam's razor at our disposal, it is more likely that Mr. P was somebody else.

In 2001, a Belgian researcher located a copy of A.M.O.R.C.'s Pronunziamento Number One in the New York public Library. On this copy can be found a curious handwritten annotation which adds a suggestion that A.M.O.R.C. derives its lineage from the O.T.O.[23].

23 It must be mentioned that there are some Rosicrucian authors who believe that the handwritten annotation on the document may have been deliberately provided by Lewis as an intentional misdirection (sometimes referred to as a *blind*). Considering the lack of evidence of Lewis's employment of misdirection, this would appear rather unlikely.

Appendix One

The series of letters between Robert Vanloo and an A.M.O.R.C. Archivist discussed the possibility of a connection between Lewis, Crowley, and the O.T.O. The primary focus was on exploring whether A.M.O.R.C. obtained authority or lineage from the O.T.O. The A.M.O.R.C. Archivist robustly refuted the suspected O.T.O. lineage, but the reverberations resulting from this interaction coupled with the story of the strange man on the ship have left a lasting impact throughout many Rosicrucian groups and online message boards. Furthermore, considering that this document is housed in a public Library, it remains plausible that someone else, with the intention of undermining Lewis, could have inserted this annotation. Given the opposition Lewis encountered during the initial phases of A.M.O.R.C, such a possibility cannot be dismissed.

Another connection often cited by those who wish to stretch a connection between the founding of A.M.O.R.C. and the O.T.O. is in the shared use of an image between the groups. Whilst some nuances differ, the image generally features a dove, chalice, cross, and Egyptian-style eye. The O.T.O. would use this as their society's lamen. In 1930, a very similar version of this image would appear on an A.M.O.R.C. document called, *Liber 777*. However, A.M.O.R.C.'s use if this image is less to do with communicating a connection with the O.T.O. by appropriating their symbol and more to do with A.M.O.R.C. utilising an image from a Toulousain Rosicrucian, namely Joséphin Péladan. It was in the works of Péladan that variations of this image first appeared in the early 1890's. Considering one of the purposes of Liber 777 is to provide a method to attune with an invisible Rosicrucian field of energy not bound by time or space, it would make sense for Lewis to have authorised its use. Within this context, the selection of Péladan's image would become significant as it signifies a connection to a pre-existing Rosicrucian tradition, one rooted in Toulouse, the very Rosicrucian lineage that Lewis claimed descent. To date, there is no evidence to suggest that A.M.O.R.C. derives its lineage, in whole or in part, from the O.T.O.

In the *Confessio R.C. Fraternitatis* version of the Toulouse legend Lewis states that the lodge he was initiated into had not been used for over sixty years, although, it had on occasion been visited by French Freemasons as recently as the 1890's. Later in the same communication, he states that the exoteric body had ceased to exist from 1880. Whoever Lewis communicated with in Toulouse, it is clear that he was dealing with a dormant group that had not been active since approximately 1840-1880, placing it firmly within the time-period of the Rosicrucians of Toulouse already mentioned in the chapter above.

A.M.O.R.C. does maintain correspondence between H. Spencer Lewis and a prominent photographer and photolithographer from Toulouse named Clovis Marie Charles Lassalle (1864-1937). A letter from Lassalle to Lewis dated 26 August 1909[24] was preserved in Lewis's personal archives bearing the inscription *important historical documents*.

Lassalle's photos of historical sites were often used by the Archaeological Society for the South of France and he was an acquaintance of Firmin Boissin; both of these points placing him with the Rosicrucians of Toulouse. In the Confessio R.C. Fraternitatis version of the Toulouse legend, Lewis would mention that a man name *Lasalle* assumed *Mastership of the Ceremonies* and had instructed him to not attempt to re-establish the order in America until 1915.

The Donjon plays a key role in the Toulouse legend. Lewis would visit the Donjon just prior to his initiation. This was the location of the archives of the Order Rosae Crucis. It was here where Lewis met the Grand Archivist and was informed that, due to his conduct, a decision had recently been made to allow him to meet the Grand Master and Imperator in the Holy Temple. The Archivist was also the Archivist of a small group of French Freemasons.

---

24 This would have been received whilst Lewis was in France and may have remained unopened until his return.

Appendix One 359

In one version of the Toulouse legend, there is a reference to a *Fr. Donjon*, which gives a suggestion that *Donjon* may refer to a person.

In a Toulouse newspaper, *L'Express du Midi* from 18 September 1937, we find a curious obituary for Clovis Lassalle. It is signed off by *The Dungeon Watcher* (French: *Le Guetteur du Donjon*).

Collaborative efforts between myself and Lyonnaise researcher, Francis Meinsohn have recently revealed the identity of *Fr. Donjon* from H. Spencer Lewis's A Pilgrim's Journey to the East legend as Rozes de Brousse (1876-1960). De Brousse was a journalist, poet, lawyer, as well as Permanent Secretary of the Floral Games Academy. He worked in the tower of the Toulouse Capitole building. This building also happens to be where the city's archives are located which Lewis would have consulted with his father.

Lewis does provide a name for his initiator, Count Raynaud Emil[25] de Bellcastle-Ligne. There is no evidence showing any man by the name of Count Raynaud Emil de Bellcastle-Ligne in Toulouse or the surrounding areas, leaving us to believe this is a pseudonym.

Certainly, with all the nobles associated with the Rosicrucians of Toulouse, we have no shortage of Counts. *Belcastel* (not *Bellcastle*) is not an uncommon name and we can forgive Lewis for his own admittedly rudimentary French language skills.

Baron Gabriel de Lacoste de Belcastel (1821-1890) was a local of Toulouse. He was a skilled orator and statesman and in 1850 his speech entitled Discourse on Progress (French: *Discours sur le progress*) earned him the *Golden Wild Rose* prize at the Floral Games Academy. He would later be nominated a Maintainer of the Floral Games Academy in 1853. He was also a companion of the Academy of Sciences, Inscriptions and Belles-Lettres. Baron Gabriel's writings reveal his staunchly conservative Catholic beliefs, his opposition to Republicanism, and his disdain for Freemasonry. While these

---

25 Lewis nearly always used the name, *Count Raynaud E. de Bellcastle-Ligne*. The only location found where we find the name *Emil* is in a document entitled, '*The Ancient and Mystical Order Rosae Crucis in the United States of America: Its History, Purposes and Symbolism*' on page 9. It is not known why *Emil* was shortened to *E.* although there is a plausible theory.

characteristics align with those of a Toulouse Rosicrucian, it seems that if he was indeed a Rosicrucian, he did not share the same enthusiasm for hermetic philosophy and spagyric medicine as his contemporaries. Additionally, Baron Gabriel passed away nineteen years prior to Lewis's arrival. However, Baron Gabriel did have a nephew, Joseph de Belcastel (1860-1942) who lived in Toulouse when Lewis visited in 1909.

The Imperator of the Confraternity of the Rose-Cross (C.R.+C.) Gary L. Stewart conducted his own research on this matter which he offered to C.R.+C. Magi. He proposes that Lewis met Joseph de Belcastel and his wife in Toulouse and that Joseph introduced Lewis to the remnants of the Order Rosae Crucis. According to Stewart, Lewis would disguise Joseph's name as *Grand Master Lasalle.* Following this meeting, Lewis would then have a rare psychic initiation which was conducted by Baron Gabriel.

Although this is an interesting theory, it would be more likely that Lewis, when referring to Grand Master Lasalle in a private document intended only for select senior A.M.O.R.C. members, was referring to the Clovis Lassalle discussed above, who we now know was a contemporary of identified Rosicrucians of Toulouse. However, Stewart's theory does provide a justification for why Lewis chose the name Belcastle/Belcastel when referring to his initiator in public facing documents. Nevertheless, it is certainly possible that Lewis had come across many important noble family names during his research and attached the name Bellcastle as a pseudonym for his initiator.

It may be more likely to consider that Lewis's initiation was a psychic initiation facilitated by Clovis Lassalle and at least two other unnamed individuals.

So we have evidence for a pre-existing group of Rosicrucians in Toulouse. We know that H. Spencer Lewis visited Toulouse attempting to find out more about the Rosicrucians. And we know that H. Spencer Lewis made contact with Clovis Lassalle; a gentleman who had intimate connections with Boissin and the dormant Rosicrucians of Toulouse. So why would Lewis go to such great lengths to disguise his Rosicrucian contacts? Let us consider that it is common practice in many initiatory rites to not name your initiator until after their death. Additionally, many of the Rosicrucians of Toulouse were eminent people of society and were occasionally active politicians who would have desired to remain private for obvious reasons.

However, there is one more very curious avenue to be explored.

In 1909, Toulouse would also receive a visitor from London. This was Marcus Worsley Blackden.

Blackden was a member of the S.R.I.A.[26] and possessed a deep fascination with ancient Egypt, and unlike many of his peers, he approached the study with genuine academic rigour. His experience involved working on archaeological sites which contributed to several scholarly works, including a paper upon the hieratic graffiti in Tell El-Amarna, the former capital of the heretical Pharaoh Akhenaten.

Blackden believed that a large part of the ancient Egyptian *Book of the Dead* actually contained,

> ...*fragments of Initiatory Ceremonial for the benefit of the Living, rather than Priestly practices for the benefit of the Dead.* (Blackden, 1914)

Blackden also maintained that one chapter of the book was an initiatory ritual providing the candidate an entrance into the Egyptian mystery tradition. Being unsatisfied with the available translations, Blackden provided his own personal translations to the Book of the Dead from three papyri preserved in the British Museum and modified it in such

---

26 Blackden was raised in Freemasonry on 10 February 1902 in St Marylebone Lodge No. 1305 alongside his friend and confidante, Arthur Edward Waite. They would later be admitted into the S.R.I.A. together on the same night of 10 April 1902. In addition, Blackden had been a member of the Hermetic Order of the Golden Dawn and later aligned himself with Waite in leading the Independent and Rectified Rite following the Order's internal schism. They would however have a falling out over a disagreement regarding the authenticity of the Cipher Manuscripts. They eventually reunited during a friendly encounter in Southampton in 1924 (Davis, 2017).

a way as to make it read as a ritual script. This he presented as *Ritual and Mystery of the Judgement of the Soul*. It is certainly possible that Blackden was positioning himself to become a head of an initiatory society that would make use of his Egyptian styled ritual.

In January 1909, Blackden's research would be read at a Metropolitan College meeting of the S.R.I.A. However, Blackden would not attend this meeting, deciding instead to prematurely cease all his public esoteric pursuits. This was likely to settle down with his new wife whom he married in the following month. Following the wedding ceremony Blackden and his newlywed would journey on a honeymoon to Toulouse. Although Blackden would not have met Lewis in Toulouse (who arrived seven months later in September), it is curious to speculate if Blackden may have crossed paths with any of the other Rosicrucians of Toulouse during his journey.

A summary of Blackden's *Ritual and Mystery of the Judgement of the Soul*[27] is as follows:

The candidate appears as a recently departed soul and arrives at the portal of the *Temple of Osiris*. The door is blocked by Anubis who questions the candidate regarding his purpose. Satisfied with the response, Anubis conducts the candidate through the portal. Anubis escorts the candidate through a darkened passageway, stumbling past many horrors and dangers before arriving at the gate of the *Pillared Hall of the Two Truths*. Anubis enters through the gate and announces the candidate to the members inside. The members inside the Hall order Anubis to admit the candidate within but only after having received from the candidate proof of their worthiness via knowledge and peculiar symbols. Once inside the Hall, the candidate proclaims his innocence and good life. His heart is weighed against the feather of Truth to ascertain his honesty. Having been found of sinless heart, Thoth announces the candidate *True of Voice* and the members assembled therein chant, *Come! Come in Peace!* The Initiate is further examined and then must unlock the door that leads to the *Temple of*

---

27 This would be later published the Societas Rosicruciana in Anglia (S.R.I.A.) in 1914.

Appendix One

Osiris. Upon crossing the threshold into the Temple of Osiris, the Initiate is conducted towards Osiris; the Master of the Temple. As an award for his advancement he is told, *Lo! Thy bread shall be in the Eye of God and thy strong drink shall be from the Eye of God.* He is then taken to the Throne of Osiris who bestows upon him his award, making of the candidate as like a god[28] and told that he shall forever be a follower of Horus. The new Initiate is then provided with an explanation of the various gods and their duties within the Temple. The ceremony is finally closed with a prayer (Blackden, 1914).

Members of A.M.O.R.C. who have been initiated into the First Temple degree may observe more than a few similarities between Blackden's ritual and A.M.O.R.C.'s First Degree Initiation ceremony. This curiosity becomes even more intriguing when we consider that H. Spencer Lewis not only visited Toulouse in 1909 but also made a stop on his return journey in Southampton. Southampton was a major maritime hub in the U.K. and is still actively used for both commercial shipping and passenger vessels today. But this was also the town where Blackden had chosen to settle down with his new wife. Lewis would also record having visited the British Museum whilst docked here.

As can be seen, there are still considerable gaps remaining in our understanding of A.M.O.R.C.'s formative years and I look forward to conducting more research into this area.

---

28 "*May he hear what ye (Osiris) hear, may he see what ye see, may he stand up as ye stand up, may he sit down as ye sit down*" (Blackden, 1914).

APPENDIX TWO:

ROSICRUCIAN ALCHEMY

By Fra AMA

Our world today is curiously paradoxical. We are surrounded by information and yet it is so challenging to find answers. There is perhaps no other subject more misrepresented in our modern times than that of Alchemy. Yet, between the sixteenth-nineteenth centuries >4500 books were written upon the subject. Yet if you were interested in the subject only 20 years ago, you would be lucky to find a handful of resources. Now, not only can we find copies of many of these old writings, but we can also find countless other books that claim to contain the secrets and mysteries of alchemy many of which are simply contemporary authors using the cryptic and enigmatic language of alchemy to promote their own personal narratives. During the middle-ages, the term *Puffer* was often applied to pseudo-alchemists or charlatans who applied alchemical imagery and terminology to market their own miracle cures and gadgets. It would appear that this *Puffery* is all too common in the 2010's-2020's as well.

And yet, in the eighteenth century when Freemasonry was being established, we find the greatest intellectuals of the time discussing the *Art of Transmutation*. Indeed, the very first historically known Rosicrucian society (*Orden des Gold- und Rosenkreuz*) was an alchemical society, where candidates were expected to be proficient in laboratory alchemy. We could simply pass off all the physical alchemy as being a simple metaphor for more metaphysical pursuits, but then we would be doing a great injustice to the tremendous advances made in science and medicine achieved through practical alchemical work. So, what was this work? Is there any truth to some of the amazing alchemical claims? Could alchemists really turn metal into gold; cure any disease; and provide the key to immortality? And why should any of this be relevant to us in the twenty-first century?

History of Alchemy

It is likely that the term alchemy derives from the ancient Egyptian word for Egypt (𓆎𓏏𓊖 transliterated to *Kemet*). This Egyptian word literally means *Black Earth* and alludes to the fertile black soil of the Nile where new life would spring from the old each season. This word would later be used by Arabs as *al-kīmīā* which became the Arabic word for chemistry. It might seem surprising to some that we have to travel this far back in time to understand the writings of alchemists in the fifteenth, sixteenth, and seventeenth centuries, but it is important as many alchemists throughout history claimed that their alchemical wisdom was derived, at least in part, from the writings of a wise Egyptian sage known as Hermes Trismegistus. It is unknown whether Hermes Trismegistus was a real person or a mythical figure. Nevertheless, there are a wealth of writings which are attributed to him. Most of these writings were written during Hellenistic Egypt (Ptolemaic dynasty) from 305bce. The subjects covered in these hermetic texts include philosophy, cosmogony, astrology, and magic.

From a scholarly perspective, hermetic texts can be divided into two broad categories: *The Technical Hermetica* and *The Theoretical Hermetica* (Copenhaver, 2000, p. xxxii)

The Technical Hermetica

As its name would suggest, this division of the hermetica deals with technical subjects, such as science, astrology, botany, medicine and magic.

The Technical Hermetica flourished during the Islamic period, which is why Islamic alchemists were much more proficient with physical alchemy, bringing about massive advances in chemistry, medicine and physics.

Some examples of some Technical Hermetic texts include:
- Cyranides;
    - A magical-medical text.
- Myriogenesis;
    - An astrological-magical text.
- The Emerald Tablet;
    - An unusual short text of unknown origin. This is where we get the phrase *That which is above is like that which is below; and that which is below is like that which is above; to accomplish the work of the One thing'*

The Theoretical Hermetica

The Theoretical Hermetica is by far and large the more popular division of hermetic texts and it makes up the bulk of hermetic writings. The Theoretical Hermetica deals with cosmogony, ontology, good and evil, salvation, and the relationships that exist between Man, Nature, and God.

Some examples of Theoretical Hermetic texts include:
- Greek Tractates;
    - Greek dialogues written during Hellenistic Egypt from ~305bce. However, there is abundant evidence to suggest that these writing were originally composed much earlier and may have formed a portion of the curriculum of the ancient Egyptian Mystery School Tradition.
    - These dialogues are usually what people are referring to when they discuss *The Corpus Hermeticum* or *The Hermetica*.
- Asklepius (sometimes referred to as *The Perfect Sermon*)

Whilst these divisions serve us well to appreciate the journey of hermetic wisdom from ancient Egypt to today, we should keep in mind, that to the hermetic philosopher, these divisions are completely arbitrary. Hermetic philosophy was originally understood as a single holistic philosophy.

Collectively, the hermetic texts discuss the relationships existing between man, the universe, and God. One of the common themes within these texts is that the universe was created, and is sustained, by the Mind of God (often called *Nous*). The hermetic texts describe Man as a microcosm of God, and as such, our own mind is considered a divine faculty which can be utilised to understand our Self and to transform the world around us.

It was these hermetic writings that formed the basis of alchemy. In many ways, we could consider alchemy to be a practical application of hermetic philosophy. For the next several centuries, this alchemical tradition was nurtured in Alexandria. Some notable alchemists during this period include Mary the Jewess and Zosimus of Panopolis. After Alexandria, alchemy was raised to new heights in the Middle-East, particularly Iran and Iraq, where it was used to underpin scientific advances in chemistry, physics, and medicine. Some notable alchemists during this period include Jabir ibn Hayyan (*Geber*), Muhammad ibn Zakariya al-Razi (*Rhazes*), and Ibn Sina (*Avicenna*).

However, aside from a couple of lesser known (although, not insignificant) alchemical texts (such as Turba Philosophorum) we do not get many alchemical texts arriving in Europe until the Renaissance when an Italian monk named Marsilio Ficino translates much of the Corpus Hermeticum. During this period, Europe is abuzz with hermetic philosophy and esoteric thought. It is also at this time that we find many notable alchemists that have now become popular names in esotericism such as Paracelsus, whose legacy would go on to influence the Rosicrucians and many later alchemists of the Middle-Ages. In fact, the first Rosicrucian manifesto (the Fama Fraternitatis) attributes the wisdom of Paracelsus among the many treasures found within the tomb of Christian Rosenkreuz.

Appendix Two

After Paracelsus, alchemy gains much of the character that we come to associate with it today. In the following 150 years, metallurgists, physicians, and natural philosophers write thousands of books upon the subject; all hastened by new advancements in printing technology. Even until the mid-eighteenth century, alchemy is still being discussed, particularly by Freemasons. This interest would culminate in the founding of The Order of the Golden and Rosy Cross (German: *Orden des Gold- und Rosenkreuz*) in the 1750's, where alchemy is the primary topic of discussion. However, in general, alchemy begins to lose its appeal. The quantity of alchemical writing reduces dramatically and interest in alchemy outside of these specialist groups all but wanes.

However, in the mid-nineteenth century, occult subjects experience a revival in Britain and France and with this occult revival, alchemy receives renewed attention. This is particularly influenced by the author Éliphas Lévi who writes in his cornerstone text, *Transcendental Magic*,

> *Behind the veil of all the hieratic and mystical allegories of ancient doctrines, behind the shadows and the strange ordeals of all initiations, under the seal of all sacred writings, in the ruins of Ninevah or Thebes, on the crumbling stones of the old temples, and on the blackened visage of the Assyrian or Egyptian sphinx, in the monstrous or marvellous paintings which interpret to the faithful of India the inspired pages of the Vedas, in the strange emblems of our old books of alchemy, in the ceremonies at reception practised by all mysterious societies, traces are found of a doctrine which is everywhere the same, and everywhere carefully concealed.* (Lévi, 1910, p. 3)

It is possible to see in this quote some correspondence being made between various esoteric and religious traditions. This comparative esotericism not only revitalises alchemy, but would go on to influence Martinism, the Golden Dawn, Theosophy, and of course, Rosicrucianism. Levi's works would inspire such notable people as

Papus and Joséphin Péladan. For perhaps the first time, we begin to see alchemy merge with ritual, mysticism, and magic. But this alchemic renaissance comes at a cost. Alchemy loses much of its identity that it had developed over the centuries, and it begins to be conflated with other traditions. Much of the alchemy studied during this period would have been close to unrecognisable to the alchemists of the middle-ages.

From here, the flood gates open and alchemy is ascribed to all manner of meta-narratives. Some of these meta-narratives simply use the allure of alchemical imagery and symbolism to market books and gadgets. It is no wonder that many start to see alchemy as a frivolous pseudoscience.

The purpose of this small history lesson is not to impress upon you at length and detail the milestones of each advancement in alchemy. Rather, what I wish to emphasise is the journey of alchemy from a hermetic philosophy inspired from the ancient Egyptian mystery schools; to inspiring great men and women to do great things in medicine and science; and at each step, not just imparting part of its own wisdom, but also absorbing a fragment of the tradition of the time as it travels down the winding path to us today. It is this journey that helps us to appreciate some of the symbols that are used in alchemy. This journey should also impress upon us that alchemy is adaptable. The fact that it can survive for so long, that it can be applied to art, science, philosophy, medicine, and spirituality tells us that whatever alchemy has to say, it must be fairly important and powerful. We might therefore assume that alchemy is something terribly complex and something that only an advanced mind could readily understand.

But then we hear from Paracelsus who states that,

> *Any one can at pleasure learn this Art in Alchemy, since it is so simple and easy; and by it, in a short time, he could make any quantity of silver and gold.*[1]

And to achieve progress in Alchemy, one only needs to be,

> *..truthful, simple, patient and persevering*[2].

---

1   *Coelum Philosophorum*
2   *A Short Catechism of Alchemy*. Although this text's attribution to Paracelsus is questionable.

Philosophy of Alchemy

If you are so inclined, you can read through Paracelsus' works. His importance cannot be understated, especially to the world of medicine. This was a time when balancing humors via blood-letting and purging was a standard medical treatment; and Paracelsus dared stand against the medical authority of the time and suggest doctors *not* bleed patients into unconsciousness; that they should keep wounds clean; that fresh food, water, and air are conducive to good health...*how radical*! It was also Paracelsus who introduced Salt to the alchemical trinity of Salt, Sulphur, and Mercury.

If you were to read Paracelsus' works, you may find the above quotes regarding the simplicity of alchemy as being rather hypocritical. Indeed, his books are quite complex. But we could talk about our Rosicrucian/Masonic/Mystical journey rather similarly. Afterall, all you need to be a great Man is the Volume of the Sacred Law and an earnest desire to better yourself. This is simple. This is true. But it says nothing about the journey each of us must take as sojourners towards the *Greater Light*. It does not emphasise the *effort* required nor our *participation* in the work.

Principles of Alchemy

I'll do my best to simplify some of the fundamental tenets of alchemy and remove some of the archaic terms. These points should not be considered as authoritative. Keep in mind that there was no single school of alchemy, no universal alchemical philosophy, and no overarching authorities on the subject. Alchemists often disagreed with each other and occasionally they changed their opinions over the course of their own lives. Some alchemists even contradicted themselves within their own works! Nevertheless, these tenets I have set out below are almost universally agreed upon by many alchemists of note. You may also notice that when we peer behind the cryptic language and symbolic imagery, we find a philosophy that is quite unchanged since the original hermetic writings.

1. **All creation comes from one indivisible source**
   All creation is emanated from one indivisible divine source and all things still have a spark of the divine contained within them. This spark was commonly referred to as *Spirit* by alchemists. This is true for all things, whether they be considered *living* or *non-living*. In fact, to many alchemists, all things were considered to be alive as a result of this spark. Therefore, plants, planets, metals, animals, people, and minerals were all considered as living things and proof of life was perceived within their movement and forms, even if some things (such as rocks and metals) move slower than us.

2. **God creates by limiting his own infinity**
   That as creation emanates away from the divine source, it becomes more material. We therefore have a spectrum or *hierarchy* of being. A wise man is more superior to a dull man. Similarly, there are some metals which are superior to other metals. Naturally, gold is the most superior of metals. This concept can be more easily visualised using the below illustration by Dr Robert Fludd. Fludd illustrated this principle by a single-stringed musical instrument called a *Celestial Monochord*. We can appreciate from this image that the different realms of creation (such as the animals, vegetables, minerals, angels, etc) are simply like different octaves upon a universal scale. You will also note on this image that the string is being tuned by the hand of God.

3. **Law of correspondence**
   Continuing with Fludd's Celestial Monochord, we can appreciate that the different octaves of creation share a sympathetic relationship (or resonance) just like musical notes. Just how there is a sympathetic relationship between C_4 (middle-C) and C_5, there is likewise a sympathetic relationship between planets, colours, musical notes, organs, and metals. For instance, Mars shares a sympathetic relationship (or rules over) iron. Alchemists combined this knowledge with the humoral theory of medicine to affect health.

4. **Nature is in a state of perfecting itself**
   Many alchemists believed that all things were desiring to return to their source and all things evolved over time. This longing for return was due to the spark of divinity contained within all things. However, this spark was covered up by *dross*. The process of evolution was to remove the dross to expose the divinity within. Some things expressed this divinity more than others. Gold was a more perfect metal than was copper. This analogy also applied to humans with wise men being more *pure* than a non-wise man. The wise man did not necessarily have more divinity, rather he had less *dross* allowing the Spirit within to shine forth in its splendour. This is an important distinction. Left to its own devices, Spirit would still evolve, or *spiritualise matter*, but to hasten this process and to help it reach its zenith, the alchemist would need to intervene.

5. **The Alchemist as Natures assistant**
   Extending upon the previous point, whilst all things slowly advanced towards their evolutionary summit, this process would take a long time. Inferior metals, such as lead and tin, if left in the earth long enough, would eventually rarify to gold, but this would take a very long time. The alchemists job therefore was to assist Nature and hasten this process. Many alchemists considered themselves to be Nature's assistant, and by extension, a servant of God. Many considered alchemy to be a spiritual work and were devoutly religious. To the alchemist therefore, religion and spirituality was not a matter of imposing God onto the worshipper, rather religion and spirituality brought the worshipper to the presence of God within. This also reconciles the seeming points of difference between physical and spiritual alchemy. They were not separate works; rather they are outward and inward effects of a single work.

According to the alchemist, by understanding the basic laws that govern their beings, and by extension the entire universe, we may learn to recognise the divine presence resident in all organisms. The alchemical work was directed at isolating, purifying, and manipulating this divine presence to assist Nature in her rectification.

This assisting of Nature is what is referred to as *transmutation*. Alchemical transmutation therefore does not involve destroying or ignoring impurities, rather, it involves working with them to transmute them into something more noble. The alchemist did not begin his work by placing *perfect* things into his crucible.

As you can see from these basic alchemical principles, alchemy is a holistic philosophy. It should be appreciated how this single philosophy can be applied to seemingly distinct subjects such as science, art, and medicine. The balance between physical and transcendental alchemy is perhaps best summarised by the phrase *Ora et Labora*. The alchemist viewed *Man* as but a microcosm of *Nature* and Nature but a microcosm of the *Universe*, with all three of these spheres sharing intimate relationships through a sympathetic resonance.

The Philosopher's Stone

The pinnacle of the alchemical process was something occasionally referred to as *The Philosopher's Stone*. This can be quite a challenging concept to understand, but let's return to our first principle regarding alchemical philosophy; that all things have contained within a spark of the Divine often called *Spirit*. Theoretically, if an alchemist could remove all the dross from their starting material and isolate Spirit, then they would be left with an undifferentiated spark of divinity, replete with all the faculties of its divine source. Therefore, the alchemical process when applied to a metal, would yield gold; when applied to a plant, would yield a healing panacea able to cure any disease; and when applied to man, would allow him to become a living expression of Spirit, or in other words, attain *Illumination*.

From this perspective, each of the great avatars throughout time could be considered a veritable living Philosophers Stone able to transmute those of whom they inspire.

Appendix Two

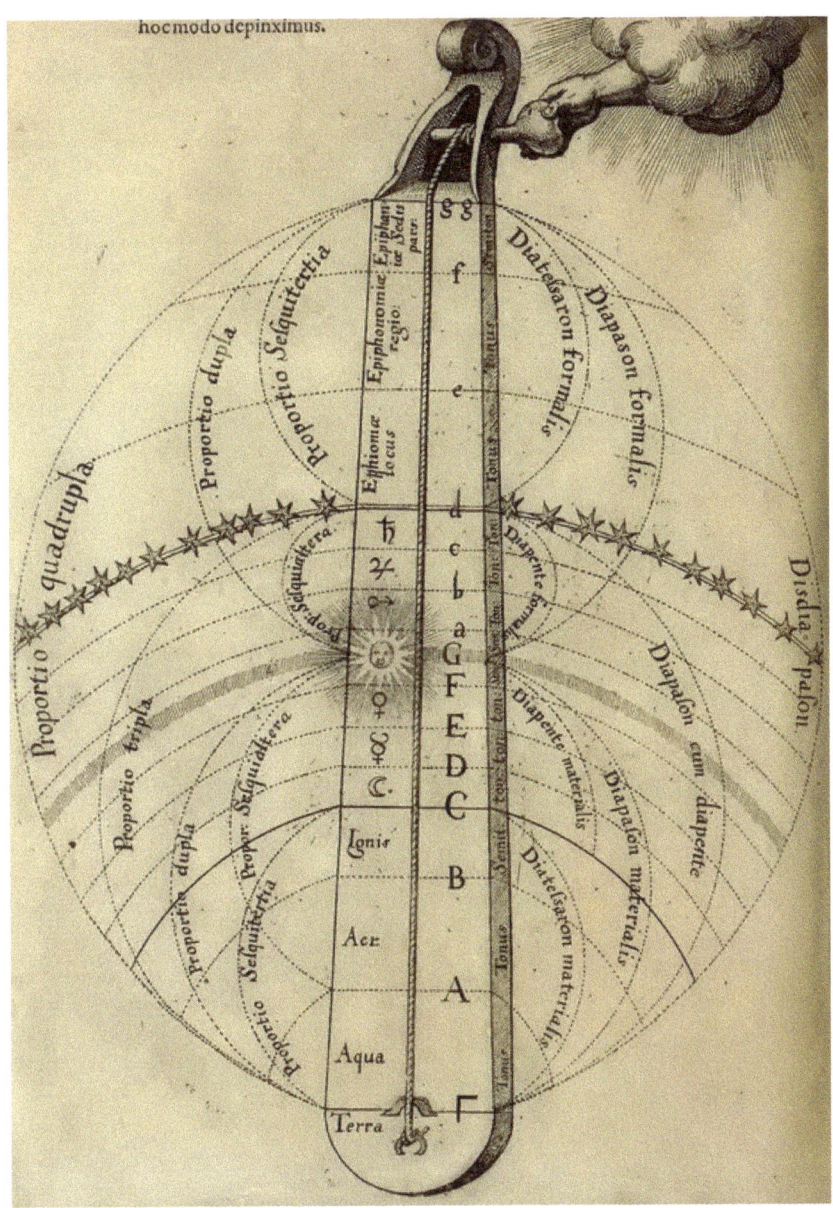

Robert Fludd (1574-1637) envisioned the universe like a long single string instrument called a Monochord. All natural phenomena were like octaves on this giant instrument. And just like a musical instrument, sympathetic resonance occurred between certain notes.

APPENDIX THREE:

THE ROSE AND THE CROSS

The Rose

Light veiled in shadow,
A seeker walks the path.
The hidden door appears,
Voice calls from silence.

Wisdom lost is found,
Symbols mark the way.
Seven stars illuminate,
A Master waits unseen.

A hand extends in darkness,
Fire stirs the heart.
The unseen voice speaks,
The heart remembers its name.

and the Cross

Voice calls from silence,
The hidden door appears.
A seeker walks the path,
Light unveiled.

A Master waits unseen,
Seven stars illuminate.
Symbols mark the way,
Wisdom lost is found.

The heart remembers its name,
The unseen voice speaks.
Fire stirs the heart,
A hand extends in darkness.

INDEX

A

Across the Atlantic........................ 257
Advancement of Learning, The ... 113
Agartha............................156-8
Alchemy .4, 7, 49, 77, 155, 201, 205, 214-5, 223, 226-8, 237-8, 313-7, 321-5, 334-5, 365-74
A Letter from the Brothers R.C. . 12-3
Alighieri, Dante.............................. 199
Alveydre, Saint-Yves d'.................155-8
A.M.O.R.C. ... 12-3, 36-9, 94-8, 104, 116, 122-8, 139-43, 166-8, 175-7, 219-26, 258-72, 316, 319, 326-7, 339, 345-63
An Adventure Among the Rosicrucians 170, 224
Anatomy of Melancholy, The 96-7
Ancient and Primitive Rite of Memphis-Misraim, The.........................261
Andreae, Johannes Valentinus.......6 6 , 77, 85-6, 88-104, 200-3
Andrea, Raymund............................ 261
Angelology 182
Angels...181
Anthroposophical Society, The.... 172, 341
Anthroposophy 35
Antonia of Württemberg, Princess..............................89-91
Archaeological Society for the South of France, The (French: La Société archéologique du Midi de la France) 320
Artificial Intelligence............. 273, 277
Asiatic Brethren of St. John the Evangelist in Europe, The (German: Die Brüder St. Johannes des Evangelisten aus Asien in Europa)........................ 238, 314-7
Astrology 31-2
Authentic message from the Knight and Brother Initiates from Asia (German: Authentische Nachricht von den Ritter- und Bruder-Eingeweihten aus Asien)............317
Auxiliary languages.......................... 348

B

Baconian Theory............................95-8
Bacon, Sir Francis....94-103, 113, 257
Balbiani, Prince 321-2
Banks, Mary Henrietta AKA Stacey, May Banks..... 166, 346-7, 355-6
Barbarossa, Emperor Frederick 40-2

Belcastel, Baron Gabriel de Lacoste de 359
Belcastel, Joseph de 359
Besant, Annie 128, 166
Besold, Christoph 87-92
Blackden, Marcus Worsley 248, 338, 361-63
Blavatsky, Helena Petrovna 84, 155-73, 194, 347
Böhme, Jakob 73-6, 314
Boissin, Firmin AKA Brugal, Simon 321-6, 358-60
Book M 22, 26-7
B.O.T.A. 103, 137, 263
Brother of the Third Degree 224
Brousse, Rozes de 327, 359
Bulwer-Lytton, Edward 127, 160, 215-23, 292
Burton, Robert 96-98

C

Cagliostro 321-23
Cambridge Platonists 330
Case, Paul Foster 103-4, 137-38, 142, 262-67
Catharism 319
C.B.C.S. 150
Celestial Hierarchy, The 177-81
Chemical Wedding of Christian Rosenkreuz in the Year 1459, Analysis of 65
Chemical Wedding of Christian Rosenkreuz in the Year 1459, The 12, 16, 57-9, 65-89, 103, 144, 199-203
Christianopolis 97
Cipher Manuscripts 247
Cloaks, Daggers, and Crosses 241
Cloud, Rosicrucian 140
Cloud upon the Sanctuary, The 136-7
Clymer, Reuben Swinburne 258-62, 339
Cole, Thomas 120
Companion of Christian Rosenkreuz (C.C.R.) Award 115

Comte de Gabalis, The 5, 209, 217, 223-4
Confessio Fraternitatis 12-16, 45-68, 89, 103-7, 131, 135, 138, 144, 199, 211, 234
Confessio Fraternitatis, Analysis of 51
Consideratio Brevis 45-6
Cosmic Masters 175-7
Court de Gébelin, Antoine 324
C.R.+C. 270, 360
Crowley, Aleister 248-9, 258-62, 337-8, 356
Crown of Thorns 275

D

Damcar 21, 27, 40, 49
Day C.   23
Debussy, Claude 328
Dee, John 45, 236
Demiurgus College 245
Dew   205
Didactic Literature 210
Discourse on Progress (French: Discours sur le progress) 359
Divine Comedy, The 199
Divine Feminine, The 73
Djinn 225
Dorbon Aîné 157
Du Mège, Alexandre 323-4
Dunning Jr, C. R. 215
Dweller on the Threshold 216-23

E

Echoes in the Chamber 271
Eckartshausen, Karl von 136
Ecker und Eckhoffen, Hans Heinrich von 238, 316
Elder Brothers 116, 138, 171-6, 207, 340-1
Elementals 22, 27, 221-4
Élus Coëns 151-4
Encausse, Gérard AKA Papus 110, 154, 15-8, 328, 370

Esoteric School of Theosophy 341, 347
Externsteine 37-40

F

Fama Fraternitatis 6-7, 12-41, 58, 67-8, 75, 89, 95, 99, 103-10, 113, 122-4, 131-2, 138, 144, 199-204, 211, 221, 225, 233, 276, 288-91, 368
Fama Fraternitatis, Analysis of 25
Farr, Florence 337
Felt, George H. 164
Floral Games Academy, The (French: Académie des Jeux Floraux) 320, 326, 359
Fludd, Robert ... 8, 83-4, 110, 127, 144, 148, 200-2, 233, 323, 372
Förner, Friedrich 235
Fräulein Sprengel 336
F.R.C 258, 262, 339
Freemason Patent (German: Freimaurerpatent) 239, 318
Freemasonry .. 128, 150-4, 154, 166, 195, 196
Friends of Saint-Yves, The 157-8
F.U.D.O.F.S.I. 262
F.U.D.O.S.I. 262-4

G

Garver, Will L. 224
Germelshausen, Christian von 41
Gnostic Church of France, The 256
Gnosticism 109, 151
Golden Fleece 61, 73
Gould, Sylvester Clark 334
Great White Brotherhood, The 154, 165, 176-7
Gretser, Jacob 235
Guaita, Stanislas de 250-3
G.u.R.C. 129, 237-9, 311-8

H

Hall, Manly Palmer 96-7, 194, 225
Hallmark Four: Rosicrucian Masters 143
Hallmark One: Service 110
Hallmark Three: The Invisible College of the Rosicrucians 131
Hallmark Two: The Rosicrucian Pulse 118
Hartmann, Franz 15, 110, 127, 169-70, 224-5, 263, 316, 341
Haslmayr, Adam 7
Hayyan, Jabir ibn AKA Geber 368
Heindel, Max ... 100-3, 138, 142, 171-5, 194, 340-4
Helmont, Jan Baptist van 314
Hermeticism ... 69, 109, 129, 151, 328, 334-5, 366-7
Hess, Tobias 87-92
Het Rozekruisers Genootschap (English: The Rosicrucian Society) 343
Himmler, Heinrich 39
H.O.G.D 28-30, 103, 129, 206, 245-9, 263, 335-8
Holy Guardian Angel 143
How to become a mage (French: Comment on devient mage) 325
Hughan, William James 241, 330-1
Hund, Baron Karl Gotthelf von ... 150, 316

I

Illuminati 236-9, 317-8, 353
Initiatic power of esoteric narrative 228
Invisibility, Rosicrucian 118, 132-5, 138-42, 234
Invisible College 285
Invisible Fraternity and its Visible Critics, The 233
I.R.R 248, 338

J

Jinarājadāsa, Curuppumullage 166
Judge, William Quan 162-4

Index

K

Kabbalah 4, 151, 155, 315, 321, 328, 334-5
Kabbalistic Teaching Painting of Princess Antonia of Württemberg....... 90
Khunrath, Heinrich.................. 54, 313
Knights of the Faith........................ 326
Knights of the Golden Cross (Italian: Cavalieri dell'Aurea Croce).... 314
Kortholt, Christian......................... 234

L

Lapasse, Viscount Louis-Charles-Édouard de........................... 110, 243, 320-7
Lassalle, Clovis Marie Charles..... 358-60
Latin Decadence, The (French: La Décadence Latine) 250
Lévi, Éliphas.................... 225, 252, 369
Lewis, Harvey Spencer...... 122-42, 176-7, 205-6, 241, 258-68, 327, 331, 345-63
Lewis, Ralph Maxwell........... 265, 352
Libavius, Andreas........................ 8, 234
Little, Robert Wentworth....... 218, 241, 330-3
Lost Rosicrucian Secret, The..... 189, 283, 294
Lumen de Lumine.............................13
Lutheranism and Rosicrucianism 234

M

Mackenzie, Kenneth R. H. 127-30, 331-2
Mahatma Letters to A. P. Sinnett, The... 165
Maier, Michael........ 7, 8, 81, 110, 127, 144, 202-3
Mailänder, Alois .... xii, 168-171
Manhattan Mystic Circle 347-8
Martinism....... 151, 154, 159, 255, 329, 369
Martinist Order (French: Ordre Martiniste) 329

Mathers, Samuel Liddell MacGregor 245-9, 335-8
Menippus...87-8
Mercure François.............................. 132
Mersenne, Marin 8
Mesmer, Franz Anton 110
Mirror of Wisdom of the Rosy Cross, The (Latin: Speculum Sophicum Rhodostauroticum) 12, 212
Mission of India in Europe, The (French: Mission de l'Inde en Europe)............................ 155-88
Mögling, Daniel AKA Schweighardt, Theophilus............................212
Monas Hieroglyphica................. 45, 60
Münter, Friedrich 238, 317

N

Neoplatonism 109
Neo-Templery of Genoude and Lourdoueix 326
New Atlantis, The 94-8, 100, 257
New York Institute for Psychical Research................................ 346

O

O.K.R.+C. 251-3, 319, 328-9
Olcott, Henry Steel 162-4
Oneal Haye, Anthony..... 242-3, 330-2
Order of the Catholic and Aesthetic Rose-Cross of the Temple and the Grail (French: Ordre de la Rose-Croix Catholique et Esthétique du Temple et du Graal).....................252-4, 328
O.T.O................................260-2, 356-7

P

Parabola...12
Paracelsus........52, 221-4, 323, 368-71
Pasqually, Martinez de 151-4
Pegasus of the Firmament, The (Latin: Pegasus firmamenti) 12

Péladan, Adrien 110, 252, 325
Péladan, Joséphin .. 112-4,   250-6,
    325-8, 357
Pfeffer, Ulrich 314
Philippe, Nizier Anthelme 110, 254-6
Philomatic Society of Verdun, The (French: La Société philomathique de Verdun) 348
Philosopher's Stone, The 374
Pike, Albert............... 199
Planis-Campy, David de 323
Plummer, George Winslow AKA Frater KHEI 334
Primitive World analysed and compared with the Modern World (French: Monde Primitif, analysé et comparé avec le monde modern) 324
Prince Karl of Salm-Reifferscheidt 239
Pseudo-Dionysius the Areopagite 177-83
Pseudo-Gualdi 314
Pullen, Henry Burry 337

R

Randolph, Paschal Beverly ... 258, 339
Razi, Muhammad ibn Zakariya al- AKA Rhazes 368
Rectified Scottish Rite 153
Red Cross of Constantine and Rome 332
Reformation and Rosicrucianism 121
Reuss, Theodor 260-1, 356
Richter, Samuel AKA Renatus, Sincerus......................237, 313
Rite of Strict Observance 150
Rose-Cross, The........................... 199
Rosenkreuz, Christian ...19-21, 24-38
Rose of Sharon....................69-71
Rosicrucian Community............ 286
Rosicrucian Cosmo-Conception, The 101-2, 171-3, 194

Rosicrucian Fellowship, The ... 1 0 0 - 3 , 116, 138, 171-6
Rosicrucian Home, A..................... 287
Rosicrucian in his Nakedness, The (German: Der Rosenkreuzer in seiner Blöße) 239, 317
Rosicrucian Masters 117,   143-7, 168, 175, 185-6
Rosicrucian Master, The 185
Rosicrucian Rivalries in Belle Époque France............................... 250
Rosicrucians of Toulouse, The....... 311, 319, 320, 325, 349, 354, 358, 359, 360, 362
Rosicrucian Source Works, How many........................... 11
Rosicrucian Source Works, Manifesto, Treatise or allegory? 14
Rosicrucians vs the Illuminati, The 236

S

Saint-Martin, Louis-Claude de 153-4
Saint-Yves d'Alveydre, Alexandre....... 253
Salons de la Rose+Croix 252, 328
Schweighardt   Constantiens, Theophilus................. 133
Schweighardt, Theophilus........... 212-4
Secret Doctrine, The ...155, 157, 162, 166
Secret Symbols of the Rosicrucians, The (German: Geheime Figuren der Rosenkreuzer) 69, 74-6, 316-8
Sheath of the Sword of the Spirit, The (Latin: Theca gladii Spiritus).. 87-9
Silence after the Cries, The (Latin: Silentium Post Clamores) 12
Sina, Ibn AKA Avicenna 368
Societas Rosicruciana..... 71,   99-100, 113-5, 126-30, 185, 218-9, 241, 244, 311, 330-334, 362
Societas Rosicruciana in America, The........................ 334
Song of Solomon....................71-2
Sophia....................73-5

Sovereign Pyramid of the Friends of the Desert (French: Souveraine Pyramide des Amis du Désert) 320
Spener, Philip Jacob 90
Sprengel, Fräulein 247-8
Steiner, Rudolf 35, 127-8, 172-3, 341-2
Sub-Rosa 196
Summum Bonum 83, 200-1
Supreme Vice, The (French: Le Vice Suprême) 250
Symbolist movement 328
Synarchy 155-7, 253-4

T

Tarot 71, 76, 155
Temple and the Vault, The 241, 246
Temple of the Rosy Cross, The 166-7
Testamentum 314
Themis Aurea 7, 81-2
Theosophical Society, The 84, 128, 154-5, 158-9, 162-74, 195, 340-1, 347
Thun, Prince Pietro Vigilio 322
Tower of Olympus 62-65
Treasure of Treasures (Latin: Thesaurus Thesaurum) 314
T.R.F. 116, 138, 171-6, 207, 340-3
Triumphal Palm of the Miracles of the Catholic Church, The (Latin: Palma Triumphalis Miraculorum Ecclesiae Catholicae) 235
True and Invisible Rosicrucian Order, The 103
Tübingen Circle, The 92

U

Underhill, Evelyn 338
Urim and Thummim 315

V

Vaughan, Thomas AKA Philalethes, Eugenius 12-3, 46, 141-2, 146, 149
Vault of C.R.C 30, 122, 368
Villars, Abbé Henri Montfaucon de 209, 223

W

Wachtmeister, Countess Constance ... 162
Waite, Arthur Edward 248
Westcott, William Wynn .... 1 1 0 , 126-30, 244-9, 331-8
White, William Henry 332
Willermoz, Jean-Baptiste 153-4
Woodford, Rev. Adolphus Frederick Alexander 247, 336
Woodman, William Robert 110, 126, 218, 245-7, 335-7

Y

Yarker, John 218

Z

Zanoni 5, 215-9, 223, 292

LIST OF IMAGES

Cover	Designed by Mitch Savage-Charman.
Page 20	The title page of the *Fama Fraternitatis*. Sourced from https://upload.wikimedia.org/wikipedia/commons/a/a8/Fama_fraternitatis.jpg. Public domain.
Page 38	Rosicrucian Digest, Vol. 15, No. 6, 1937. Sourced from https://archive.org/details/IAPSOP-rosicrucian_digest_v15_n6_1937_jul. Public domain.
Page 38	Externsteine, 2022. Sourced from https://upload.wikimedia.org/wikipedia/commons/e/e0/Horn-Bad_Meinberg_-_2022-05-02_-_Externsteine_%28DSC04581%29.jpg. Public domain.
Page 42	A sculpture of Frederick Barbarossa taken from the Kyffhäuser Monument. Sourced from https://upload.wikimedia.org/wikipedia/commons/a/a7/Monument_barbarossa.jpg. Public domain.
Page 46	Title page of the combined, *Secretioris Philosophiae Consideratio brevis a Philipp à Gabella Philosophiae St. conscripta, et nunc primum una cum Confessione Fraternitatis R.C. in lucem edita Cassellis. Anno post natum Christum MDCXV.* Sourced from https://babel.hathitrust.org/cgi/pt?id=ucm.5327358319&seq=3. Public domain.
Page 50	Title page of *The fame and confession of the Fraternity of R.C., commonly, of the Rosie Cross*. Sourced from https://archive.org/details/fameconfessionof00vaug/page/n9/mode/2up. Public domain.

Page 59	Title page of *The Chemical Wedding of Christian Rosenkreuz in the Year 1459*. Sourced from https://archive.org/details/chymischehochzei00rose/page/n3/mode/2up?view=theater. Public domain.
Page 60	Contrasting the *Hieroglyphic Monad* of John Dee (1591), *Consideratio Brevis* (1615), and *The Chemical Wedding of Christian Rosenkreuz in the Year 1459* (1616). Sourced from https://archive.org/details/monashieroglyphi00deej/page/94/mode/1up and sources included above. Public domain.
Page 70	Red King and White Queen from the *Rosarium Philosophorum*. Sourced from https://www.gla.ac.uk/myglasgow/library/files/special/exhibns/month/april2009.html. Public domain.
Page 72	From *The Secret Symbols of the Rosicrucians*. Coloured and adapted by author. Public domain.
Page 81	Michael Maier. Sourced from https://upload.wikimedia.org/wikipedia/commons/3/34/Michael_Maier_portrait.jpg. Public domain.
Page 83	Robert Fludd. Sourced from https://www.britannica.com/biography/Robert-Fludd. Public domain.
Page 85	Johann Valentin Andreae by the German engraver Melchior Küsel. Sourced from https://picryl.com/media/andreae-johann-valentin-6254e1. Public domain.
Page 89	The central image of the triptych commissioned by Princess Antonia of Württemberg often referred to as *The Kabbalistic Teaching Painting of Princess Antonia of Württemberg*. Sourced from https://commons.wikimedia.org/wiki/File:Teinach_lehrtafel_hauptbild.jpg. Public domain.

Page 92	Cover of, *The Rosy Cross Unveiled* (1980) by Christopher McIntosh, published by Aquarian Press. This would later be republished under the name, *The Rosicrucians: The History, Mythology, and Rituals of an Esoteric Order* (1997), by Red Wheel/Weiser.
Page 98	The curious footnote that has led many to incorrectly attribute a connection between Andreae and Bacon. Sourced from https://archive.org/details/anatomyofmelanch00burt/. Red underline added by author. Public domain.
Page 101	Sir Francis Bacon by John Vanderbank. Sourced from https://en.wikipedia.org/wiki/Francis_Bacon#/media/File:Francis_Bacon,_Viscount_St_Alban_from_NPG_(2).jpg. Public domain.
Page 111	*The apostles Peter and John laying hands in ordination.* Illustration, 1873. Unknown author. Sourced from https://upload.wikimedia.org/wikipedia/commons/8/85/Peter_and_John_laying_their_hands_on_the_disciples.jpg. Public domain.
Page 114	*Salon de la Rose + Croix* by Carlos Schwabe (1866-1926). Sourced from https://commons.wikimedia.org/wiki/File:Salon_de_la_Rose%2BCroix_lithographie.jpg. Public domain.
Page 120	*The Course of Empire*, by Thomas Cole. Sourced from https://upload.wikimedia.org/wikipedia/commons/1/1a/Cole_Thomas_The_Consummation_The_Course_of_the_Empire_1836.jpg. Public domain.
Page 124	*The Little Brown Casket* (1920). Sourced from https://iapsop.com/ssoc/1920__anonymous___the_little_brown_casket.pdf and upscaled with A.I. Public domain.
Page 127	William Wynn Westcott. Sourced from https://upload.wikimedia.org/wikipedia/commons/5/54/William_Wynn_Westcott_PNG.png. Public domain.

Page 133	*The Mirror of the Wisdom of the Rosy Cross*, published by Theophilus Schweighardt Constantiens. Sourced from https://upload.wikimedia.org/wikipedia/commons/a/a5/Templeofrosycross.png. Upscaled using A.I. Public domain.
Page 147	*The Annunciation* by Fra Angelico (c. 1426). Sourced from https://commons.wikimedia.org/wiki/File:Fra_Angelico_-_The_Annunciation_-_WGA0455.jpg. Public domain.
Page 148	This image is taken from the second tractate of Robert Fludd's *Utriusque Cosmi maioris scilicet et minoris metaphysica, physica, atque technica Historia*. Public domain.
Page 150	Baron Karl Gotthelf von Hund. Sourced from https://upload.wikimedia.org/wikipedia/commons/e/e4/Carl_Gothelf_von_Hund_und_Altengrotkau.jpg. Upscaled using A.I. Public domain.
Page 152	Seal attributed to Martinez de Pasqually. Sourced from https://upload.wikimedia.org/wikipedia/commons/e/e4/Seal_of_Martin%C3%A8s_de_Pasqually.jpg. Upscaled using A.I. Public domain.
Page 157	Saint-Yves d'Alveydre. Sourced from https://commons.wikimedia.org/wiki/File:Saint-Yves_d%27Alveydre.jpg. Public domain.
Page 161	Helena Petrovna Blavatsky. Sourced from https://upload.wikimedia.org/wikipedia/commons/e/ea/Hours_with_the_ghosts%2C_or%2C_Nineteenth_century_witchcraft_-_illustrated_investigations_into_the_phenomena_of_spiritualism_and_theosophy_%281897%29_%2814591793778%29.jpg. Upscaled using A.I. Public domain.

Page 160	Blavatsky recalls her memorable night. Sourced from https://upload.wikimedia.org/wikipedia/commons/4/49/Picture_of_H.P.Blavatsky.jpg. Upscaled using A.I. Public domain.
Page 167	Taken from *Ritual of the Mystic Star (4th edition)* by C. Jinarajadasa (Theosophical Publishing House, Adyar, 1951). Public domain.
Page 170	Taken from *In the Pronaos of the Temple* By Franz Hartmann. Sourced from https://archive.org/details/inpronaostemple00hartgoog/page/n105/mode/1up?view=theater . Public domain.
Page 172	Max Heindel. Sourced from https://upload.wikimedia.org/wikipedia/commons/0/0a/Max_Heindel.jpg. Public domain.
Page 177	H. Spencer Lewis. Sourced from author's private collection.
Page 184	Angelic Hierarchy of Robert Fludd. Sourced from https://commons.wikimedia.org/wiki/File:R._Fludd,_De_integra_macrosmi...;_hierarchy_of_angels_Wellcome_L0016200.jpg. Public domain.
Page 187	*The Light of the World* (1853) by William Holman Hunt. Sourced from https://upload.wikimedia.org/wikipedia/commons/b/bc/Hunt-light-of-the-world.jpeg. Public domain.
Page 197	*The Soul of the Rose* (1908) by John William Waterhouse. Sourced from https://upload.wikimedia.org/wikipedia/commons/c/c4/John_William_Waterhouse_-_The_Soul_of_the_Rose%2C_1903.jpg. Public domain.
Page 198	Temple of Jupiter in Split, Croatia. Sourced from https://commons.wikimedia.org/wiki/File:Pentagramma_Croatia_05.jpg. Public domain.

Page 200	This stylised Rose-Cross appears on the front page of a Rosicrucian work *Summum Bonum* by Robert Fludd. Sourced from https://archive.org/details/robert-fludd-summum-bonum-1629. Public domain.
Page 204	This stylised version of the Rose-Cross comes from the title page of the 1681 version of the Fama Fraternitatis. Sourced from https://archive.org/details/b28759345/page/n3/mode/2up. Public domain.
Page 216	*Zanoni* (1888). Sourced from https://archive.org/details/zanonilytt00lyttuoft/page/n5/mode/1up?view=theater. Public domain.
Page 220	*Knight, Death and the Devil* (1513) by Albrecht Dürer. Sourced from https://upload.wikimedia.org/wikipedia/commons/0/0a/Albrecht_D%C3%BCrer%2C_Knight%2C_Death_and_Devil%2C_1513%2C_NGA_6637.jpg. Public domain.
Page 227	An alchemical mandala-like image from Basil Valentine. Sourced from https://upload.wikimedia.org/wikipedia/commons/2/2f/Fotothek_df_tg_0008255_Theosophie_%5E_Alchemie_%5E_Hermetik_%28cropped%29.jpg. Public domain.
Page 229	*Magdalene with the Smoking Flame* (c. 1640) by Georges de La Tour. Sourced from https://upload.wikimedia.org/wikipedia/commons/b/ba/Georges_de_La_Tour_-_Magdalen_of_Night_Light_-_WGA12337.jpg. Public domain.
Page 234	Clouds of invisibility. Sourced from https://upload.wikimedia.org/wikipedia/commons/1/15/A_young_naked_man_on_a_cloud%2C_holding_his_hand_to_his_heart._Wellcome_V0025920.jpg. Public domain.

Page 240	The Urim and Thummim of G.u.R.C. Pictured here in MS.4808 (1737) from the Wellcome collection in London. Sourced from https://wellcomecollection.org/works/m3fnrxg3/items?canvas=246. Public domain.
Page 254	Joséphin Péladan. Sourced from https://commons.wikimedia.org/wiki/File:Portrait_du_S%C3%A2r_P%C3%A9ladan_-_photographie_Walter_Damry.jpg. Public domain.
Page 255	Master Philippe of Lyon. Sourced from https://upload.wikimedia.org/wikipedia/commons/6/6c/Nizier_Anthelme_Philippe_%28Ma%C3%AEtre_Philippe_de_Lyon%29_1849-1905.jpg. Public domain.
Page 260	Clymer, R. S. (1935). *An Expose of the Imperator of A.M.O.R.C.* [Brochure]. The Rosicrucian Foundation. Public domain. National Membership Defense Committee. (1935). *AMORC White Book D* [Brochure]. The Rosicrucian Order, AMORC. Public domain.
Page 264	F. U. D. O. S. I. (Fédération Universelle des Ordres et Sociétés Initiatiques). (1946, November). *F.U.D.O.S.I. (An International Journal of the Ancient and Honorable Esoteric Orders)*, *1*(1). Upscaled with A.I. Public domain.
Page 227	Rosicrucianism in the digital age. Designed using Microsoft Copilot A.I.
Page 375	Cosmic Monochord of Robert Fludd. Sourced from https://archive.org/details/utriusquecosmima01flud/page/n97/mode/1up. Public domain.
Page 378-9	Central image sourced from https://archive.org/details/b28759345/page/n3/mode/2up. Public domain. Vines designed by author using A.I. and Adobe Illustrator.

www.ingramcontent.com/pod-product-compliance
Lightning Source LLC
Chambersburg PA
CBHW042112100526
44587CB00025B/4027